MW01015355

How to access the supplemental web resource

We are pleased to provide access to a web resource that supplements your textbook, *Sustainable Tourism.* This resource offers videos from the field, a tool for developing your career goals, a business planning workbook, a sample business plan and planning worksheets, learning aids from the textbook, and more.

Accessing the web resource is easy!
Follow these steps if you purchased a new book:

1. Visit **www.HumanKinetics.com/Sustainable Tourism**.

2. Click the <u>first edition</u> link next to the book cover.

3. Click the Sign In link on the left or top of the page. If you do not have an account with Human Kinetics, you will be prompted to create one.

4. If the online product you purchased does not appear in the Ancillary Items box on the left of the page, click the Enter Key Code option in that box. Enter the key code that is printed at the right, including all hyphens. Click the Submit button to unlock your online product.

5. After you have entered your key code the first time, you will never have to enter it again to access this product. Once unlocked, a link to your product will permanently appear in the menu on the left. For future visits, all you need to do is sign in to the textbook's website and follow the link that appears in the left menu!

→ Click the Need Help? button on the textbook's website if you need assistance along the way.

How to access the web resource if you purchased a used book:

You may purchase access to the web resource by visiting the text's website, **www.HumanKinetics.com/Sustainable Tourism**, or by calling the following:

800-747-4457 . . . . .U.S. customers
800-465-7301 . . . . .Canadian customers
+44 (0) 113 255 5665 . . . . European customers
08 8372 0999 . . . . Australian customers
0800 222 062 . . . . .New Zealand customers
217-351-5076 . . . . .International customers

For technical support, send an e-mail to:
support@hkusa.com . . . . U.S. and international customers
info@hkcanada.com . . . . Canadian customers
academic@hkeurope.com . . . . European customers
keycodesupport@hkaustralia.com . . . . . Australian and New Zealand customers

HUMAN KINETICS
The Information Leader in Physical Activity & Health

09-2015

Product: Sustainable Tourism web resource

Key code: PATTERSON-7W42NW-OSG

This unique code allows you access to the web resource.

Access is provided if you have purchased a new book. Once submitted, the code may not be entered for any other user.

HUMAN KINETICS WEB RESOURCE

SUSTAINABLE TOURISM

BUSINESS DEVELOPMENT, OPERATIONS, AND MANAGEMENT

Carol Patterson, CMA

President, Kalahari Management Inc.
University of Calgary

HUMAN KINETICS

Library of Congress Cataloging-in-Publication Data

Patterson, Carol, 1957-
    Sustainable tourism : business development, operations, and management / Carol Patterson.
        pages cm
    Includes bibliographical references and index.
    1. Sustainable tourism--Economic aspects. 2. Tourism--Management. I. Title.
    G156.5.S87P37 2015
    910.68'4--dc23

                                                        2015009207
    ISBN: 978-1-4504-6003-3 (print)

The web addresses cited in this text were current as of March 2015, unless otherwise noted.

Acquisitions Editor: Gayle Kassing, PhD; **Developmental Editor:** Jacqueline Eaton Blakley; **Managing Editor:** Anne E. Mrozek; **Copyeditor:** Annette Pierce; **Indexer:** Dan Connolly; **Permissions Manager:** Dalene Reeder; **Graphic Designer:** Fred Starbird; **Cover Designer:** Keith Blomberg; **Photograph (cover):** Art Explosion; **Photographs (interior):** Photos on pp. 126, 134, 137, and 140 by Rainer Martens; photo on p. 92 by Bernard Wolff Photography; photo on p. 40 © Human Kinetics; photo on p. 53 Dob's Farm/fotolia.com; leaf icon photo © Stockakia/Dreamstime.com; all other photos by Carol Patterson; **Photo Asset Manager:** Laura Fitch; **Photo Production Manager:** Jason Allen; **Art Manager:** Kelly Hendren; **Associate Art Manager:** Alan L. Wilborn; **Illustrations:** © Human Kinetics, unless otherwise noted; **Printer:** Sheridan Books

The video contents of this product are licensed for private home use and traditional, face-to-face classroom instruction only. For public performance licensing, please contact a sales representative at www.HumanKinetics.com/SalesRepresentatives.

Printed in the United States of America   10 9 8 7 6 5 4 3 2 1

The paper in this book is Forest Stewardship Council™ certified.

Human Kinetics
Website: www.HumanKinetics.com

United States: Human Kinetics
P.O. Box 5076
Champaign, IL 61825-5076
800-747-4457
e-mail: humank@hkusa.com

Canada: Human Kinetics
475 Devonshire Road Unit 100
Windsor, ON N8Y 2L5
800-465-7301 (in Canada only)
e-mail: info@hkcanada.com

Europe: Human Kinetics
107 Bradford Road
Stanningley
Leeds LS28 6AT, United Kingdom
+44 (0) 113 255 5665
e-mail: hk@hkeurope.com

Australia: Human Kinetics
57A Price Avenue
Lower Mitcham, South Australia 5062
08 8372 0999
e-mail: info@hkaustralia.com

New Zealand: Human Kinetics
P.O. Box 80
Mitcham Shopping Centre, South Australia 5062
0800 222 062
e-mail: info@hknewzealand.com

E6014

CONTENTS

PREFACE

The Mexican architect Héctor Ceballos-Lascuráin coined the term *ecotourism* in 1983. It provided a possible solution to a dilemma that confronted travelers and tourism professionals: travel, while bringing benefits to the consumer, was causing harm to the communities that hosted it. Ecotourism offered guiding principles for a form of tourism that minimized environmental impacts while maximizing benefits to the local communities. People embraced the new concept and looked for ways to develop new eco-products or incorporate the ecotourism philosophy into their business.

As a pioneer in the ecotourism development field, I have had a ringside seat as one of the most exciting developments in the tourism field in the last 50 years has unfolded. The birth of ecotourism was a heady time, especially for emerging destinations such as Costa Rica or east Africa, where consumers already associated the travel experience with nature. In North America, progress was slower. I worked with many communities wanting to incorporate principles of ecotourism into their strategic plans or with tourism businesses that wanted to develop new tourism products. But there was an unexpected problem. Travelers from the United States and Canada who eagerly traipsed to Central America to sleep in a rainforest lodge hesitated to book an ecotourism holiday nearer to home. To quote one business owner, "Customers were afraid there would not be enough outdoor adventure and too much indoor adventure in the form of uncomfortable beds, Spartan meals, or the need to 'suffer' in the quest for sustainable tourism!"

Obviously, a different approach was required for developing North American ecotourism. While still concerned with managing a triple bottom line of financial, environmental, and cultural outcomes, North American organizations focused on the visitor experience or experiential travel. They highlighted how principles of ecotourism made better holidays—for example, lower guide-to-client ratios or more chances to meet locals. As a result, nature and culture-based adventure tourism grew.

For a few days in 2002, North America was ground zero for the sustainable tourism movement. People from over 132 countries gathered in Quebec City to mark the International Year of Ecotourism and discuss ways to make one of humankind's most popular pastimes, travel, more gentle on the earth and the communities that host it. The result was the Quebec Declaration on Ecotourism, a set of UN-level recommendations for the development of ecotourism activities in the context of sustainable development. The hope was that governments, nongovernmental agencies, and tourism organizations would use this framework to guide the development and operation of tourism.

Fast-forward a decade later. Ecotourism is joined by geotourism, responsible tourism, volunteerism, and sustainable tourism, among others, in the lexicon of tourism jargon as we green the world's tourism industry. No common international standard for sustainable tourism has been created and there are no national standards in Canada or the United States. Businesses search for best practices and implementation strategies, and the successful tourism professional will be someone with insight and skill in this field.

If you are wondering whether sustainable tourism is the same as ecotourism or whether all adventure tourism is sustainable, you are not alone. I have yet to meet a traveler or business owner who wants to harm the environment, but it is easy to find evidence of negative environmental impacts from tourism. It would appear that the challenge is in the implementation of sustainable tourism practices, but as I show in figure 1, I believe ecotourism principles and the World Tourism Organization (UNWTO) Global Sustainable Tourism Council Criteria (discussed at length in chapter 1) should be at the heart of all tourism development.

Against the backdrop of sustainable tourism development, we see the main components of ecotourism experiences: nature tourism, cultural and historical tourism, educational tourism, and volunteerism. Mass, or urban, tourism is on the opposite end of the spectrum but is still a part of sustainable tourism, often leading innovation in energy efficiency and waste management.

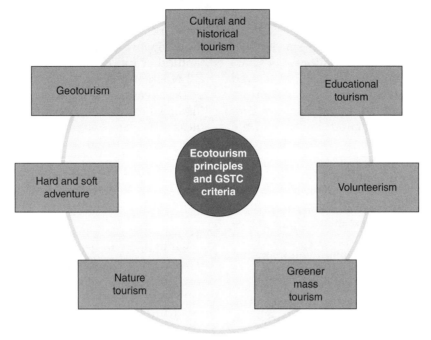

Figure 1   Principles of ecotourism and the UNWTO Global Sustainable Tourism Council Criteria should be at the heart of all tourism development.

Hard and soft adventure describe the level of effort and risk that accompany travel activities, and soft adventure can cross several tourism components. Experiential tourism has grown out of the emphasis on the experience economy and emphasizes unique or high-quality interactions between travelers and their physical or cultural environment. Geotourism, actively promoted since 2002 by National Geographic as a way to protect a place's character in addition to adhering to the principles of sustainable tourism, focuses on tourism that sustains or enhances geographical character. So one could say that all tourism should be geotourism because it is important to protect the landscape—urban or natural—where tourism occurs.

As you might guess, if we have this much trouble defining sustainable tourism, then it is also difficult to implement sustainable tourism practices and it is becoming increasingly difficult. Tourism has spread to the world's most remote locations. Technology creates new activities each year, and more cultures want a say in tourism growth. What is green in one location may not be in another. What is simple in a policy document is difficult to implement in the field. And with the need to fly to most tourism destinations, some would question whether the accompanying carbon emissions make all travel unsustainable.

PREPARING FOR A CAREER IN TOURISM

For you to succeed in this field, you will need to understand the complexity of sustainability issues and approach solutions with innovative ideas and often an entrepreneurial focus. The ecotourism industry (and its related components) is dominated by small to medium-size businesses and emerging destinations. You will find yourself grappling with problems for which there are few procedure manuals and where your ability to connect with people in government, volunteer groups, and business may be the difference between celebrating success or looking for a new career.

This book can help you stack the odds in your favor. By sharing the lessons of others who share your vision of a more sustainable tourism industry, this book provides a framework to build the skills you need for success.

I got involved in ecotourism because I met many people developing tourism businesses with great passion for the outdoors or wildlife, but little passion for business. Working on a financial forecast or selling their tours to customers was about as enticing to them as giving a pill to a sick cat. I realized that I could complement the skill gaps of many tourism operators. I liked business and could make a contribution to the behind-the-scenes elements of tourism. I had passion for the business of sustainable tourism and was willing to sacrifice financial rewards in conventional fields for the smaller budgets of emerging tourism organizations.

Tourism has evolved and grown since I entered the field. People now talk about the triple bottom line balancing environmental, social, and economic success; some add climate change to the mix. To successfully balance these complex matrices, everyone needs business skills. You cannot contribute to biodiversity conservation or cultural preservation if you run out of money in your first year of operations. This book will help you develop business skills in the context of principles of sustainable tourism.

You will also learn how major events like the 2008 Great Recession affected ecotourism and sustainable tourism. You might be surprised to hear there were many positive outcomes! The book's emphasis is on sustainable tourism in the United States and Canada. Differences exist in how ecotourism is viewed in other countries, and the fact that tourism development occurs against a backdrop of established economies and other forms of tourism not always found in emerging destinations poses different challenges.

The information shared in the book is reality-tested. While you will learn how the UNWTO's framework shapes sustainable tourism, you will also develop key competencies in critical thinking, innovation through unique combinations of common elements, financial analysis, strategic planning, relationship building, and marketing.

ORGANIZATION

You will likely find yourself working for an entrepreneur who wants you to act like a business owner. This means tackling problems and suggesting improvements from a broad perspective. The 13 chapters in this book are structured to give you an overview of business operations in sustainable tourism that will help you build this broad perspective. Chapter 1 offers an orientation to the sustainable tourism industry and why you should be incorporating sustainability criteria into your business. Chapters 2 through 4 help you assess new ideas against sustainable criteria, develop a strategic plan, and develop tourism products to increase your chances of success. You will also learn about the standards to which other tourism businesses aspire. Chapters 5 through 8 will teach

you about the most valuable skill in tourism: how to market and reach your customers, including how to work with social media, the travel trade, and other tourism partners. Chapters 9 through 12 teach you the nitty-gritty about making your ideas a reality. You will learn how to manage your financial resources, mitigate risk, prepare a business plan, ensure great customer service, and hire the right people for the job.

SPECIAL FEATURES

From start to finish, this book is designed to help you master the wide-ranging knowledge you'll need in order to prepare for a career in sustainable tourism. **Learning outcomes** and key points are summarized at the beginning of each chapter, serving as a framework that you build on as you read through the chapter. **Sidebars** throughout each chapter highlight businesses or destinations demonstrating good practices for sustainable tourism businesses. These sidebars offer an inspirational and informative view of how principles of sustainable tourism affect the daily practice of real businesses. Although many of the examples focus on North America, they are supplemented with examples from international destinations to provide global context for sustainable tourism in the United States and Canada.

Throughout the book, you will be periodically prompted to stop reading and do exercises called **ecochallenges**, which offer a chance to consider sustainable tourism concepts within the context of personal values and beliefs. These exercises vary in length and complexity; some offer a few questions that call for a short written reflection, while others challenge readers to search the Internet or talk to people in the sustainable tourism industry. All of them are carefully written and placed with the intent of providing a meaningful personalized learning experience for each user.

Each chapter closes with learning aids that check for and reinforce understanding. The **glossary** and **review questions** highlight key terminology and concepts from the chapter. A **video case study** points you to the web resource, where you may view a short video on a topic relevant to the chapter and answer reflection and discussion questions on your own or in a group.

Finally, a section called **Your Business Plan** guides you in applying the chapter's content to your own business plan. This section corresponds to a business-planning workbook in the web resource that you can use throughout a class term as a substantive class activity. As you are learning about marketing your business and managing finances, for example, you'll work your way through questions and forms in the business-planning workbook that allow you to flesh out what marketing and finances will look like for the business you envision. The chance to envision a new sustainable tourism business and research detailed requirements for product development, marketing, finances, operations, and risk management can build valuable business skills. Completing all of the business-planning workbook assignments will result in a finished business plan at the end of the term. A sample business plan is also provided in the web resource to help you envision a completed plan.

In addition to the video case studies and the business-planning workbook, the web resource accompanying this book also includes the following:

- A guide to creating a tourism career you love, which includes tips for identifying hidden opportunities and networking methods and increasing your chances of success

- A list of helpful web links for further learning about sustainable tourism

- Templates for business planning, such as cash flow forecasts and operating budgets

- Microsoft Word versions of the book's review questions, discussion questions on the video case studies, Your Business Plan sections, and glossary terms (with and without definitions) that you may download so you can complete assignments electronically.

When the book refers to online resource content, you'll see the icon. Together, this book and web resource provide an interactive path to success in the sustainable tourism business.

eBook
available at
HumanKinetics.com

ACKNOWLEDGMENTS

This book would not exist if not for the vision of Gayle Kassing. Her thoughtful assessment of the tourism industry and the needs of educators were the guiding light for the book's content. I would also like to acknowledge the contribution of Jackie Blakley. Her wise counsel during editing kept me moving forward and her suggestions improved the work's format and clarity. Thank you to Carol Kline and Miles Phillips for your thoughtful reviews of early drafts. Your feedback kept the book's focus on providing practical knowledge for the next generation of tourism leaders.

Finally, I would like to thank my husband, Colin, for his moral and practical support as I squeezed more time out of our lives to complete this project. He has given me the freedom to write and the chance to interact with the many tourism professionals who have helped shape ideas in this book.

HOW TO USE THIS BOOK AND WEB RESOURCE

This book and corresponding web resource at www.HumanKinetics.com/SustainableTourism work together to give instructors and students a flexible way to interact with and respond to the concepts taught.

The centerpiece of the web resource is the business-planning workbook, which lets students plan their own sustainable tourism business throughout the semester as they learn about business development and operations. For students who want to start a business after graduation, the business planning workbook and the other exercises in the book will help to develop a business plan. Those who have no specific plans to start a business can develop a concept for a fictional business to use in working through the workbook; consider modeling the fictional business after a real business you have experience with or that operates nearby. It may be helpful for students to work in teams as they develop a business plan. This allows for the division of labor and the pooling of knowledge. Download the Word document called Business Planning Workbook from the web resource and save it; then simply complete assignments in the workbook as they are discussed in the chapters and assigned by the instructor. A sample business plan is included in the web resource.

Creating a Career You Love is a guide to identifying how your personal interests and passions can be aligned with potential opportunities in the sustainable tourism business. Even if you do not think you will work in the tourism field, your instructor may ask you to read this document and complete the exercises to build job search skills you will need after graduation. As you work through this document, you will identify your career goals, begin to articulate what you want in a career, and take steps to research potential career paths and align your skills with businesses that need them.

Video case studies are presented in the web resource. These brief clips highlight issues and questions related to topics covered in the chapters; at the end of each chapter you'll be directed to watch a particular video and answer questions about it. The questions are in the book and in the web resource; they might be used for individual reflection or group discussion according to the instructor's preference.

Blank templates are included for some forms discussed in the book:

- Resource inventory
- Pricing worksheet
- Sales forecast spreadsheet
- Operating budget worksheet
- Cash flow worksheet

You may download these documents for use in business planning.

The web resource also provides the book's learning aids—glossary terms (with definitions to serve as study sheets, without definitions to serve as quizzes), review questions, video case study questions, Your Business Plan questions—in Word format. In this way, you may download and complete assignments and easily e-mail them to instructors or upload them into a learning management system. Of course, the completed exercises may also be printed out and turned in as hard copies.

A list of websites with free information on sustainable tourism is provided in the web resource to streamline your research as you probe issues raised in this book.

1

INTRODUCTION TO SUSTAINABLE TOURISM

|||||||||||||| LEARNING OUTCOMES |||||||||||||||

After reading this chapter, you will be able to do the following:

- Understand the need to make the tourism industry sustainable

- Describe the history of sustainable tourism

- Define sustainable tourism and related forms of tourism

- Summarize common characteristics of travelers interested in sustainability

- Explain several trends contributing to the growth of sustainable tourism

- Recognize the need for sustainable tourism operators to have business-plan skills

Tourism is a complex field that encompasses hotels, airlines, attractions, and natural areas, among other sectors. Because of its size, the tourism industry has environmental impacts. With good planning and policies, these impacts can be mitigated. To develop the skills to make tourism sustainable, you need to understand the relatively short history of sustainable tourism and the terms used by travel professionals so you have an understanding of problem solving.

Sustainability is benefitting from new research, some of which creates debate. In this chapter, you will learn about trends that are spurring growth in sustainable tourism and why there is still much for tourism professionals to learn. This chapter introduces business planning to help you acquire the skills for developing and implementing strategies in sustainable tourism.

WHY SHOULD TOURISM BE SUSTAINABLE?

Some people regard vacations or holidays as the one time every year they can act selfishly. Freed from the constraints of everyday life, they leave the lights on, stay up late, eat dessert with every meal, drink more than normal, and try new experiences in an attempt to learn more about themselves or at least to post a photo of a first-time experience on Facebook. Asking travelers to think about planetary health seems like a long shot.

Air travel creates substantial amounts of greenhouse gases.

But sustainable development cannot be overlooked when people travel. Tourism is one of the world's largest industries. The World Tourism Organization (UNWTO) attributes 235 million jobs, 5 percent of direct global GDP, and 30 percent of the world's export of services to international tourism (UNWTO 2012). And the industry can have a negative effect on the environment. For example, one of the biggest single contributors to climate change is aircraft emissions, a large component of most vacations. The United Nations estimates that air traffic contributes 2.5 percent of the production of carbon dioxide, one of the greenhouse gases (UNEP 2014).

With a large industry, there is potential for large contributions to sustainability. One medium-size hotel can save 72,000 gallons (272,000 L) of water annually just by asking guests to reuse towels (Rogers 2014). It seems the time for the tourism industry to adopt principles of sustainable development is here.

HISTORY OF SUSTAINABLE TOURISM

You might wonder where the impetus to "green" the tourism industry came from. Although people have been traveling for thousands of years, leisure travel for the average person is a relatively recent phenomenon. As table 1.1 shows, the United Nations only started its world tourism statistics in 1950. International arrivals in that year were 25 million; by 2012 they exceeded 1 billion (UNWTO 2013).

With international tourism arrivals breaking 1 billion and many more people traveling domestically, tourism is a large industry with significant social, economic, and environmental impacts. Some of those impacts, such as increasing understanding across cultures, are positive, but others, such as pollution or overuse of sensitive environments, harm the things travelers go to see or experience!

Since the 1970s, several global initiatives have had implications for the tourism industry. As shown in table 1.1, a World Conservation Strategy was issued in 1980. Shortly thereafter, the term *ecotourism* became popular. In 1987, many world leaders focused on the issues facing their countries, noting that many were the result of unplanned development. Their discussions resulted in the Brundtland Report, *Our Common Future*, and defined **sustainable development** as "development that meets the needs of the present without compromising the ability of future generations to meet their own needs" (WCED 1987). The Brundtland Report recognized that many of the problems facing government leaders result from interlocking crises. It also recognized

Table 1.1   Timeline of Sustainable Tourism

1950	UN World Tourism Organization statistics begin (25 million international tourists recorded).
1970	Sept. 27 declared as World Tourism Day.
1976	World Tourism Organization becomes an executing agency of the United Nations Development Programme.
1980	International Union for Conservation of Nature issues World Conservation Strategy.
1983	Héctor Ceballos-Lascuráin popularizes the term ecotourism.
1987	Brundtland Report, Our Common Future, issued by World Commission on Environment and Development, defines sustainable development.
1990	The International Ecotourism Society is founded.
1992	Earth Summit in Rio de Janeiro led to release of Agenda 21, the Rio Declaration on Environment and Development; sustainable development goal was agreed to by world nations.
1994	World Travel and Tourism Council launches voluntary Green Globe certification program.
2000	United Nation initiative results in establishment of Millennium Development Goals.
2002	International Year of Ecotourism is declared.
2003	UNWTO becomes the United Nation's specialized agency for tourism.
2003	First International Conference on Climate Change and Tourism held in Djerba, Tunisia.
2007	Coalition of 27 organizations come together under UN umbrella to develop Global Sustainable Tourism Council Criteria. Davos Declaration on sustainable tourism actions to combat climate change comes from second International Conference on Climate Change and Tourism.
2011	United Nations releases Towards a Green Economy: Pathways to Sustainable Development and Poverty Eradication (known as the Green Economy Report).
2012	GSTC launches sustainable tourism criteria for destinations.

that solutions require input from all parts of society.

Building on the work of the Brundtland Report was the United Nations Conference on Environment and Development held in 1992 in Rio de Janeiro. Called the Earth Summit, it brought 172 governments and 2,400 nongovernment representatives together to find ways to change global attitudes toward development.

Coming out of the summit were the following documents:

- **Rio Declaration on Environment and Development**, which recognized that people are at the center of concerns for sustainable development. It acknowledges that states have the sovereign right to exploit their own resources but suggests that it must be done in a way that meets the needs of current and future generations.
- **Agenda 21** is a nonbinding, voluntary plan for sustainable development. Canada and the United States are signatories to Agenda 21, but opposition to the plan has

been increasing in recent years, especially among U.S. conservative political organizations. The Republican National Committee adopted a resolution opposing Agenda 21. Glenn Beck, media personality and political commentator, and Harriet Parke wrote a book, *Agenda 21*, which compares Agenda 21 principles to George Orwell's prophecies in *1984*.

- The **Statement of Forest Principles** was the first global consensus on forests and outlined a series of principles for sustainable forest use.
- The **United Nations Framework Convention on Climate Change** was agreed to by 130 countries and included new resources for meeting convention goals, more technology transfer to developing countries, and an institutional mechanism to manage climate change.
- The **United Nations Convention on Biological Diversity** was an attempt to develop a global strategy for conserving biological

diversity. It was not signed by the United States over fears that it would threaten control over developed nation's conservation dollars (Meakin 1992).

In 2000, global leaders built on Agenda 21 guidance for sustainable development by establishing Millennium Development Goals. All United Nations member states agreed to these goals, with the goal of achieving them in 2015:

- Eradicating extreme poverty and hunger
- Achieving universal primary education
- Promoting gender equality and empowering women
- Reducing child mortality rates
- Improving maternal health
- Combating HIV/AIDS, malaria, and other diseases
- Ensuring environmental sustainability
- Developing a global partnership for development

(UNWTO 2012)

By 2014, many targets had been met to reduce poverty, improve access to drinking water, and improve lives of slum dwellers. Targets such as access to technologies, debt relief, and more participation by women in politics show progress, while malaria, tuberculosis, and access to HIV treatment will surpass targets (United Nations 2014). Work is under way to develop a set of new goals to be agreed to by world leaders in 2015 (United Nations 2014).

Although some goals may not seem directly related to tourism (for example, few travelers take a trip with the goal of ending world hunger), the way in which tourism is developed can have a significant impact on host communities. For example, in Honduras, the Mayan ruins at Copán are a UNESCO World Heritage Site and received over 150,000 tourists in 2006, but only 5 percent of people in Honduras were working in tourism. With the help of nongovernmental organizations and the UNWTO Sustainable Tourism – Eliminating Poverty Initiative, work was undertaken from 2008 to 2011 to establish links between small businesses, mainly run by women, and larger businesses like the Hotel Marina Copán. Over 300 people benefitted from the creation of jobs and reduced economic leakages, thus advancing progress on the Millennium Development Goals through tourism (UNWTO 2012).

In a parallel movement to the United Nations' work around sustainable development was the creation of **ecotourism**, ecologically sustainable tourism that fosters environmental and cultural understanding, appreciation, and conservation. The International Ecotourism Society was founded in 1990 with the goal of growing ecotourism through membership services, education and training, and partnerships. Proponents of ecotourism felt that the benefits of preserving environments for tourism could compete with more consumptive uses of resources. For example, after the world's largest shark sanctuary was established in the central Pacific by the Marshall Islands, researchers found that "a single shark brings in US$1.9 million to the tourist economy over its lifetime versus U.S.$108 it is worth if caught once and brought ashore." They also estimate that shark ecotourism brings in U.S.$18 million annually to the economy (or 8 percent of national GDP) (Polcer and Buchl Perez 2012, p. 17). The United Nations declared 2002 the International Year of Ecotourism.

The United Nations made the World Tourism Organization its specialized agency for tourism in 2003, and the first international conference on climate change and tourism was held the same year. This was part of several global initiatives to apply sustainable development principles throughout the tourism industry, principles such as the following (Lane 2013):

- Holistic, cross-sectoral planning and strategy making
- The importance of preserving essential ecological processes
- The need to protect both human heritage and biodiversity
- The requirement that development be carried out so that it does not deplete resources for future generations

One of the most significant initiatives was the creation of the Global Sustainable Tourism Council (GSTC) and the development of GSTC Criteria. The GSTC was formed in 2008 when a group of more than 50 industry leaders and UN representatives came together to create a global, multistakeholder organization focused on promoting sustainable tourism (GSTC 2014). The main focus of the GSTC has been the development of GSTC Criteria to set standards for industry members and provide specific actions for tourism organizations to turn global goals into action.

After three years of public consultation, GSTC released its Criteria for Hotels and Tour Operators in 2012 and entered the second phase of public consultation on GSTC for Destinations (GSTC 2013). The complete standards can be found in on the GSTC website.

WHAT DO WE CALL IT?

One of the biggest debates in the tourism industry in recent history has revolved around what to call tourism that incorporates sustainability principles and who is part of it. One of the benefits to come from the development of the Global Sustainable Tourism Council Criteria is the creation of common language among tourism professionals. By describing sustainability with specific criteria for tour operators, hotels, and destination managers, everyone has a better idea of what constitutes best practices for this industry. Regardless of whether they describe their business as adventure travel, accommodation, ecotourism, educational tourism, or geotourism, tourism professionals can use these standards.

Some of the terms related to sustainable principles are described in table 1.2. If you look at the definitions, you will see notable differences; for example, nature-based tourism is distinguished by the setting and does not focus on the ethics that are inherent in responsible tourism. Geotourism broadens the principles of sustainability to include the sense of place. Community-based tourism places more emphasis on the involvement of people from rural or economically marginalized areas and less on the type of product.

Many of these differences revolve around scope, but at the heart of these definitions are several common themes:

- Minimizing the negative environmental and social impacts of travel
- Maximizing the economic impacts for host communities
- Providing a meaningful experience for the traveler with educational opportunities or chances to engage with local people
- Involving local communities in the planning of tourism

These themes are consistent with the principles of sustainable tourism described earlier. So it can be assumed that each contributes to a more sustainable tourism industry.

Sustainable tourism is developed and operated in a way that meets the current needs of travelers and host communities without compromising the requirements of future generations. This book includes the research done for the related fields of ecotourism, nature-based tourism, adventure travel, community-based tourism, responsible tourism, and others as each builds toward sustainability. The broader scope will give you a better understanding of the travelers seeking these experiences, the levels of visitor satisfaction, and other aspects of tourism development and operation.

Table 1.2 Tourism Definitions

Term	Definition
Adventure travel	A form of nature-based tourism that incorporates some risk, higher levels of physical exertion, and often the need for specialized skill
Community-based tourism	Tourism in which local residents (often rural, poor, and economically marginalized) invite residents to visit their communities with the provision of overnight accommodation
Ecotourism	Ecologically sustainable tourism that fosters environmental and cultural understanding, appreciation, and conservation
Geotourism	Tourism that sustains or enhances the geographical character of place: its environment, culture, aesthetics, and heritage and the well-being of its residents
Nature tourism (or nature-based tourism)	A broad term that includes a range of tourism experiences, including adventure tourism and ecotourism, and aspects of cultural and rural tourism, and is distinguished by its natural setting
Responsible tourism	Tourism focused on making places better for people to live and better places to visit
Sustainable tourism	Tourism that takes full account of its current and future economic, social, and environmental impacts, addressing the needs of visitors, the industry, the environment, and host communities

Table 1.3   Tourism Organizations Potentially Applying Principles of Sustainable Tourism

Category of tourism product	Subcategories	Examples
Tour packages	Inbound Outbound Culture-based Nature-based Adventure-based Historical Educational Experiential	Europeans biking through Napa Valley New Yorkers on safari in Africa Tour of Inuit community Bird-watching walk Trekking in Nepal Tour of Gettysburg Tour of reclaimed logging sites Expedition to North Pole
Festivals	Wildlife	Festival celebrating migration of Sandhill cranes
Accommodations	Hotels Lodges Bed and breakfasts Backcountry cabins Tented camps	Hotel and convention center Backcountry lodge with hiking and skiing B&B near bird-watching hotspots Hut-to-hut cross-country skiing Tented river camp offering canoe trips
Guiding services	Interpretative talks Step-on services Safety orientation Dramatic presentations	Evening horticultural talk Cultural interpretation for tour bus passengers Bear safety courses Re-create historical characters at historic sites
Attractions	Zoos and aquariums Museums Historic sites and parks	Internationally accredited zoo Science center Cave dwellings at Mesa Verde
Transportation	Automotive rentals Airlines Boats Cruises	Van rentals for tour operators Flights for domestic and international tourists Whale-watching tour Expedition cruise to Antarctica
Government	Parks and tourism Fish and wildlife Economic development Destination marketing	Visitor management at Arches National Park Determining catch limits for fishermen in Florida Building tourism infrastructure in Montana Creating marketing materials for Las Vegas
Food services	Restaurants Catering Banquets	Organic meals with local products Picnic lunches for day hikers Conference gala for engineering association

If you are considering a career in sustainable tourism, you may wonder how these definitions and principles translate to job postings. As you can see in table 1.3, sustainable tourism covers a range of businesses and government organizations. To be successful, these organizations require employees who are able to balance profit and environmental and social goals.

NEED FOR SUSTAINABLE TOURISM

The field of sustainable tourism will become more complex. While there is a consensus on the need to balance a triple bottom line of economic, social, and environmental factors, it is possible we may need to factor in climate change. At the UNWTO Davos Conference on Tourism and Climate Change in 2007, it was recognized that tourism has an important role in combatting climate change and it was recommended that adoption of sustainable tourism policies was urgent. The UNWTO is demonstrating leadership by compensating for the greenhouse gas emissions from its own operations (UNWTO 2009).

The need for action will grow as travelers become aware of the environmental impact of air transport. Air travel produces 19 times the greenhouse gas emissions of trains and 190 times more than ships. One return trip by air from Florida to the United Kingdom produces the greenhouse gas emission equivalent to an average year of driving (McCarthy, Woolf and Harrison 2005). One study found that the majority of carbon dioxide emissions from long-haul travel comes from the air travel not the ground activities (Strasdas 2012).

According to the Intergovernmental Panel on Climate Change (IPCC), aviation accounts for approximately 2 percent of human-generated global carbon dioxide emission, the most significant greenhouse gas. IPCC expects aircraft emissions to increase to 3 percent of global carbon dioxide emissions by 2050, even with technology improvements in the airline industry (USGAO 2009).

Although steps have been taken to reduce environmental impacts, they may not be enough. Modern aircraft are about 70 percent more fuel efficient per passenger than they were 40 years ago, and commercial aviation uses less energy to transport a single passenger a single mile, a measure of energy intensity. The experts consulted by IPCC believe that "future technological and operational improvements are likely to help reduce emissions from commercial aircraft, but likely not enough to fully offset estimated market growth" (USGAO 2009, p. 22).

So what can we do as tourists, knowing that our love of travel is contributing to climate change?

Some would suggest we stay home, saving our air travel for infrequent, long visits with family. Others propose that tourists get involved in reducing emissions by traveling via mass transportation or choosing to arrive by train instead of by jet.

For those who continue to fly, organizations have sprung up to sell carbon offsets. A **carbon offset** is the reduction of carbon emissions by the creation of emission reductions elsewhere; the idea being that if you cannot stop flying, you can support organizations that reduce greenhouse gases by planting trees or investing in alternative-energy technology.

A quick scan of the Internet will show that several organizations sell carbon offsets by planting or protecting forests in tropical countries. One innovative Canadian farmer has found a way to save the family farm by generating carbon offsets. Brad and Rebecca Rabiey of The Carbon Farmer (see Green Stay Option in this chapter) have partnered with one of the hotels in the Fairmont chain to offer travelers a greener stay.

WHO ARE THE TOURISTS?

Few, if any, travelers want to harm the environment. In fact, people are looking for more lifestyle products that have fewer environmental impacts

Travelers interested in sustainability are often active on their vacations.

Green Stay Option

"Would you like our Green Stay option?" queried the clerk at the Fairmont Hotel Macdonald. Because I'm an ecotourism specialist, I'm all for green initiatives, but some are just greenwashing. I want something that actually helps the environment, and this program fits the bill. Edmonton's Hotel MacDonald is part of the Fairmont family; the World Travel and Tourism Council and the World Tourism Organization have recognized its green partnership program.

The Green Stay program includes paperless checkout, less-frequent linen changes, free parking for hybrid vehicles, and a tree planted and cared for in your name by The Carbon Farmer, an Alberta-based carbon offset provider.

Mandy Quon, Hotel Macdonald sales manager, explained further, "The trees are planted near Manning, Alberta, by Brad Rabiey. This is a third-generation farmer who is giving back to the environment by replanting trees."

I found it ironic that a farmer would replant land his grandparents worked hard to clear, but there is a long-term strategy behind The Carbon Farmer.

Brad, a biologist, and his wife, Rebecca, a social worker, believe that sustainability is an environmental and societal challenge, so they took their professional training back to the family farm in 2007 and set to work on a new kind of crop.

Brad and Rebecca plant trees instead of wheat or barley. The carbon absorbed by the trees is sold as offset credits to businesses and people wanting to reduce their carbon footprint.

The Fairmont Hotel Macdonald became a partner in 2009 after Mandy heard about the program and saw a fit with the Fairmont's commitment to sustainability. For each hotel guest choosing the Green Stay option, one tree is planted; for every three trees planted, one metric ton of carbon emissions is offset.

This purchase contributes to the planet's sustainability and that of an Alberta farm. "We certainly see The Carbon Farmer and our trees as enhancing the sustainability of our farm. The goal is ensuring our third-generation farm is well-positioned for the generations to come," Brad says.

Some people have criticized Brad and Rebecca's decision to replant cleared land. "But when people learn that we are focusing on areas of key habitat potential or marginal farm land, we turn most of the skeptics into supporters," Brad explains, "We hope to partner with other landowners very soon to plant trees on their land and help ensure they can take advantage of this market opportunity and at the same time benefit the environment. This is indeed a business model that can be used by other farmers."

So if you want to reduce the negative impact on the environment when you travel, look for a hotel with a carbon-offsetting program like the Fairmont Hotel Macdonald's. Or do it yourself by buying credits from a carbon offsetter.

Courtesy of the *Red Deer Advocate*.

---

or that support local economies. Therefore, it would be reasonable to assume that people want to take that interest in sustainability on vacation, but perhaps that is not the case.

Which travelers are participating in sustainable tourism? In some of the earliest studies of ecotourism, research indicated that experienced ecotravelers were likely to be middle aged or older, college educated, and traveling with a spouse (HLA and ARA 1994). Several studies showed that people searching for this type of travel had higher incomes (Eagles and Cascagnette 1995; Blarney and Hatch 1998).

Since then, we have seen the interest in sustainable tourism broaden. The 2012 National Travel and Tourism Strategy found that "nature-based, culture-based, heritage and outdoor adventure travel represent a significant segment" of Americans traveling abroad (Task Force on Travel and Competitiveness 2012, pp. 6-7).

These travelers searching for the unusual and the authentic can be a lucrative market for tourism organizations. Interestingly, international travelers to Costa Rica, a predominantly ecotourism destination, spend more on a trip (U.S.$944) versus those spending time in France (U.S.$666), a more conventional, mass-market tourist destination (Blanke and Chiasa 2011).

According to a 2012 survey by TripAdvisor, a travel website with more than 60 million unique

Fun in the Sun or a Clear Conscience?

How important is reducing climate change to you? Would you be willing to stay home or alter your plans because of greenhouse gas emissions? Calculating your carbon footprint brings the sustainable tourism concept alive. If you fly, realize that you are part of the problem and why the need for sustainable tourism is growing. Assessing your own carbon footprint will also help you understand the moral values that influence travel and the difficulties in changing traveler behaviors.

Do you know how much carbon your next vacation will generate? Calculate your estimated emissions on a CO_2 calculator like the ones listed here.

- Terrapass: www.terrapass.com/carbon-footprint-calculator-2
- The Carbon Farmer: www.thecarbonfarmer.ca/carbon-calculator/#

Once you know your estimated emissions, ask yourself the following questions:

- Do you want to reduce the amount of carbon emissions?

- If you do, are you willing to forgo the trip? Can you switch your method of transport?
- If you are not willing or able to reduce your carbon emissions, would you buy carbon offsets? How much would you be willing to pay? Would you require certification of a program before you would buy carbon offsets?

There is no right answer to these questions, but answering them will give you insight into how difficult it is to make travelers aware of environmental issues and to alter behaviors, especially when your vacation time may be regarded as time to shuck normal obligations and indulge in mindless behavior. You might also realize why there is a difference between the amount of concern about environmental issues travelers report and the green behaviors they actually display on vacation. Watch the video on glacier calving in the web resource to see a situation in which tourists wondered whether they had seen the effects of climate change and the questions it raised.

monthly visitors, the green travel trend is gaining momentum. Of their members, 71 percent indicated they plan to make more eco-friendly choices in the next 12 months, compared to 65 percent who did so in the past 12 months (TripAdvisor 2012).

Eco-conscious travelers have also shown themselves to travel more than the average consumer. With more than 75 percent taking at least two vacations away from home during the last year and another 22 percent taking five to eight vacations a year, they far exceed the national average (Roth 2010).

But it is not just the leisure traveler who is interested in sustainable travel. A 2008 survey found that 95 percent of business travelers think that lodging providers should undertake green initiatives and 90 percent take their concern on the road, saying they believe they are "some shade of green when staying at a lodging facility" (Deloitte Development 2008 p. 4).

It is clear that many tourism organizations will find their customers interested in greener travel products and the environmental practices of tourism suppliers. Consumers who have become accus-

tomed to recycling, reducing and reusing at home may bring these habits with them when they travel.

TRENDS IN SUSTAINABLE TOURISM

Several trends appear to be creating more demand for sustainable travel products and greater incentives for tourism organizations to adopt principles of sustainable tourism. These include the following:

Greater Interest in Experiential Tourism

In their popular book *The Experience Economy*, Joseph Pine and James Gilmore explained that experience is the missing link between a company and its customers. They believe that staging experiences lets businesses make a memorable impression on their clients and secures long-term loyalty. Introduced by Pine and Gilmore in 1999, the concept of experiences has spread to tourism and many companies now offer experiential tourism.

With easy access to information, travelers have a greater awareness of social and environmental issues and many are searching for authentic experiences, wishing to be "involved as participants, not spectators, and seek a variety of optional experiences" (Dwyer 2008, p 39).

A recent Internet search of the term *experiential* tours yielded more than 2 million results, proof that the tourism industry has embraced the concept, and it appears this interest will continue. As people have more interest in travel and the money to travel, they are looking for more "new and interesting experiences through an ever-broadening array of activities" (Dwyer 2008, p. 34).

Often this interest in experiences requires tourism organizations to develop products that have a greater connection to local communities or immersion in nature environments. These items are easier to deliver using sustainable tourism criteria.

Efforts to Battle Nature Deficit Disorder

Our world is increasingly urbanized. By 2020, more than 60 percent of people will live in cities (Dywer 2008). Already we are seeing a great disconnect from nature as more people live in cities than in rural areas. Richard Louv coined the term **nature deficit disorder** to describe the reduced time people spend outdoors and the associated behavior and health problems, and discovered that children are choosing to play indoors because "that's where the electrical outlets are" (Louv 2006, p. 10).

With some researchers estimating that children spend the equivalent of a full-time job watching television, texting, or playing video games, there are concerns that children are headed for ill health as their physical activity level and time outdoors decrease (Shapley 2012).

One of my video projects tackled the issue of nature deficit disorder by combining dance and the outdoors to encourage young people to find time for nature. You can see this video, "Naturescapes," by visiting my YouTube channel at www.youtube.com/reinventure.

Fortunately, with the creation of several campaigns and organizations such as Children & Nature Network and No Child Left Inside, there is a national back-to-nature movement for children and it seems to be working. A 2011 survey by the Children & Nature Network shows "the number

Children need to be introduced to outdoor adventure to create the next generation of nature-loving travelers.

of children and youth getting outdoors in nature through the efforts of the Network members has tripled in two years" (Children and Nature Network, 2012, p. 1).

These efforts will create more potential customers for nature-based travel. And given the educational component of many of these programs, it is likely these future travelers will be thinking about the environmental impact of their travels.

Popularity of Nature-Based Travel

It is not just children who are increasingly interested in nature. Outdoor activities such as hiking, camping, wildlife watching, and snorkeling are trending upward (Center for Responsible Travel 2013).

The U.S. Department of Commerce tracks U.S. residents' international travel patterns and in 2011, over half of the 22 million people traveling for leisure participated in nature, culture, and heritage activities such as visiting historical sites and national parks and engaging in water sports, camping, and hiking (U.S. Department of Commerce 2012).

The National Survey of Fishing, Hunting, and Wildlife-Associated Recreation, undertaken every five years, shows a dramatic increase in wildlife-related outdoor recreation from 2006 to 2011 (U.S. Fish & Wildlife Service 2012). This growth will put more pressure on natural areas and require the creation of more sustainable tourism policies and practices.

Generational Changes

SNV Netherlands Development Organisation (2009) looked at the environmental attitudes across different generations of travelers. Baby Boomers, people born between 1946 and 1964, are reaching retirement age and finding more time for travel. They prize travel and are increasingly aware of environmental issues. Gen-Xers, people born between 1961 and 1981, are environmentally conscious and want to influence the world with their spending habits. The children of Baby Boomers, Gen-Y or Millennials, are knowledgeable and passionate about the environment.

Interestingly, a study on green actions at hotels showed that Baby Boomers act greener than younger segments. Millennials were least likely to turn off lights or conserve water. But

Millennials were the most likely to pay more for green accommodation, and they were more likely to purchase carbon offsets, research environmentally friendly accommodation, and participate in volunteer or eco-travel (Deloitte Development 2008).

Fortunately, each generation is influencing the other with an increasing concern for the environment. Tourism organizations may improve sales by promoting their sustainability practices. Conversely, organizations that are seen to be harmful to the environment may suffer backlash.

These trends along with world events will shape the future of sustainable tourism. Your success will depend on your ability to meet changing consumer expectations with sustainable products.

MEETING THE CHALLENGE

It is exciting to be part of a tourism movement that is relatively young. To achieve the goals that the UNWTO has set out will require the contribution of people from all areas of the tourism industry. You will contribute more if you have developed practical skills for sustainable tourism businesses.

One way to learn and gain these skills is to create a **business plan**, a document that explains in detail how a business will achieve its goals. Even though you may not own a business, you might be asked to act like an entrepreneur by your employer. If you work in the nonprofit world or for a government agency, you will need to sell ideas to a donor or funding agency. The information gathered and analyzed in a business plan can be used on a smaller scale to justify new programs or products. So learning to create a business plan will be a useful exercise regardless of your career goals.

If you are undertaking a business plan as part of your coursework, you should refer first to chapter 13 for an overview of the business-planning process. As you work through the book, you will find information in each chapter to help you complete your plan. You will also find a sample business plan, business plan worksheets, and spreadsheets for forecasting and calculating prices.

SUMMARY

The concept of sustainability is prominent in the news; every day there is a story that touches on the issues of climate change, loss of traditions, increased pollution, or habitat destruction, among others. As one of the largest industries in the world, tourism cannot stand apart from efforts to incorporate sustainable principles into all facets of development and operation. As consumers of travel products and services, tourists must participate in the change. Some travelers actively seek companies demonstrating good sustainable practices; others may assume sustainability is the responsibility of business. As a future employee in this field, you need the skills to lead and manage sustainability initiatives in your organization. Reality-tested strategies will be critical in your success, so take the time to work on the ecochallenges in the book and, if appropriate, build a business plan for a sustainable tourism business.

GLOSSARY

adventure travel—A form of nature-based tourism that incorporates some risk, higher levels of physical exertion, and often the need for specialized skill.

carbon offsets—The reduction of carbon emissions by the creation of emission reductions elsewhere.

community-based tourism—Tourism in which local residents (often rural, poor, and economically marginalized) invite tourists to visit their communities with the provision of overnight accommodation.

business plan—A document that explains in detail how a business will achieve its goals.

ecotourism—Ecologically sustainable tourism that fosters environmental and cultural understanding, appreciation, and conservation.

geotourism—Tourism that sustains or enhances the geographical character of a place: its environment, culture, aesthetics, and heritage and the well-being of its residents.

nature deficit disorder—The reduced time people spend outdoors and the associated behavior and health problems.

nature tourism—A broad term that includes a range of tourism experiences, including adventure tourism, ecotourism, and aspects of cultural and rural tourism, that is distinguished by its natural setting.

responsible tourism—Tourism that makes places better for people to live and better places to visit.

sustainable development—Development that meets the needs of the present without compromising the ability of future generations to meet their own needs.

sustainable tourism—Tourism that takes full account of its current and future economic, social, and environmental impacts, addressing the needs of visitors, the industry, the environment, and host communities.

REVIEW QUESTIONS

1. Describe three reasons tourism should be sustainable.
2. List the Millennium Development Goals. Choose one goal and give an example of how sustainable tourism practices might be used to help achieve it.
3. Which travelers are most likely to use sustainable tourism practices? Why?

4. What barriers prevent organizations from using sustainable tourism practices? What barriers exist for travelers wanting to reduce their impact while on the road?

||||||||||||||||||||||| VIDEO CASE STUDY ||||||||||||||||||||

Visit the web resource to view the video "Glacier Calving." After watching the video, answer the following questions:

1. Do you think the glacier calving seen in the video is evidence of climate change? Why or why not?

2. Captain Fred Rodolf of Lu-Lu Belle Glacier Wildlife Cruises did not feel the unusually high volume of ice calving from the glaciers was a result of climate change. What was his argument for this?

3. What role do tourism business owners and guides have in identifying the effects of climate change? In educating tourists about the issues of climate change?

4. What effect do you think seeing this unusual glacier calving had on tourists on the Lu-Lu Belle? Do you think it would influence their behaviors after the cruise if they were concerned about climate change? Explain the reasons for your answer.

|||||||||||||||||||||||||| REFERENCES |||||||||||||||||||||||

Blanke, J., and T. Chiasa. 2011. The travel and tourism competitiveness report 2011: Beyond the downturn. www.weforum.org/issues/travel-and-tourism-competitiveness/index.html.

Center for Responsible Travel. 2013. The case for responsible travel: trends and statistics. Washington, D.C.

Children & Nature Network. 2012. Grassroots Leadership Survey: Findings of the 2011 Questionnaire http://www.childrenandnature.org/downloads/2011Grassroots_Survey-Summary.pdf.

Deloitte Development. 2008. The staying power of sustainability: Balancing opportunity and risk in the hospitality industry. http://www.deloitte.com/assets/dcom-unitedstates/local%20assets/documents/us_cb_sustainability_190608(1).pdf.

Dwyer, L. 2008. Megatrends underpinning tourist to 2020: Analysis of key drivers for change. CRC for Sustainable Tourism Pty Ltd. http://www.sustainabletourismonline.com/awms/Upload/Resource/bookshop/80046%20Dwyer_TourismTrends2020%20WEB.pdf.

Eagles, P.F.J., and J.W. Cascagnette. 1995. Canadian ecotourists: Who are they? Tourism Recreation Research 20(1): 22-28.

Ecotourism Australia. 2014. www.ecotourism.org.au.

Global Sustainable Tourism Council website http://www.gstcouncil.org/about/gstc-overview/our-history.html accessed February 16, 2015.

Global Sustainable Tourism Council. 2013. Global Sustainable Tourism Council Criteria and Suggested Performance Indicators for Destinations. Version 1, 10 December 2013. http://www.gstcouncil.org/images/Dest-_CRITERIA_and_INDICATORS_6-9-14.pdf.

Global Sustainable Tourism Council. 2012. Global Sustainable Tourism Council Criteria and Suggested Performance Indicators for Hotels and Tour Operators. Version 2, 23 February 2012. http://www.gstcouncil.org/images/pdf/HTO-CRITERIA_and_INDICATORS_6-9-14.pdf.

HLA Consultants, and ARA Consulting Group. 1994. Ecotourism – Nature, Adventure, Culture: Alberta and British Columbia Market Demand Assessment Prepared for Canadian Heritage, Industry Canada, British Columbia Ministry of Small Business, Tourism and Culture, Alberta Economic Development and Tourism, and the Outdoor Recreation Council of British Columbia.

Lane, B. 2013. Sustainable development and sustainable tourism: Business, the community and the environment. https://www.google.com/url?sa=t&rct=j&q=&esrc=s&source=web&cd=2&cad=rja&uact=8&ved=0CCYQFjAB&url=https%3A%2F%2Fwww.ecu.edu%2Fcs-acad%2Fsustainabletourism%2Fupload%2FLaneLecture10_02_08.doc&ei=3wD-VPiPE8apNq-Fg-gK&usg=AFQjCNFW5WsSdlpWlu2b1SShcDp9wDexrA&bvm=bv.87611401,d.eXY.

Louv, R. 2006. *Last child in the woods*. Algonquin Books of Chapel Hill. Chapel Hill, North Carolina.

McCarthy, M., M. Woolf, and M. Harrison, M. 2005. Revealed: The real cost of air travel. *The Independent*, May 28. www.independent.co.uk/environment/revealed-the-real--cost-of-air-travel-492356.html.

Meakin, S. 1992. The Rio Earth Summit: Summary of the United Nations Conference on Environment and Development. Science and Technology Division. Government of Canada. November. http://publications.gc.ca/collections/Collection-R/LoPBdP/BP/bp317-e.htm.

Pine, J.B., and J.H. Gilmore. 2011. *The experience economy*. Harvard Business Press, Boston, Massachusetts.

Polcer, S., and A. Buchl Perez. 2012. Fin-win situation. *Hemispheres Magazine*, January 2012. Brooklyn, New York. The market for responsible tourism products. p. 17.

Rogers, R. 2014. Reusing hotel towels: Nitty-gritty. *Stanford Magazine*. https://alumni.stanford.edu/get/page/magazine/article/?article_id=29072.

Roth, T. 2010. CMIGreen Traveler Study Report 2010. Vol. 1. San Francisco: CMIGreen Community Marketing. www.greenlodgingnews.com/downloads/cmigreentraveler2010v1.pdf.

Shapley D. 2012. Kids Spend nearly 55 hours a week watching TV, texting, playing video games. The Daily Green, Jan. 20. www.thedailygreen.com/environmental-news/latest/kids-television-47102701?click=main_sr.

Strasdas, W. 2012. Ecotourism's carbon footprint: The case of Namibia. Presented at the Ecotourism and Sustainable Tourism Conference, Sept. 19.

Task Force on Travel and Competitiveness. 2012. National Travel and Tourism Strategy, Department of Commerce and Department of Interior. Washington, DC, pp. 6-7.

TripAdvisor. 2012. TripAdvisor survey reveals travelers growing greener. April 19. www.multivu.com/mnr/49260-tripadvisor-eco-friendly-travel-survey-voluntourism-go-green.

United Nations Environmental Programme. 2014. Environmental impacts of tourism: global level. www.unep.org/resourceefficiency/Business/SectoralActivities/Tourism/TheTourismandEnvironmentProgramme/FactsandFiguresaboutTourism/ImpactsofTourism/EnvironmentalImpacts/EnvironmentalImpactsofTourism-GlobalLevel/tabid/78777/Default.aspx.

United Nations. 2014. The millennium development goals report. www.un.org/millenniumgoals/pdf/MDGReport2014_PR_Global_English.pdf.

United States Government Accountability Office. 2009. Aviation and climate change. June. www.gao.gov/new.items/d09554.pdf.

U.S. Fish & Wildlife Service. 2012. 2011 national survey of fishing, hunting, and wildlife-associated recreation. December. https://www.census.gov/prod/2012pubs/fhw11-nat.pdf.

U.S. Department of Commerce. 2012. Profile of U.S. resident travelers visiting overseas destinations: 2011 outbound. http://travel.trade.gov/outreachpages/download_data_table/2011_Outbound_Profile.pdf.

World Commission on Environment and Development. 1987. *Our common future*. Oxford: Oxford University Press. p. 27.

World Tourism Organization (UNWTO). 2009. From Davos to Copenhagen and beyond: Advancing tourism's response to climate change. http://sdt.unwto.org/sites/all/files/docpdf/fromdavostocopenhagenbeyondunwtopaperelectronicversion.pdf.

World Tourism Organization (UNWTO). 2012. Annual report. http://dtxtq4w60xqpw.cloudfront.net/sites/all/files/pdf/annual_report_2011.pdf.

World Tourism Organization (UNWTO). 2013. International tourism to continue robust growth in 2013. Jan. 28. http://media.unwto.org/en/press-release/2013-01-28/international-tourism-continue-robust-growth-2013.

World Tourism Organization (UNWTO) and European Travel Commission. 2011. Handbook on Tourism Product Development, Madrid, Spain. p. 11.

STRATEGIC PLANNING FOR A SUSTAINABLE TOURISM BUSINESS

| LEARNING OUTCOMES |

After reading this chapter, you will be able to do the following:

- Understand why strategic planning is essential for success

- Complete the main steps of a strategic plan

- Distinguish feasibility from viability

- Explain why it is important to involve host communities in planning

- Comprehend the relationship between business planning and strategic plans

As a future business owner or tourism professional, you must plan if you are to survive. Some of your planning will be short term, for example, determining how many sandwiches are needed for tomorrow's canoe trip. If you want a government grant or need a bank loan, you must look further ahead. Your banker will want your **business plan**, a description of your business, its goals, and the way you will reach your targets.

But before you do any of that, you need to think about why your business exists. The first planning you do should be the **strategic plan**, where you look at your organization's long-term focus and goals, and define your strategies to reach them. Strategic planning is one of the key roles of senior managers and board members. In a strategic plan, you take the opportunity to step back from daily

activities and ponder your values and define your core business.

Most tourism professionals quickly realize this is an industry reliant on effective marketing. Well, good marketing depends on good planning. If a person lays the groundwork with a well-thought-out strategic plan and an annual business plan, the marketing will be more effective and the business will thrive. Failing to plan might mean unexpected situations from which a business cannot recover. Ignore it at your peril!

A person may think a small or medium-size tourism organization does not need strategic planning or that the process is a waste of time. I have heard people say, "My business is too small for strategic planning" or "This is just a bunch of theoretical planning with no real use." It is understandable that the process intimidates people, so this chapter explains the benefits of strategic planning and a practical way to approach the process. You will learn how to develop a strategic plan that outlines realistic options for growth. And if you go on to work in an existing business that has never undergone strategic planning, you will see how creating a strategic plan and reviewing it regularly can help your business identify where it is succeeding, new opportunities for growth, and ways to overcome barriers that may be holding you back.

WHAT IS A STRATEGIC PLAN?

A strategic plan is usually created when an organization is started and is updated every three to five years. Tourism development works best if a strategic plan is completed for a community or region and an entrepreneur creates his or her own strategic plan in the context of the community's strategic plan. By building the strategic plan with an eye to the tourism for a larger area, a critical mass of tourist attractors can be created. If a strategic plan is created at the community level, the participation of a cross section of stakeholders can help identify the following:

- Possible negative impacts
- Mitigation strategies
- New sustainable tourism opportunities
- Branding opportunities
- Related business opportunities
- Ways to build community support

The planning process can be an excellent way to involve your community in developing sustainable tourism. By asking people for their input, you can identify a broad range of opportunities not just for yourself but for other entrepreneurs as well. For example, if you develop a tour company that leads natural history hikes into remote areas, it could create opportunities for local artisans to make and sell crafts. If you are building an eco-lodge, you could purchase your supplies locally. This may encourage local farmers to grow additional or special crops to supply your needs. You can create employment opportunities for people skilled in interpretation or knowledgeable in local history, culture, and ecology. A group of tour companies can create opportunities for service companies that can offer guide training, booking services, and website development.

People love to hear good-news stories or accounts of community partnerships, so talk about your tourism ideas and the planning process. Don't worry that you may generate competition by discussing your business plans. Having similar tour operators in your area can strengthen your position by providing greater choice for tourists and the capacity to handle additional clients. If you can also market together, your marketing budget will go further. If you look at shopping centers, this is the principle under which they work. One store on its own will not attract as many customers as a group of stores. It becomes even more powerful when a common theme is maintained.

This premise also applies to sustainable tourism products. For example, communities in central and southern Alberta, Canada, lived in the tourism shadow of Banff and Jasper National Parks for many years. To attract tourists to communities too small to attract long-haul tourists, the Alberta government created a larger tourism brand, the Canadian Badlands, which incorporated rural character, paleontological and aboriginal features, and outdoor adventure possibilities. This concept has evolved into a community partnership of more than 64 municipal governments. Since its inception, Canadian Badlands has poured money and talent into building a world-class destination. It has created strategic plans for clusters of communities, funded product development, mapped driving itinerary for independent travelers, facilitated training, and offered cooperative marketing opportunities. This investment in tourism infrastructure has created a second iconic tourism draw within the province and shows how government, communities, and businesses can work together.

The **strategic planning process** focuses on the values, mission, and goals of the organization. It looks at the needs of the company's customers and the physical, cultural, and political setting to determine the most viable development strategies. It places less emphasis on financial information and forecasting than a business plan does. When the strategic plan is completed, an organization should understand where to put its resources and be ready to develop its business plan. The organization should involve as many people as possible in the process of developing the strategic plan; multiple viewpoints should be represented. Inviting input from other organizations or disciplines will help develop a fuller understanding of sustainability issues. Technol-

Figure 2.1   Strategic planning process.

ogy improvements to reduce environmental impacts appear often; having a cross section of people contributing ideas helps identify the best sustainability strategies.

The strategic planning process used for this book is shown in figure 2.1. In the next sections, we explore each phase of the strategic plan in detail.

CREATE A MISSION STATEMENT

The first step is to create a mission statement or refine your existing mission statement. A **mission statement** describes what your business does, how it does that, for whom, and why. It clarifies your primary customers, your core business, and the location in which you operate. It should also incorporate your values related to sustainability. Your mission statement tells the world (and yourself) what the essence of your business is. During the strategic planning process, some businesses will also prepare a **vision statement**, a description of what the organization wants to become.

Usually mission statements are short, a paragraph or even one sentence. An example of a mission statement is "Green Hiking Tours provides outstanding natural history trips for domestic and international travelers. We use expert guides and visit undiscovered destinations to impart a sense of stewardship for the environment." This mission statement tells the reader the following:

- What they do: provide outstanding natural history trips
- How they do it: by using expert guides and visiting undiscovered destinations

- Who their target customers are: domestic and international travelers
- Why they do what they do: to impart a sense of stewardship for the environment

If you have a mission statement for your business, compare it against the example. Or select one for a company with which you are familiar. Determine whether the mission statement reflects the values and competitive strengths of the organization as you understand them. If you do not feel there is a good match, chances are the mission statement needs revising.

As you work on your strategic plan or start to develop a business plan, your mission statement will guide you in decision making. For example, if you are tempted to emulate other successful companies and their business models, comparing their situation against your own can make clear why their model would not work with the values and customers you describe in your mission statement. Or you might be implementing your strategic plan when someone offers you an unsolicited opportunity. For example, perhaps you have planned to offer backcountry ski trips for overseas visitors but are being asked to offer soft adventure trips to South America for outbound travelers. It might be a good option for your organization, but evaluating it will be easier if you can refer to your mission statement and start the decision making with a clear idea of where you are going and what you value.

With a clear vision of where you want to take your organization, it is time to evaluate your setting and determine what opportunities and challenges you will face. In the next section, we

Ecochallenge
Mission or Mishmash?

Mission statements sound good in theory but are notoriously difficult to create and even harder to implement. How well have your favorite businesses done?

Visit the website of three tourism companies you like. Can you find their mission statement? Many companies do not proclaim their mission, but if you check the About section, it will explain what is important to them. They may describe their values or what makes them unique. For example, Quark Expeditions does not say it operates cruise liners; instead it operates Polar Adventure Ships.

You can also try searching for the company's mission statement on the Internet. If it is a large hotel or publically traded company, you might find mention of the mission statement in business articles.

Compare your perception of the company to the mission statement. Do you think the mission statement accurately conveys the company's purpose or tourism experience? Are you surprised by the claims made? Can you see how difficult it is to ensure that the ideas and values of the mission statement are reflected in all aspects of a business?

review the external environment with the objective of finding as many opportunities as possible.

CONDUCT AN EXTERNAL REVIEW OF THE ENVIRONMENT

An important step in the planning process is assessing the physical, economic, and political setting in which you operate. It helps you define the products you can offer and suggest areas of operational challenge. Completing a resource inventory will make you aware of the types of tourism products and experiences that are possible in your area. It will also help identify resources that might be too sensitive to support tourism activities.

Perform Resource Inventory

A **resource inventory** is list of natural, cultural, and man-made features in your community or operating area that can be used to develop a tourism product. You will want to consider the following:

• Natural or scenic attractions: These include natural features, for example, mountain ranges, beaches, and safe harbors, but might also encompass man-made features that enhance recreational opportunities such as hiking trails or bird-watching blinds. It can also include political features, for example, protected areas that restrict consumptive (e.g., hunting) or motorized activities and provide good wildlife-viewing opportunities.

• Historical attractions: You might want to include modern history experiences, for example, museums or battle sites, but you can also include ancient history of first peoples or even paleontological evidence.

• Cultural or social attractions: These might be historical in nature, or you might find that living culture can attract tourists and should be added to the resource inventory. Social activities such as music festivals might be considered local entertainment but could also be of interest to tourists.

• Accommodations: Without accommodations, it is difficult to develop more than a one-day tourism experience. List all accommodations, existing and potential, on your resource inventory. Be creative if you are short of facilities. Hunting lodges, nursing homes, residential schools, even jails and churches have been converted to tourist lodging where hotels were scarce.

• Restaurants: Travelers need to eat, so look for food service facilities that provide good food at hours suitable for travelers. List all possibilities on your inventory.

• Interpretive services: Guided tourism products often generate more economic benefits than self-guided trips, but without guides or interpreters you will find it difficult to develop these products. Identify existing guides and people who, with training, such as historians or birdwatchers, could offer interpretation for your business.

• Transportation: If people cannot get to your destination, your business will suffer. Identify transportation links to and within your community. Look for transportation providers, such as bus companies, you can hire to provide some of your transportation services. Information from the inventory will be useful in identifying possible issues later in the planning process.

• Infrastructure: Focus on the infrastructure that affects your ability to offer a tourism experience. For example, if your driving route has no washrooms, you will need to lobby government or business to provide facilities. As well, mobile communication is becoming increasingly important to today's travelers, so make sure you have access to wireless networks.

• Human resources: As populations in North America age and move to cities, you might encounter labor shortages in rural or wilderness settings. If your business will operate in one of these areas, identify labor sources on your inventory. Perhaps you can partner with a local college to develop an internship program or distance learning.

Use the resource inventory form in table 2.1 to analyze what infrastructure and natural, historical, and cultural features might form the basis of a tourism experience. A blank copy is provided in the web resource. As you identify a natural, historic, or cultural feature in your area, add it to the inventory. Note unique features found in your community; these may be the basis of your competitive advantage or shape your marketing messages.

The next step is to complete the column Appeal to Visitors. You must decide whether the resource will appeal to tourists in the local or regional area, who are coming from a one- or two-hour drive away, or whether it is more unique and will draw people from farther away. Indicate the appeal using the following codes:

• L = Local or regional. Appeal is relatively low, attracting people within a two-hour drive of your business.

• S = State or provincial. Appeal is moderate, attracting people within the boundaries of your state or province, or if you are located close to a state border, within an eight-hour drive of your business.

• N = National. Appeal is high, attracting people willing to travel across the country to visit your business.

• I = International. Appeal is very high, attracting people from other countries.

Your understanding of the tourism marketplace is critical during this step as you decide whether your business or community can offer an attraction appealing enough that a traveler will undertake a long journey in the face of competing tourism organizations. For example, it is unlikely someone will fly 12 hours to tour a small museum for an hour. So this museum is assessed as having local or regional appeal, even though a traveler from a great distance away might enjoy it if they happened to be in the neighborhood. Conversely, you can assume that if an attraction has very high appeal attracting international visitors, then local, state, and national travelers would also enjoy it.

The following questions can be helpful as you complete this part of the inventory:

• Is interpretation available for this feature? More interpretation will usually mean it will appeal to a greater number and variety of travelers.

• Is this resource rare? Be honest, but explore creative options before answering. Sandhill cranes are not rare, but Nebraska gets hundreds of thousands of them. The sheer volume of cranes that migrate through forms the basis for several natural festivals each spring.

• Does another business or community offer something similar? If you have a lot of competition, your appeal to visitors may be lessened.

• What types of activities and destinations are popular with travelers? Chapter 1 discussed several trends; you can find more trend information from your local destination marketing organization and state or provincial tourism department. Use this information to decide whether today's travelers favor what you offer. If they do not, perhaps you can update your business. Note ideas in the last column.

If you have lived in the region a long time, it can be difficult to accurately assess what resources will have the greatest appeal to national or international visitors. It is easy to overlook something that you take for granted. For example, I worked with several communities in eastern Arkansas on a resource inventory. The residents were proud of their cultural heritage but could not see how the nearby swampland could attract tourists other than hunters. These bottomland hardwoods, sometimes called The Big Woods, became a tourism hotspot for bird-watchers when someone reportedly sighted the ivory-billed woodpecker. Considered extinct, hope that a remnant population might exist attracted people from around the United States.

Table 2.1 Resource Inventory

Resource	Unique features	Rating of appeal to visitors:*	Descriptions and problems
NATURAL OR SCENIC ATTRACTIONS			
Beaches		Local or regional	Cold, algae bloom
Bird species	300 species	International	
Bird-watching sites		Local or regional	Poor parking
Canyons			
Caves			
Cliffs			
Climate			
Deserts	Hot, dry		
Fishing		State or provincial	Good fly-fishing
Forests		National	Logging conflicts
Fungus			
Geological formations	Hoodoos	State or provincial	Minor defacing
Hiking trails	Uncrowded	State or provincial	Maps not distributed
Islands			
Lakes			
Lichen	Vast wetlands	State or provincial	Low local awareness of potential
Mammals			
Mountains		National	Funding needed
Nature trails	See two mountain ranges	National	Multiple-use conflicts
Parks and protected areas			
Plants		State or provincial	
Rivers	Class III rapids	National	
Waterfalls		State or provincial	
Wilderness		Local or regional	Few, hard to access
Other		State or provincial & national	
HISTORICAL ATTRACTIONS			
Indigenous sites			
Interpretive centers			More work needed
Museums			
Other		Local or regional	
CULTURAL AND SOCIAL ATTRACTIONS			
Festivals			
Special events		State or provincial & intornational	Major birding festivals
Traditional lifestyle		State or provincial	Community-orientated
Other			

Resource	Unique features	Rating of appeal to visitors:*	Descriptions and problems
ACCOMMODATIONS			
Bed and breakfasts			
Campgrounds	Great views	State or provincial	Off beaten path
Hostels		State or provincial & national	Limited RV sites
Hotels			
Inns		International	Boutique hotel
Lodges		State or provincial	
Motels		Local or regional	Upgrading required
Other			
RESTAURANTS			
Casual			
Ethnic		Local or regional	Need more visitors
Fine dining		Local or regional	
Health		National	Focus on local ingredients
Theme			
Specialty			
Other		State or provincial	
INTERPRETIVE SERVICES			
Bus tours			
Dramatic presentations			
Guided walks			
Guiding services			
Talks		State or provincial	Offered on some paddling trips
Video		National	Provided by parks services, limited number
Other	Text		
RETAIL			
Souvenir shops			
Artisan shops or galleries			
Store for supplies, food, hardware			
TRANSPORTATION			
Airline service	Private aircraft only	Local or regional	150 miles to nearest commercial airport
Animal transport			
Boat service	Hunting outfitters	State or provincial	Traditional activity
Bus service			
Ferry service			
Helicopter service	Rentals	State or provincial	
Rail service			
Other	Local tours	State or provincial	Need more interpretation

(continued)

Table 2.1 *(continued)*

Resource	Unique features	Rating of appeal to visitors:*	Descriptions and problems
INFRASTRUCTURE			
Communication services	One Internet cafe		
Medical services	One regional hospital		
Police services			Low crime, large area, slow response time
Roadways	Scenic byway	Local or regional & national	Able to reach all areas
Sewage systems	Adequate for existing population		
Other			
HUMAN RESOURCES			
First-aid personnel			
Guides			
Hospitality workers			
Marketing			
Support staff			Need more
Interpreters		State or provincial	Hard to find and keep staff
Other			Need more cooperative marketing programs

The chance to see the unusual will bring tourists from great distances, so you need to carefully assess what the real tourism attractors are for your region. Perhaps it is a way of life. Or maybe you have something intangible that you can market in the increasingly urban world, such as quiet, darkness (see sidebar Finding the Dark), or a place where neighbors know each other by name. You might need an unbiased opinion at this stage of your planning, so consider hiring a tourism consultant. Business owners also approach local universities or colleges, asking tourism students to undertake special projects, thereby providing inexpensive talent to the business owner and real-world experience to the student.

If the geographic area you are reviewing for the inventory is small, or if you do not believe you have many resources to attract national or international travelers, consider partnering with other organizations. If you can create a larger critical mass of attractions by clustering or grouping resources by activity or geography, you are likely to be more successful. By creating a tourism experience that keeps people in the area longer, you make it worthwhile for people to travel longer distances.

Assess Government Regulations

Government directs individual and business activities through legislation, rules, codes, and ordinances. It protects common environments for use by all people and sets minimum standards for the operation of business. Being familiar with regulatory requirements is extremely important for sustainable tourism businesses.

If your business involves the construction of a major facility, you will likely be subject to an **environmental impact assessment (EIA)**. If you will only conduct tours, you might be relieved of many EIA requirements; however, you will always want to review the effects of any proposed activity to prevent harm to the physical ecology or local culture. As well, your business will likely require a business license and might need to meet requirements for technical skills, first aid, and area knowledge.

First, determine the regulatory requirements for your area. Contact the agencies that may have jurisdiction where you plan to operate. Often this involves federal, state or provincial, and municipal governments. You might cross department or functional boundaries and find you are dealing with planning, tourism, environment, and fish and wildlife departments.

Finding the Dark

My dad passed away almost three years ago, but I can imagine his reaction to hearing that Canada has its first dark-sky preserve. "What the heck is a dark park? Isn't every park dark after the sun goes down?" he likely would have asked.

In his day, parks were dark after sunset but that is no longer the case in Canada and the United States. I remember flying over the eastern United States and wondering what caused the unlit areas I could see below me. Power outages? I puzzled at the contrast between the dark spots and the well-lit areas around them. It suddenly hit me that the only areas without lights weren't forests or parks, but large bodies of water. Everything else was lit up like a department store before Christmas.

Now Jasper National Park has created the world's largest dark-sky preserve, where the amount of man-made light is minimized. Canadians can beat their chests with pride knowing Canada has the largest number of certified dark-sky preserves in the world and a rigorous set of standards to safeguard them.

Protecting night skies is good for nocturnal wildlife as shown by the successful reintroduction of black-footed ferrets into Grassland National Park Dark Sky Preserve. Darkness is also creating new science through the emergence of scotobiology, the study of how biology is affected by darkness. And of course, stargazing is better with a dark sky.

But does anyone besides an astronomer care whether there are still places that experience real darkness? After all, brightly lit streets give muggers fewer places to ply their trade. But nature feels closer at night and there is something invigorating about darkness, or at least there is if you're not looking for a missing house key.

Unfortunately, our kids are losing the connection to this aspect of nature. If you're not sure what I mean, ask a young child to go out in the dark for fun and watch his or her reaction. While visiting a cabin in the Columbia Valley well out of the reach of streetlights, I asked my city-dwelling nephew, Adam, whether he'd like to go for a walk to see what real darkness looks like. He looked like I'd suggested we play in traffic. "No, I'm serious," I stressed, "When have you ever been someplace where there is no light at all? Don't you think it would be cool?" I don't remember his exact answer, but roughly translated it was "No!"

My husband and I prevailed and led a less-than-enthusiastic Adam outside for our evening adventure. I didn't want Adam thinking about things with teeth so I asked him to look at how much light was still visible. There were porch lights and yard lights and Christmas lights; we realized how hard it was to escape light pollution.

I was beginning to fear we might not find true darkness when we turned the corner and there it was. Inky blackness that covered like a blanket and caused a few tentative steps before our night vision returned. We looked up at the stars twinkling like rhinestones on an Elvis jumpsuit. Adam clutched the shovel he carried for protection even tighter. "Just in case," he said, but he admitted it was pretty cool.

If you want to visit Canada's largest dark-park preserve, go to http://darksky.org/night-sky-conservation/dark-sky-parks for a list of the best places to get away from light and best conditions for stargazing.

Courtesy of the *Red Deer Advocate*

If you are taking tourists into state or national parks, you will often need special permits or licenses. Activities that do not occur in protected spaces or are of short duration and low risk might not need a permit. While some activities might not need a permit, a similar activity in another jurisdiction or in an area with a different protection status will.

Researching your regulatory requirements is an area in which it pays to be thorough. You do not want to start construction on a fly-fishing lodge near a state park, only to find out you have not complied with fishery legislation or regulations for other states downstream of your camp.

You might find you cannot get approval for your idea or the cost of undertaking an EIA is too great. By identifying obstacles early, you might be able to alter the location or nature of your business to make it feasible. This is sometimes called **fatal-flaw analysis** because it identifies obstacles that, if not overcome, would make it impossible to proceed.

Dealing with bureaucracies can be time consuming and costly. Be realistic in setting deadlines. If you are counting on getting approval to operate in an area within a few weeks or months and the process actually takes a year or two, you need alternative cash flow sources and need to delay your marketing efforts to prevent customer disappointment.

The amount of time needed to obtain approvals varies with the scope of your tourism product and the extent of community support you have achieved. Talk to other operators early in the process; you may be surprised to find it can cost hundreds or thousands of dollars to deal with regulatory requirements.

Be watchful of new legislation that might require you to have a permit where none was needed previously. You can provide input by attending hearings or talking with government and community representatives so that your business is not adversely affected by unrealistic requirements.

Analyze Competitors

As part of your strategic plan, you need to understand who is already offering similar tourism experiences and the business strategies they employ. This step requires you to evaluate your competitors; learn what products they offer, who their customers are, how they market, and what their business' strengths and weaknesses are. Their strengths can show you one way to profit in the tourism industry, but by understanding their weaknesses, you create competitive advantages.

For example, there may be companies offering canoeing trips, but perhaps no one is offering trips with a historical slant. Discover Banff Tours in Canada's Rocky Mountains offers traditional voyageur canoe experiences and provides historical anecdotes as part of the trip. This feature allows Discover Banff Tours to appeal to history lovers as well as to adventure seekers and can generate interest from travel writers because it is unique.

Take time to identify both your **direct competitors**, companies offering experiences very similar to yours, and **indirect competitors**, companies offering different experiences but competing for consumers' leisure time and discretionary income. An amusement park may not seem like a competitor, but if it offers a leisure product to your potential clients, it is a competitor. Find out what price your competitors charge, their strategies for marketing and customer service, and any unique product characteristics they offer.

Understanding your competitors and how to distinguish your product from theirs will become important if you are seeking bank financing or investors. Often bank managers or loan officers are not experts in tourism. If anything, they may know enough about tourism to feel it is a high-risk area. You will need to explain why you are different from other tourism businesses. With a focus on sustainability, you may also encounter skepticism from bankers. Be sure to explain the paybacks from your green policies.

Many nature-based tourism businesses require a relatively small investment in equipment and working capital, an advantage when dealing with banks. On the other side, the small tangible asset base means that banks do not see much collateral on which to base a loan. Explaining how your business is different from others will demonstrate your ability to generate sales revenue and, ultimately, the cash flow to repay lenders.

CONDUCT AN INTERNAL REVIEW OF YOUR BUSINESS

Once you have looked at the external environment, you will need to review your internal environment and identify your strengths and weaknesses. A helpful tool at this point of the process is the **strength, weakness, opportunity, threat (SWOT) analysis** taught in many business courses. This is a concise accounting of the pluses and minuses of your business.

Many organizations use a brainstorming session among key employees to complete their SWOT. By gathering people from different departments, you can come up with a wide range of strengths, weaknesses, opportunities, and threats. An example of a SWOT analysis for an adventure business is shown in figure 2.2.

Start by identifying your organization's strengths. A strength is something your business possesses that provides a competitive advantage or helps it function better. For example, you might have the most skilled white-water rafting guide in the state or maybe you have a permit to operate in a national park, which is difficult to obtain.

Move onto your organization's weaknesses, those things that you do not do well or where you lack resources. Also look for ways to turn weaknesses into strengths. For example, many small operators find that a shortage of money is

Strengths	Opportunities
* Access to full range of trained guides * Close to international airport * Permits to operate in three national parks * Partnership with hotel company for cross promotion	* No new permits are being offered in national parks, therefore existing ones will have greater value * Creation of several social clubs in neighboring cities provides a potential market * Currency fluctuations are attracting more international visitors * Research indicates baby boomers are looking for more active vacations
Weaknesses	**Threats**
* Short of working capital * Lack of four-season camping equipment * Website needs search engine optimization (SEO)	* May not be able to access other national parks * Areas allowing mountain biking are becoming more crowded

Figure 2.2 SWOT analysis of a soft-adventure travel company.

one of their weaknesses. On the strength side, they might have a strong knowledge of flora and fauna, or they might have exclusive guiding rights to a protected area. This can compensate for weaknesses by limiting competition and creating a niche that will establish them as a recognized provider of unique trips. Or, if you are located a long distance from an international airport, you could overcome this weakness by offering charter flights or make the trip from the airport part of the tour by adding interpretation along the way. Make sure to identify your weaknesses before your competition does. They may use your shortcomings to increase their sales.

Opportunities and threats refer to the external environment for your business; you will have much of this information from the previous step of the strategic planning process. Some examples of opportunities could be favorable economic conditions or removal of government restrictions on travel; threats could be closure of an area to travelers. Other threats you may encounter are lack of access or user conflicts. Many parks and protected areas are becoming increasingly crowded as our population grows. Park managers may choose to limit activities, for example,

motorized recreation during busy months, or they might limit the number of hikers that can use a certain trail. To discover more possible threats, read your local newspaper or check with tourism industry associations to see what issues they are discussing. Issues with political, safety, insurance, or technology implications might be threats to your business.

Although you are completing a SWOT analysis for your strategic plan, you might want to include it or key parts in your business plan. At a minimum, describe your weaknesses and corrective plans in your business plan. Savvy investors will be aware of your weak points, and a lack of acknowledgment and preparation could leave investors with the impression you are deceiving them or you have not thought through your operation. Neither of these is desirable! To develop skill in preparing a SWOT analysis, watch the video "Planning for Change" in the web resource and complete the discussion questions.

SET GOALS AND OBJECTIVES

Setting **goals**—general intentions of the direction you are taking your business—and **objectives**—specific, measurable, time-bound targets—tells you how to recognize success when it arrives. You will start with goals that are fairly broad, such as to be the leading provider of sea kayaking trips, as measured by sales, to Baja, California in five years.

To achieve your goals, establishing several smaller objectives will make the task easier. A good objective is specific and measurable wherever possible and has a time frame for completion. Selling as many kayaking trips as possible is not a well-defined objective. If this were restated as sell 15 four-day kayak trips for the spring of 2015, it would be a more meaningful objective. To test whether your objective is well written, ask yourself how you will know when you have reached your target. If you cannot describe what success will look like, you need to rework your objective.

Your strategic plan's goals and objectives will form the backbone of your business plan and drive your daily activities. Each year, or perhaps every few months, you should evaluate your progress against the targets you set in your strategic plan.

ANALYZE THE MARKET

Once you have examined your environment and your business, it is time to think about your customers. You have the best chance of meeting your strategic goals by offering the right product and selling it; to do this you must analyze the marketplace and identify unmet needs.

Information used to analyze the marketplace can come from the following sources:

- **Primary market research** consists of new surveys or interviews you conduct with customers.
- **Secondary market research** consists of publically available studies done previously for other purposes.
- **Customer feedback** is information provided by customers in a formal manner, for example, a customer satisfaction survey, or informally, for example, when guests talk to the staff.

Gathering primary market research is often too expensive and time consuming for individual businesses, but you can use secondary market research. This could consist of studies conducted by tourist associations or governments. Many are not specific to sustainable tourism, but might be relevant to your business.

Some businesses get inexpensive primary market research through local colleges and universities. Business and tourism studies departments often look for real-world projects to develop students' skills and knowledge. Although the results might have a somewhat theoretical bent, these studies can be helpful, especially in conducting visitor surveys or other labor-intensive tasks.

You may also decide to gather market information by gathering customer feedback. By asking existing or potential customers casual questions such as where they are from, how they chose a trip, or what they would like to do but cannot find in your region, you will build a better understanding of your customer base and you can use this to develop your marketing strategies.

The purpose of doing your **market analysis** is to identify the types of people or groups of travelers with similar characteristics, called **market segments**, that would be best suited for your tourism products. Market segments may be defined by demographics, activities undertaken, reasons for travel, or demographic origin. Often market segments are given a label that summarizes their characteristics and give a face to a broad group of travelers, such as serious adventurer as seen in table 2.2.

Analyzing your market by segment will help you understand the characteristics and travel patterns of tourists interested in sustainable tourism. Often researchers will include **demographic information**, or characteristics that can be quantified, such as age, household income, gender, or country of origin.

You also want to find out what types of activities members of the market segment participate in while traveling. If they are on vacation this could include activities such as hiking, skiing, wildlife viewing, or other outdoor recreation. Other activities might include attendance at a festival or cultural event, visiting friends or relatives, dining, shopping, sightseeing, learning, volunteering, gambling, or going to an amusement park.

Table 2.2 Examples of Market Segments

Segment description	Serious adventurer	Weekend recreationist	Incentive group
Age range of traveler	25-40	30-45	35-55
Origin of traveler	Germany	Colorado, New Mexico	North America
Gender of traveler	Mainly male	Female	60% male, 40% female
Reasons for travel	Physical challenge	Spending time with friends and family	Unique reward for sales representatives achieving work targets
Source of information when selecting vacation destination and activities	Referrals from friends, websites, social media	Social media, websites	Industry trade shows, referrals
Length of stay in research destination	5-7 days	1-2 days	1-2 days

Researchers also look at the length of the trip. By discovering how long people have for their vacation or how much time they spend at a single destination, tourism business owners can make sure their products can be experienced in the time available and are the right length for their market. If one of your market segments is people driving the Alaska Highway, they might be interested in just a short side trip of several hours because they have a long distance to cover in a short amount of time. You would perhaps target your advertising by distributing brochures at visitor information centers on the Alaska Highway and roads leading to it.

This example shows why market researchers often seek information about how people choose a tour. Advertising is expensive, so business owners want to make sure their money is spent wisely. Understanding where customers look when they are making their travel decision helps business owners match their marketing activities to their potential customers.

You may also want to gather information on how important principles of sustainability are to your potential customers. If green business practices are important, you want to mention them prominently in your marketing. If your customers choose their vacations based on other considerations, then perhaps it will be sufficient to mention your green policies in a less prominent part of your website.

Figure 2.3 shows an example of a market segment called incentive group. A market segment can be made up of **independent travelers**, people traveling without a guide, but it can also be groups of people such as **incentive groups**, employees being rewarded for high performance. Recreational clubs that take trips together could also be considered a market segment.

The information gained during the market analysis helps a company define its products. A tour company using the segments in figure 2.3 might decide to offer a half-day bear-awareness course to the serious adventurer market segment to better prepare these people for backpacking trips. Knowing that these people are probably independent in their travel, the price for the course needs to be low or this market segment might decide to do the training on their own.

The company needs another product for the incentive group, which wants something special for its high-performing staff. If employees are being rewarded for achieving a difficult sales target, they will expect something more elaborate than dinner and cocktails. Perhaps the tour company can offer a two-day mountain immersion experience based at a remote lodge and special talks by bear biologists or the chance to observe radio tracking of wolves.

It is important to note that in this case, the marketing for the incentive group will be aimed at the person or company organizing the experience for the incentive group, not the high performers who will participate in the tour. Selling products or services from one business to another is called **business-to-business marketing**. If you decide to target your marketing at businesses rather than individual travelers, this is a strategic choice and should be articulated in your strategic plan. If it will be a major focus of your marketing efforts, make sure it is reflected in your mission statement. Do not imply you are targeting leisure travelers when you have found it more profitable to work directly with corporations.

Identifying and analyzing your market segments focus your expenditures on product development and marketing and gives you the best return on investment. Many new entrepreneurs make the mistake of targeting everyone who ever traveled as a potential customer. Avoid that mistake in your planning process and you will build credibility with potential investors and creditors.

DEFINE YOUR PRODUCT

With an inventory of your area's resources and an analysis of the marketplace, you can begin to identify, first, the products you are able to offer and, second, the products that tourists are likely to purchase. As listed in table 1.3, tourism businesses operate across the tourism industry, including tourism attractions, accommodation and transportation providers, and tour operators. The products you define will vary depending on the type of business in which you work. A hotel might develop a weekend getaway as a product, or it could be a program aimed at female business travelers, with designated floors, extra security, and concierge services. A tourist attraction such as a museum might partner with other hotels and other attractions to create a multiday product.

If you are a tour operator and have identified an abundance of bird life as a natural asset on your resource inventory, you might develop a bird-watching tour for casual bird-watchers. You could offer a multiday tour to serious bird-watchers if you have species not easily observed elsewhere. Or if you have few unique species, you could offer adventure activities like hiking or canoeing with natural history interpretation. An economic development officer looking at the same inventory might want to create an event, such as a festival celebrating large migrations, to fill rooms in hotels or profile seasonal cuisine. You might find it helpful to use a worksheet similar to that in table 2.1 to organize your thoughts.

Be creative in identifying the possible product offerings. Think about how long the trip would be and what activities, lodging, and meals you would include. Do not forget that the preferences of your targeted market segments will determine the structure of your product and the prices you are able to charge. You might think you have enough in your area to entertain someone for a week, but if most of the people visiting your area come only for a weekend, you need to focus on a product that can be enjoyed in a weekend or spend a lot of money convincing people to stay longer.

As you define your product, test your product ideas against your market analysis. If you develop a weekend trip visiting several bird-viewing sites, overnighting at a romantic bed and breakfast, and eating a meal at an aboriginal cultural center, that will probably pass the test if your market analysis indicates that most casual bird-watchers travel as part of a couple, are interested in culture as well as nature, and are looking for a trip of one or two days.

IDENTIFY AND SELECT VIABLE STRATEGIES

At this point, you have gathered a lot of information. Now it is time to select the key **strategies,** or actions, that will guide your business toward its goals for the next three to five years. By selecting your strategies and documenting them in your strategic plan, you will have a record of your decisions. You can refer back to it as you develop your business plan or are faced with unexpected opportunities, such as a sudden cash windfall.

If you have not developed a strategic plan before, you may wonder what a strategy looks like. The following list may give you ideas for your organization, but remember that each company will be unique. The following are examples of tourism business strategies:

- Provide access to hard-to-reach areas
- Invest in green technologies

- Focus marketing on social media
- Contract with another company for transportation
- Hire only seasonal staff
- Lease all equipment
- Develop high-quality customer service and charge premium prices for it
- Create itineraries that offer multiple learning opportunities
- Become known as the company to travel with for wildlife watching
- Build comfortable camping structures to attract aging backpackers

As you select your key strategies, make sure you focus on those that are realistic and will help your business succeed. You need to make sure your ideas are feasible and viable. Assessing whether your tourism operation is feasible and viable can be painful because you might not get the answers you want. However, honesty is required if you are to avoid losing your investment.

An adage called Matsch's Law says it is better to have a horrible ending than to have horrors without end. This sums up the benefits of strategic planning: If your estimates of price and sales volumes do not generate sufficient profit to thrive or survive, it is better to look on paper for ways to increase your volume or prices than in real life. Once you have spent your life's savings or the bank's money, it is much more difficult to modify your product offering or redefine your business focus.

Feasibility

Feasibility refers to whether you can actually do all the things you need to do to establish your business. This might mean securing financing and regulatory approval. Or if you want to establish a backcountry lodge, your business feasibility will depend on approvals and permits to build and to operate. You may need to secure special technology; applied technology may affect the feasibility of your lodge. Permit approval could be contingent on developing a working waste disposal system that meets regulatory standards in a harsh physical setting. You need be able to insure your business activities, so make sure a carrier will take on your business. If insurance carriers deem your adventure activity too risky to insure or make the premiums unaffordable, you may need to alter your operations.

Tourism businesses already in existence may have an advantage over new operators, especially when it comes to regulatory issues. Some national parks limit the number of guiding permits issued, so operators holding existing permits have unique access to wilderness areas. This situation can make your business more valuable if you have these permits, but if you do not, your business idea may not be feasible.

Viability

If your business passes the feasibility test, you can determine whether it is viable. **Viability** refers to whether your business is capable of developing and growing. At this point in the planning process, you should have some idea of the market you hope to capture. Estimate your prices to give you an idea of the revenues you hope to realize.

By applying an estimate of capital and operating expenditures, you can determine whether the business is economically viable. You will need to look at both the short term and the long term. Sometimes you can generate enough revenue to cover operating costs but be unable to repay a loan or pay dividends to shareholders.

Another part of the decision-making process for sustainable tourism is determining product viability on environmental grounds. During the planning process, you might realize you need to take a lot of tours to an area to cover costs. To avoid compromising environmental principles, you may need to create an additional product to spread impact, change locations, or alter the time of year you travel.

Start to assess your business viability once you get your first high-level estimates, even if you are scratching them on the back of an envelope. As you finish your strategic plan and work on your business plan, thousands of dollars can be spent hiring consultants, doing architectural drawings, and obtaining operating approvals and permits. It is wiser to assess your chances of success sooner rather than later when large sums of money are involved.

IMPLEMENT THE PLAN

Once you have picked your strategies, organize them as you see them occurring. For example, put the strategies you want to tackle immediately under the heading One to Two Years. Put the strategies that you will track later in the Three- to Five-Year category. Try to assign responsibility for each strategy so that your plan is translated into action.

Once your business concept passes the feasibility and viability tests, you want to develop your idea further. A business plan is an effective way to do this. Developing a business plan allows you to examine your business concept step-by-step from start-up through ongoing operation. It outlines

Estimating your visitation level will help determine whether your ideas are viable because knowing how many customers you have will allow you to estimate revenue.

your business activities, marketing plans, and financial forecasts for one to five years.

A business plan identifies potential problems and needed solutions. It is also a mechanism for communicating your vision and plans to employees, investors, and bankers. In fact, without it, you will not proceed past the preliminary stages with your banker.

A business plan should be updated yearly with new marketing and operating strategies. Continued forecasting of sales and expenses will show whether your ideas are viable. As many tourism businesses operate on small profit margins, forecasting can help keep you in business.

When just starting a sustainable tourism venture, a business plan is even more critical. It forces you to look objectively at the resources needed to develop a tour or service; the laws, codes, and ordinances to meet; and the size and characteristics of the market. By understanding more about the tourism industry and putting numbers to your idea, you will have a better idea of what you are getting into.

Information on preparing a business plan is provided in chapter 13 and a sample business plan can be found in the web resource. You will also find a business-planning workbook to help you prepare your plan. Work through the "Your Business Plan" questions at the end of each chapter as you fill out the workbook.

SUMMARY

The strategic planning process in important to businesses but not urgent. It takes many hours to complete and the temptation may be to put it off or give it little attention. However, there are significant benefits to giving the strategic plan your full attention. You will have a much clearer vision of where you are going, and you will have analyzed many alternatives before selecting the one most likely to succeed. The time spent will be repaid in greater efficiency in your daily operations and greater confidence from investors, creditors, and regulatory agencies. In the next chapters, we will discuss how to translate your strategies into action.

|||||||||||||||||||||||||| GLOSSARY |||||||||||||||||||||||||||

business-to-business marketing—The selling of products or services from one business to another.

customer feedback—Information provided by customers in a formal manner, for example, a customer satisfaction survey, or informally, for example, when guests talk to the staff.

demographic information—Characteristics that can be quantified, such as age, household income, gender, or country of origin.

direct competitors—Companies offering tourism experiences very similar to another company's.

environmental impact assessment (EIA)—A review of the potential environmental impacts of a proposed activity or development along with strategies to mitigate negative consequences. Depending on the project's location or type, the assessment may be required by government legislation.

fatal-flaw analysis—An analysis that identifies obstacles that, if not overcome, would make it impossible to proceed with business growth.

feasibility—Refers to whether a business can actually do all the things it needs to do to establish itself.

goal—A general intention of the direction to take a business.

incentive groups—Employees being rewarded for high performance.

independent travelers—People traveling without a guide.

indirect competitors—Companies offering experiences different from those of the tourism businesses, but that compete for consumers' leisure time and discretionary income.

market analysis—Analysis to identify the types of people or groups, called market segments, that would be best suited for particular tourism products.

market segments—The types of people or groups of travelers with similar characteristics.

mission statement—A description of the essence of a business, including its primary customers, core business, and the location in which it operates.

objectives—Specific, measurable, time-bound targets for a business.

primary market research—New surveys or interviews conducted with customers.

resource inventory—An inventory of natural, cultural, and man-made features in a community or operating area that can be used to develop a tourism product.

secondary market research—Studies, done previously for other purposes, that are publically available.

strategy—An action that will guide a business toward its goals.

strength, weakness, opportunity, threat (SWOT) analysis—A concise accounting of the pluses and minuses of a business which requires identification of strengths, weaknesses, opportunities, and threats.

strategic plan—A list of an organization's long-term focus and goals and the strategies to reach them.

strategic planning process—The steps needed to develop a strategic plan.

viability—The capability of a business to develop and grow.

vision statement—A description of what the organization wants to become.

||||||||||||||||||| REVIEW QUESTIONS |||||||||||||||||||

1. What are three benefits to a tourism organization that can result from completing a strategic plan?

2. List some of the features that you might evaluate as part of a resource inventory. How would you decide whether they are appealing to international visitors?

3. Where can you find information on regulatory requirements for new tourism businesses? How would you use this information in a business plan?

4. Describe the main components of a SWOT analysis. Explain how this analysis would help you prepare a strategic plan.

5. What is a market segment? How does the use of market segments help a business?

6. What is the difference between business feasibility and viability?

|||||||||||||||||| VIDEO CASE STUDY ||||||||||||||||||

Visit the web resources to watch the video "Planning for Change." After watching the video, answer the following questions.

1. Give examples of technology changes that have affected travel since the Alaska Highway was built.

2. What businesses have benefited from technology changes? Which have suffered?

3. How would developing a strategic plan help a business prepare for technology changes? How might a tourism business located in Alaska today adapt to a large number of cruise ships arriving in a nearby town?

4. What information could you derive from this video that could be used in a SWOT analysis for a sustainable tourism business in Alaska?

|||||||||||||||||| YOUR BUSINESS PLAN ||||||||||||||||||

At this point in the planning process, you should start the workbook. Leave the executive summary until last, but begin gathering information for the section Products and Services. You will have identified your mission statement, goals, key products or services, and major markets in the strategic planning process. You will refine your marketing information as we work through subsequent chapters, but you can capture your initial thoughts now.

1. What differences do you anticipate in the business-planning process between an established business and one starting up?

2. What businesses similar to yours can you study to gain background information if you are starting a new business? List the information you might get from Internet searches or personal interviews.

3. Share your mission statement with other people, then describe the business you are planning. Identify areas where people do not see a match between your mission and your business activities.

SUSTAINABILITY PRACTICES FOR DEVELOPMENT AND OPERATIONS

|||||||||||||| LEARNING OUTCOMES ||||||||||||||

After reading this chapter, you will be able to do the following:

- Understand how a business might affect its environment

- Develop sustainability policies

- Incorporate sustainability policies into daily operations

- Appreciate the importance of measuring and monitoring impacts of sustainable tourism practices

One of the principles of sustainable tourism is minimizing the impact of your business on the physical environment of the host community. As more and more tourism businesses adopt sustainable practices, this principle will be one of the most difficult to deal with. Putting the "eco" in your ecotourism operation will require additional planning in the development phase, the creation of sustainability policies, changes to operating activities, and ongoing monitoring and evaluation.

You will need to spend time talking to people in your community to understand how your plans will affect their businesses or lifestyles. There may be unexpected effects or you might find unexpected allies who can contribute knowledge.

Developing a sustainable tourism business also means inspiring your customers to consume less or minimize waste. This is not always easy when

travelers are looking to spoil themselves while on holidays. This chapter highlights the areas in which you will need to make more effort as you develop and operate your business.

MINIMIZING ENVIRONMENTAL IMPACT

Although early adopters may have envisioned ecotourism as a way to promote social and economic well-being without harming the environment, many people have come to the conclusion that few tourism activities, if any, have no environmental impact. A more realistic approach is to minimize negative impacts. By taking your environmental impact into account as you plan your business and set policies, you have a better chance of reducing environmental impacts and convincing your customers you are committed to sustainability.

Greening your business might mean additional start-up and operating costs; sometimes it can be difficult to compete with companies that have different environmental standards. However, if tourism is to meet the sustainability targets set by the Global Sustainable Tourism Council, all tourism businesses will eventually need to move to more environmentally friendly business practices. In the interim, convey your commitment to sustainability to your customers; if they enjoy a better travel experience because of it, they are likely to reward you by paying higher prices.

If your tourism business will construct physical structures in a sensitive environment or operate activities in protected areas, your word that you are operating according to sustainability practices is not enough. You will often need a more formal evaluation.

Development

When starting or expanding a tourism business in a sensitive environment, often there is a legislative requirement to undertake an environmental impact assessment (EIA), a formal process to identify ecological impacts, methods to mitigate harmful effects, and monitoring programs.

Start by checking with local, regional, and federal authorities to determine whether and when an EIA is required. EIA or not, it is desirable to design your facility or operation to minimize impacts. If structures will be built, their location and form should match the environment and cause as little disturbance as possible. Operating methods should minimize harm. Communication strategies should be put in place for employees and clients so standards for environmental protection can be maintained. Perhaps most important, determine how to monitor your impact. Selecting several key criteria, such as trail erosion and the number of annual animal sightings in an area, and measuring changes in these elements will quantify your operation's impact.

If you are subject to an EIA, you will undergo a formal review to determine whether your business or businesses (if planning is being done at a community level) will adversely affect the physical environment. Requirements for an EIA will differ among governments and should be investigated early. In a project with a large impact on the environment and host community, government will expect you to proactively assess impact and solicit community input.

Construction

The ways in which you weave green business practices into your physical structures are myriad. If you are constructing a facility from the ground up, you have greater control of materials used and can influence future day-to-day operations, but older buildings can also be made more environmentally

Dinosaur Provincial Park Uses Green Building Techniques

The Dinosaur Provincial Park Visitor Centre, located in a UNESCO World Heritage Site, was expanded with an eye to minimizing environmental impacts. This meant choosing native species for landscaping and a dark-sky lighting strategy that uses shades to keep light pointed downward. Plumbing upgrades include dual-flush toilets, waterless urinals, and low-flow aerators, which allows the facility to serve 2.5 times as many visitors using the same amount of water. By working with ambient site conditions and an energy-efficient building envelope, air conditioning is not needed, even during very high summer temperatures (SABMag 2010).

Construction techniques should take into account the environment where the building will be located. Dinosaur Provincial Park Visitor Centre offers a good example.

friendly. Usually this involves retrofitting, such as replacing older windows with newer ones or reducing air leaks by improving the fit of the door. It may also require investments in new technology (see sidebar Dinosaur Provincial Park Uses Green Building Techniques).

If your business will be operating in natural areas, utilities and sewage systems should be designed for sensitive environmental conditions. Often operators will need to be creative in the development of physical buildings and operating systems because operating in remote locations, at high altitudes, or in harsh climates creates unique problems that are not met by readily available construction materials. For example, at high altitude, where weather is often cold, composting toilets will not work well enough to handle waste from a small lodge. You might be forced to develop your own technology or adapt existing technology to situations where it is unproven. Often, unique solutions mean greater costs, no guarantees from manufacturers, and a lack of bureaucratic understanding.

Although visitors will appreciate your efforts on infrastructure, it is the care you put into the design and decor of your facility that will convince them of your commitment to sustainability. Designing structures that blend into the environment instead of dominating it is visually pleasant and might improve the wildlife viewing. Using local craftsmen and artisans to decorate and furnish a facility will help match the structure to its physical and cultural environment as well as provide additional employment and a sense of pride and belonging for the community.

Tours

Even if your business will not construct physical structures, you need to consider the environmental impact of your activities and ensure you are doing all you can to minimize negative effects. For companies offering tours into natural areas, select tour destinations and routes that will withstand repeated tourism activities, and determine an appropriate activity level. An area where facilities such as pit latrines or hardened trails already exist can withstand more visitation than areas without facilities. You might discard a destination or route because it cannot support the level of visitation to make your tour viable financially. Such environmental regard distinguishes sustainable tourism organizations.

In conjunction with the physical development of your business, you should start developing your

sustainability policies. These will guide you as you transform your concept into reality.

ESTABLISHING SUSTAINABILITY POLICIES

A **policy** is a guideline outlining your business' opinion on a topic and direction to help staff achieve the organization's goals. While many larger organizations develop policies—sometimes to excess—small or medium-size organizations might not believe that developing policies is necessary. Policies are critical, however, for translating your vision and goals to your staff. The following are areas in which you should consider developing sustainability policies:

- Tour development: group size, number of trips to an environment, criteria for selecting a destination
- Tour operation: camping practices, vehicle operation, food purchases, food preparation, waste disposal
- Human resources: recruiting, training, remuneration
- Marketing: printing practices, cooperative marketing, community relations, donations, partnerships with conservation groups
- Administration: recycling, vendor selection

The detail in a policy will vary between organizations, but a simple example of a policy on group size is "ABC Tours sets a maximum tour size of 18 people for multiday trips." Successful companies such as O.A.R.S. devote time to policy making. O.A.R.S., a pioneer in U.S. river rafting, has consistently demonstrated leadership in tourism sustainability. It has developed comprehensive policies for all areas of its business. For example, its policy includes the cultural ideal, "We believe in supporting the local communities in the regions in which we travel, and actively engage with and create programs to foster sustainable, authentic preservation of those communities" (O.A.R.S. 2014). The warehouse and main office in Angels Camp, California, and its warehouse and office in the Grand Canyon are solar powered. The company practices leave-no-trace skills and ethics on its tours. It purchases recycled paper products and aims to reduce its use of paper. Establishing policies like these is helpful in communicating what good tourism practices look like to guides and other staff members. If you find it difficult to identify the policies or practices your business requires to increase its sustainability, you might find free publications like *Greening North Carolina Travel and Tourism. Tips for Sustainable Practices in Tourism* helpful (Center for Sustainable Tourism 2014).

Some owners have found they cannot afford all of their environmentally-friendly practices, at least not initially. This can cause tremendous stress if they feel they are choosing between personal values and business actions. For example, if you felt it was necessary to cancel a confirmed tour booking because a wildlife species at your destination was stressed from a bad winter and your presence would increase the stress, you will understand the difficult decisions facing sustainable tourism leaders. In some ways, managing this balance between ethics and finances is the biggest challenge for sustainable tourism organizations, but taking the time to weigh priorities and costs before drafting your policies will help your business run smoother and define your business practices in daily operations.

INTEGRATING ENVIRONMENTAL POLICIES INTO DAILY OPERATIONS

Once you have drafted your environmental policies, it is time to translate them into the daily operations. A good way to do that is to develop **operating practices**, a procedure that is created for repetitive use to achieve a desired outcome. When greening your business, it is helpful to review all the steps in the business cycle and develop operating practices in each area. Look at how you will deliver the tourism experience and monitor the impacts.

When developing your operating practices, look to organizations that have shown leadership in environmental responsibility. Many communities have conservation groups that promote the four Rs (reduce, reuse, recycle, and buy recycled) and can give advice or recommend literature to green your operation. Park service employees and your state department of natural resources will also provide information on standards. Utility companies can be helpful in suggesting ways to minimize energy usage.

You might want to spend extra time on the following areas:

- Waste management
- Recreational activities in sensitive environments
- Client education

Waste Management

Dealing with the waste created by your business is not the glamorous side of travel, but it is an important issue. If you operate in or near a city, you have infrastructure to deal with waste, although you may want to reduce the amount, perhaps through recycling, reusing, or reducing your purchases.

If you are operating in a rural or wilderness setting, you will face bigger challenges. A remote lodge cannot connect to a local sewage system; you will have to create the local sewage system and ensure it meets the requirements of the local government or park manager. If you are a nature-based business operating in a protected area or national park, you may find conventional waste disposal methods such as composting or putting garbage in a bin are not options. National parks require garbage containers that are bear proof, so outdoor composting is not an option in these situations. If you have established a policy of disposing of waste in a way that does not alter wildlife behaviors or jeopardize people's lives, you will need operating practices to ensure that happens.

As shown in the sidebar Trash to Treasures, Maho Bay Camps in the U.S. Virgin Islands demonstrated one of the most innovative approaches to waste management. Founded by Stanley Selengut, Maho Bay Camps was an ecotourism pioneer. Island locations can make it difficult to dispose of nonorganic waste. Maho Bay turned its trash into treasure by developing a glass art program that turned beer and food bottles into hand-blown art and souvenirs. As a result, people were buying "trash," creating a revenue source, and removing waste from the island. To see more about the program watch the video "From Trash to Treasure" in the web resource.

The accommodation sector has shown great leadership in many aspects of sustainability, especially in the area of energy consumption and waste management. If you have stayed in a hotel recently, you may have noticed compact fluorescent light bulbs in the fixtures or a towel program card, asking guests to hang up their towels if they do not want them replaced each

Trash to Treasures

If people had told me I'd put garbage in my suitcase before a flight home, I'd have told them they were crazy. But that was before I visited Maho Bay Camps on St. John in the U.S. Virgin Islands.

Maho Bay Camps is an ecotourism legend because of its development by its visionary founder, Stanley Selengut. A civil engineer by trade, Selengut was convinced by the St. John National Park manager in 1976 that traditional construction would lead to erosion and ultimately, destruction of the island's snorkeling opportunities. So he built wood and vinyl tent cabins, located on stilts and connected by boardwalks, to minimize vegetation disturbance. People loved the first 18 tents and there are now 114 tent cabins and the slightly more luxurious Harmony Studios for people, like me, who enjoy wooden walls and roofs.

As you might expect at a green resort, water and electricity use is minimized, but Maho Bay's trash-to-treasures program is unique. Selengut was frustrated at the island's lack of recycling programs. He hit on the unorthodox process of melting glass containers so glassblowers could turn them into art.

Apparently, different beer bottles melt at different temperatures, so reinventing the bottles as art took trial and error. Enticed to swap their skills for time at Maho, the early glassblowers persisted and churned out simple glasses and sun catchers before progressing to intricate vases.

The art gallery and gift shop now burst with vividly colored vases and trinkets, mirroring the bright songbirds and cobalt-blue waters found nearby. These treasures bear no resemblance to the beer bottles from whence they came!

If you're a self-starter and aren't scared of burns from hot objects, you can sign up for a glassblowing class. If, like me, you're a scaredy-cat, you can avoid the possibility of creating a lopsided paperweight and opt for an evening glassblowing demonstration. All you need is your credit card and a cool drink, although the experience wasn't without its hardships. After 20 minutes near the 1,200° C (2,192° F) furnace, I was debating whether to drink my wine or shower with it. Each afternoon, the masterpieces from the previous evening's demonstration are moved to the art gallery and given a prominent place next to the cash register.

Maho Bay's steep hillside location means you are always climbing stairs and the gallery's location halfway up the hill makes for a convenient rest stop. Our room was 454 stairs from the beach and, yes, I counted them. What else is there to do while you are sucking air and rhapsodizing about the invention of the elevator?

I admired the Maho Bay Camp's marketing savvy in locating such attractive merchandise where most customers stop to reinsert their lungs in their chest. The temptation to add more bling to your bag was hard to resist. When I discovered that the trash-to-treasures program generates U.S.$200,000 in revenue and keeps 20 tons of garbage and 32,000 bottles each year out of the landfill, I caved.

I felt almost virtuous as I shopped, which is how I came to customs on my return to Canada with a suitcase full of "trash." "What did you buy?" asked the customs officer. "Some glass art," I replied, smug in the knowledge that my treasures would never see a landfill.

Courtesy of the *Red Deer Advocate*

day. These steps save hotels money and reduce the amount of energy used and waste created. Fairmont Hotels & Resorts was one of the first hotel chains to launch sustainability initiatives through their Green Partnership program, which focuses on energy and water conservation, waste management, and community outreach programs with local groups and partnerships (Fairmont Hotels & Resorts 2013). Aspects of the program include the following:

- Eco-Meet: Clients hosting meetings can select from several options to reduce the ecological footprint of their event.

- Carbon management program: Carbon dioxide is monitored and tracked and goals for reduction are set.

- Green cuisine: Where possible, local, organic, fair trade, and sustainable food is used for menu items.

- Waste management: Recycling and reduction strategies are used across many hotel functions.
- Energy and waste conservation: Retrofits and improvements in lighting, bathroom fixtures, and so on have been implemented.
- Partnerships: Locally, Fairmont Olympic Hotel partners with National Geographic and Seattle Climate Action Plan. Nationally, Fairmont partners with organizations such as WWF and its Climate Savers program and the U.S. Environmental Protection Agency and its Energy Star program.

The Fairmont chain has enrolled all of its golf courses with the Audubon International Cooperative Sanctuary program to develop integrated management plans with the goal of achieving Audubon International certification.

The following results are impressive:

- Ninety-five percent of seafood purchased is from sustainable sources.
- Approximately 26 tons of food waste are diverted from landfills every six months.
- Every month, 33,000 pounds (15,000 kg) on average of mixed recycling are diverted from landfills.
- Over 4 million gallons (15 million L) of steam condensate from in-house laundry machines are saved and reused (Fairmont Hotels & Resorts 2013).

Imagine the contribution to UNWTO sustainability if all hotels adopted sustainability practices like these!

Recreation Activities in Sensitive Environments

Many tourism businesses conduct outdoor activities, some in natural areas. Several organizations have created excellent guidelines for outdoor recreationists that build on principles of sustainability and can be adopted by tourism organizations. A leader in this field is the Leave No Trace Center for Outdoor Ethics in Boulder, Colorado. According to its website, this is the most widely accepted outdoor ethics program used on public lands. The training builds on the seven principles of Leave No Trace:

- Plan ahead and prepare.
- Travel and camp on durable surfaces.
- Dispose of waste properly.
- Leave what you find.
- Minimize campfire impacts.
- Respect wildlife.
- Be considerate of other visitors.

Leave No Trace Center for Outdoor Ethics 2014

The principles of Leave No Trace seek to prevent and minimize our impact on wildlife and ecosystems.

By sharing this information with your clients, you are helping future generations to enjoy our wild places. As more people live in cities, modeling good behavior will help people travel in wilderness settings as good environmental stewards and neighbors.

Another organization that helps recreationists enjoy the outdoors with less impact is the National Outdoor Leadership School (NOLS). Its website offers information on courses, publications, and research on best practices. Outdoor retailers like REI in Seattle or MEC in Canada provide training on how to use gear and recreate in the outdoors safely while respecting wildlife and wild spaces.

Client Education

Educating your clients on the proper way to behave while traveling is a good sustainability practice. Even if your tourism experiences focus on culture instead of nature, people will enjoy their trip more if they understand local etiquette. No one wants to find out after their trip that pointing something out with their finger is a rude gesture, like in Bhutan, where the only polite way to point is with your thumb.

Avoid these problems by educating clients through pretrip information. Nature Encounters Tours and Travel specializes in adventure travel to Asia and Africa and provides several opportunities for trip participants to talk to trip leaders before the trip. They can learn about the destination's ecology and culture. In addition to explaining what equipment and clothing is necessary for a safe and enjoyable nature experience, guides describe the unique features of the host community and sensitize travelers to expected behavior, for example, explaining how to deal with children who beg for money.

People cannot demonstrate sensitivity to natural and cultural environments if tour operators and guides do not take the time to explain what constitutes good behavior. For example, if a guide tells his or her clients they can gauge whether they are too close to an animal by noting whether their presence is changing animal behavior, they will know when they are crowding wildlife. The American Society of Travel Agents (ASTA) has developed travel behavior guidelines for its agents to share with their customers. These commandments are basic and useful for orienting people before they travel. They are shown in figure 3.1.

Some companies write a **code of ethics** to explain the behavior they expect from tourists.

Last Frontiers, a travel company specializing in travel to Latin America, outlines its expectations of its clients on its website though a code of ethics for travelers. It describes what good practice looks like on tour and the things the company asks people to do (drink local beer instead of imported and use humor when bargaining) to enhance their overall experience (Last Frontiers 2013):

- Travel with a genuine desire to learn more about the people of your host country. Acquaint yourself with local customs and be aware of the feelings of other people, thus preventing what might be intrusive behavior on your part.

- Your pretrip research can be continued by asking questions while you are there. Any attempt to learn even a few words of the relevant language will make this a more rewarding experience for all involved.

- Realize that often the people in the country you visit have time concepts and approaches different from your own.

- Don't treat people as part of the landscape, they may not want their picture taken. Put yourself in their shoes, ask permission first, and respect their wishes. Many people love to see images of themselves, so if you are somewhere remote with your digital camera then do show the locals the pictures you have just taken of them with the wonders of modern technology!

- Do not make promises to people in your host country unless you can carry them through.

- Ensure that your behavior has no impact on the natural environment. Avoid picking flowers, removing seeds, damaging coral, and even buying souvenirs such as shells and skins. Understand that there can be no guarantees when it comes to wildlife, all sightings are a bonus.

- Try to put money into local people's hands: drink local beer or fruit juice rather than imported brands, and buy and eat locally produced food. When you are shopping, even where bargaining is expected, do inject humor and remember a low price almost certainly means a lower wage for the maker.

- If you want to take gifts, make sure they are appropriate (for example there are few dentists in remote communities, so sweets are not recommended).

- If you want your experience to be a home away from home, it may be foolish to waste money on traveling!

Courtesy of Last Frontiers.

Figure 3.1
Putting Sustainability Into Practice

Ten Commandments of Ecotourism

1. Respect the frailty of the earth. Unique and beautiful destinations may not be here for future generations to enjoy unless all are willing to help in its preservation.

2. Patronize those (hotels, airlines, resorts, cruise lines, tour operators, and suppliers) who advance energy conservation; promote water and air quality; provide recycling; manage waste and toxic materials safely for people and the environment; practice noise abatement; encourage community involvement; and provide experienced, well-trained staff dedicated to strong principles of conservation.

3. Learn about and support conservation-oriented programs and organizations working to preserve the environment and the local culture. Consider a vacation where you could volunteer to help the local community during a portion of your vacation.

4. Walk or use environmentally sound methods of transportation whenever possible.

5. Encourage drivers of public vehicles to stop engines when parked and not idle.

6. Leave only footprints. Take only photographs. No graffiti! No litter! Do not take away "souvenirs" from historical sites and natural areas.

7. To make your travels more meaningful, educate yourself about the geography, customs, manners, and cultures of the region you visit. Take time to listen to the people. Encourage local conservation efforts.

8. Respect the privacy and dignity of others. Inquire before photographing people.

9. Do not buy products made from endangered plants or animals, such as ivory, tortoise shell, animal skins, and feathers.

10. Always follow designated trails. Do not disturb animals or plants or their natural habitats.

Courtesy of American Society of Travel Agents.

If you decide to develop a code of ethics for your business, remember that your guides need to reinforce the concepts throughout the trip for maximum effect. On a personal level, consider whether a code of ethics would influence your behavior while traveling.

Ecochallenge
Would a Code of Ethics Change Your Behavior?

Most people do not want to offend people or harm the environment on vacation, but occasionally, innocent behavior can have harmful effects. Have you ever caused harm or offense by something you did while on vacation? Review the code of ethics Last Frontiers shares with its customers. Did you see anything that would change your behavior on future trips? Have you encountered companies that have a code of ethics? Do you think they are a good idea?

Education does not have to stop at the end of a tour. Having visited an area, people often develop a personal interest in the conservation issues that face a region and may look for opportunities to donate money, goods, or time. People returning from the Calgary Zoo's tour to Ghana's Wechiau Community Hippo Sanctuary have helped bring clean drinking water, install solar-powered LED lighting, and build a school for primary education (Equator Initiative 2012).

Providing information on area organizations can link the travel experience back to the traveler's regular life and build partnerships with the host community. It can also give customers a reason to travel again with your company.

ASSESSING IMPACTS

As you build your operating practices, consider how you will measure the effectiveness of your sustainability initiatives. Travelers who have been asked to assess the industry's effectiveness at adopting sustainability practices rate it as poor.

CMIGreen's Green Traveler Study in 2009 found the travel industry's sustainability practices need work. The study found that "too many travel companies are doing little or nothing to minimize their environment impact; other businesses' highly touted recycling and conservation efforts were viewed as superficial 'greenwashing'" (Roth 2010).

If you don't want your efforts labeled greenwashing, you must determine which performance indicators relate to your business, acceptable standards, and a way to measure them. For most businesses, this means selecting indicators of energy use or waste generated. Monitoring change to wildlife populations or environmental conditions can be undertaken if you own or lease large tracts of land, but in most cases, this work is done by government land managers.

If you are working in a tourism business, try the assessment shown in figure 3.2. Rating high in all areas is a sign that your organization has already thought about its environmental policies and practices. If your organization did not rate as well, continue to look for ways to improve. Remember that as more businesses adopt sustainability practices, the standard expected by travelers will increase, and your efforts must keep pace.

Figure 3.2
Business Assessment of Sustainable Tourism Practices

1 = No effort made to meet criteria
2 = Initial efforts made to meet criteria
3 = Some effort made to meet criteria, still room for improvement
4 = Good effort made to meet criteria, fine-tuning required
5 = Have met criteria

1. The design and construction of your facility reflects the natural surroundings and culture of the area.   1 2 3 4 5 n/a

2. Renewable building materials were used in the construction of your facilities.   1 2 3 4 5 n/a

3. Guest areas are furnished with locally produced furniture and artwork.   1 2 3 4 5 n/a

4. You set a maximum number of clients that is compatible with the environmental sensitivity of the area.   1 2 3 4 5 n/a

5. You have a written environmental policy.   1 2 3 4 5 n/a

6. You have a code of conduct for your employees.   1 2 3 4 5 n/a

7. You have a code of conduct for travelers.   1 2 3 4 5 n/a

8. You prequalify clients.   1 2 3 4 5 n/a

9. You provide pretrip information to your customers on the specific ecosystems and cultures visited.   1 2 3 4 5 n/a

10. You educate your clients about local and international laws regarding threatened plants and animals.   1 2 3 4 5 n/a

11. You prepare customers to buy and trade local products while respecting the indigenous culture.   1 2 3 4 5 n/a

12. You check water consumption and use regulating equipment on faucets and showers.   1 2 3 4 5 n/a

13. You take an active role in environmental or conservation organizations.   1 2 3 4 5 n/a

14. You make donations to environmental or conservation groups.   1 2 3 4 5 n/a

15. Your guides are local or they work with local guides.   1 2 3 4 5 n/a

16. Local people are represented in all levels of your operations.   1 2 3 4 5 n/a

(continued)

Figure 3.2 *(continued)*

17. You provide frequent training (at least seasonally) for your staff.	1	2	3	4	5	n/a
18. You purchase food locally for your operations.	1	2	3	4	5	n/a
19. You promote the sale of local arts and handicrafts.	1	2	3	4	5	n/a
20. You encourage customers to stay on pathways.	1	2	3	4	5	n/a
21. You encourage public or group transportation for your clients.	1	2	3	4	5	n/a
22. You use gray wastewater for watering and toilet rinsing.	1	2	3	4	5	n/a
23. You use environmentally friendly soaps.	1	2	3	4	5	n/a
24. You have undertaken an energy audit.	1	2	3	4	5	n/a
25. You use equipment to regulate lighting and heating.	1	2	3	4	5	n/a
26. You use energy-saving electrical appliances, lightbulbs, and so on.	1	2	3	4	5	n/a
27. You have a recycling program.	1	2	3	4	5	n/a
28. You compost solid food waste.	1	2	3	4	5	n/a
29. You donate leftover food and outdated bedding to local non-profit organizations.	1	2	3	4	5	n/a
30. You use recycled paper and paper products.	1	2	3	4	5	n/a
31. You purchase in bulk when possible.	1	2	3	4	5	n/a
32. You avoid the use of disposable dishes, toilet articles, and so on.	1	2	3	4	5	n/a
33. You provide beverages served in recyclable containers.	1	2	3	4	5	n/a
34. You remove waste from natural areas.	1	2	3	4	5	n/a
35. You give preference to equipment that has a long life and can be repaired.	1	2	3	4	5	n/a
36. Your organization participates in a certification program for environmental commitment.	1	2	3	4	5	n/a

Make sure to tell your clients about your sustainability practices and the results of your monitoring. Many tourism operators neglect to mention their good work or believe that consumers do not notice. Not every traveler will be interested in your green practices, but for others, it could be the deciding factor in placing a reservation.

SUMMARY

By now, you probably realize that putting the eco in ecotourism takes a lot more than good intentions. After completing your strategic plan in the last chapter, you have a good idea of where your business is headed and what is important to you. In this chapter, you learned about the need for environmental policies and practices, some of which are dictated by legislative requirements, some by your vision for your business. You also saw examples of good environmental practices. As with any desired outcome, to achieve progress you need a monitoring process so you can measure your efforts. In the next chapter, we will discuss the use of standards and certification to achieve uniform sustainability measures.

GLOSSARY

code of ethics—A tour company's explanation of the behavior they expect from tourists.

operating practices—A procedure created for repetitive use to achieve a desired outcome.

policy—A guideline outlining a business' opinion on a topic and direction to help staff achieve the organization's goals.

REVIEW QUESTIONS

1. Discuss how a sustainable tourism business is different from other tourism businesses.

2. What is a policy? Provide three examples of policies that would help a tourism business meet its sustainability goals.

3. Give an example of waste management practices a tourism business could use to reduce the amount of material going to a landfill.

4. Why is educating travelers about sustainability important? List two ways tourism organizations can educate their clients on sustainable tourism.

5. Provide two indicators you could use to measure success of sustainability policies.

VIDEO CASE STUDY

Visit the web resource to watch the video "From Trash to Treasure." After watching the video, answer the following questions.

1. What steps did Maho Bay Camps undertake to reduce the amount of waste ending up in a landfill?

2. How successful do you think Maho Bay Camp was in reducing its environmental impact?

3. Describe the types of travelers you think would choose an experience like that offered at Maho Bay Camps? What kinds of travelers do you think would want more amenities?

4. Do you think Maho Bay Camps was in a unique situation or could it be replicated in another location?

5. What role does government play in waste management? What actions (e.g., policies, grants, financial incentives) might it take to help sustainable tourism businesses operating in remote locations?

YOUR BUSINESS PLAN

With the examples you have read in this chapter and your own experiences with sustainability, consider which sustainable practices you want to incorporate into the development and operation of your business. If you are not familiar with the technology that you want to use, take the time to do research. For example, if you plan to operate a tented camp with composting toilets, find out whether composting will work in the climate in which you will operate.

As part of your research, document the cost, warranties, and optimum operating environments. With this information you can prioritize the green practices you will use. Some, like recycling or purchasing recycled paper, may be easy to adopt. Others, like using alternative energy sources, might take longer to establish.

Make notes in your business plan workbook about where you will use sustainable practices in operations (section 5.0) or to distinguish your business (section 4.0) or products and services (section 2.0).

1. What challenges did you face in finding information on sustainable products or services? Are you able to estimate the additional costs and potential savings from your sustainable tourism practices? Will your benefits exceed your costs? If not, you need to include this additional cost in your financial forecasts in chapter 9.

2. Which elements of sustainable tourism practices are most important to you? Explain whether it is more important to select practices that have positive financial impacts, perhaps reducing waste management costs, or practices that are highly visible to customers, for example, placing recycling bins in hotel rooms.

3. How will you highlight your sustainable practices when you write your business plan? If you plan to use comparable businesses to illustrate an advantage, list the businesses and websites now.

REFERENCES

ASTA. 2013. Ten commandments on eco-tourism. www.asta.org/ELibrary/content.cfm?ItemNumber=4525.

Center for Sustainable Tourism. 2014. Greening North Carolina travel and tourism: Tips for sustainable practices in tourism. www.ecu.edu/cs-acad/sustainabletourism/upload/N-C-Green-Travel-Sustainability-Tips-2.pdf.

Equator Initiative. 2012. "Wechiau community hippo sanctuary Ghana." Equator initiative case studies, United Nations Development Programme (UNDP). www.equatorinitiative.org/images/stories/com_winners/casestudy/case_1348261639.pdf.

Fairmont Hotels & Resorts. 2013. Green Partnership Program. www.fairmontmeetings.com/seattle/pdf/green_partnership_program.pdf.

Last Frontiers. 2013. Code of ethics for travellers. www.lastfrontiers.com/rt_code.php.

Leave No Trace Center for Outdoor Ethics. 2014. About. http://lnt.org/about.

O.A.R.S. 2014. O.A.R.S. Responsible travel policy. www.oars.com/about_us/responsible_travel.html#b.

Roth, T. 2010. CMI Green Traveler Study Report 2010. Vol. 1. San Francisco: CMIGreen Community Marketing. www.greenlodgingnews.com/downloads/cmigreentraveler2010v1.pdf.

SABMag. 2010. LEED Canada Buildings in Review: 2001-2009. www.sabmagazine.com/uploads/editor/documents/21-LEED%20SUPPLEMENT.pdf.

SUSTAINABILITY STANDARDS AND CERTIFICATION

||||||||||| LEARNING OUTCOMES |||||||||||

After reading this chapter, you will be able to do the following:

- Understand the role of tourism standards

- Identify existing tourism standard programs

- Explain the consequences of too many certification programs

- Recognize the need for global certification programs

- Distinguish between accreditation and certification

- Understand how certification contributes to business success

Although your business may embrace concepts of sustainability, you might find it difficult to demonstrate your commitment to customers or you may find that competitors are making similar claims without evidence that they have put sustainability practices in place. Sustainability standards for industry are increasingly recognized as a mechanism to ensure the integrity of the sustainable tourism product as well as increase marketability and credibility with the traveling public. Adopting industry standards by participating in a certification program can accelerate your sustainability process by providing examples and training in sustainable tourism practices.

This chapter will familiarize you with several sustainability standards for tourism organizations. It will also outline the difficulties sponsoring agencies face in maintaining credibility and achieving consumer acceptance.

THE ROLE OF TOURISM STANDARDS

Sustainability standards are a benchmark of or target for minimum performance required by a tour operator, transportation provider, hotel, attraction, or other tourism organization to be considered sustainable or environmentally responsible. The Global Sustainable Tourism Council Criteria are an example of sustainability standards for the tourism industry. An organization or government establishes standards with input from experts in the tourism industry. If the organization is nongovernmental, it will go through **certification**, a process of assessment to confirm that standards are met. Certification is granted by an organization that has received **accreditation**, verification that an organization's standards, testing, and certification process are acceptable to the governing body; in the case of the GSTC Criteria, the accreditation is performed by the Global Sustainable Tourism Council. Once the organization running the tourism standards program is accredited, it can require program participants to undergo certification.

The widespread use of "eco" labels is difficult for consumers to understand without underlying sustainable tourism standards.

While many tourism organizations claim to operate in an environmentally sustainable manner, it can be difficult for an outsider to know what processes back up these assertions and whether a business is doing better or worse than similar organizations. Setting industry standards and certifying that businesses are meeting them can provide the following benefits:

- A commonly understood description of sustainable tourism practices
- Established standards of acceptable behavior for sustainable tourism organizations
- Measurement criteria against established criteria
- External validation of adherence to sustainable tourism practices (if audits are required)
- Consistency in the use of sustainable tourism labels or claims
- Reduced confusion among travelers looking for sustainable tourism products
- Increased marketability of tourism businesses meeting the criteria

The benefits of setting up standards have encouraged many organizations to establish their own program; usually these include the following elements:

• A description of acceptable behavior—Guidelines that specify exactly what sustainable practice looks like are usually written by experts in the field. This expertise lends credibility to certification resulting from meeting the standards.

• Descriptions of the benefits for switching to the new practices—Investing in green technology or training staff in new procedures has a cost. By providing a description of the expected savings and additional revenues from adopting sustainability practices, businesses are more likely to participate in the program.

• Training on sustainability practices—Standardized training for implementing changes will help participants ensure behavior meets standards consistently. For example, setting up a towel program in which towels are only washed if the client leaves them on the floor requires that housekeeping staff understands why the program is in place and how to respond. Some hoteliers report problems with staff wanting to replace all towels so the room looks cleaner, even though that does not meet the goal of reducing water usage.

• Ideas for sources of green technology and building materials—Providing a list of suppliers of cleaning supplies, lights, or other materials can save businesses time, and if an organization can set up bulk purchasing discounts, money.

• Expectations for how members will remain in good standing—This could include an independent audit or review, or it could be a simple agreement to operate in a way that meets the organization's code of ethics.

• Suggestions for how to add more sustainable practices each year—Even if an organization meets the minimum standards, there is room for improvement and the organization should have a multiyear plan to tackle tasks in place. With new scientific discoveries, changes in technology, and evolving consumer beliefs, it is also important to keep looking for improvements to the program.

An example of where standards have improved the tourism industry can be seen in the video on whale watching standards found in the web resource. The next section looks at existing programs in more detail.

EXISTING PROGRAMS

Using tourism standards to define acceptable behavior is not a new concept. The American Automobile Association (AAA) has been rating tourism businesses since 1937. In 1963, AAA adopted a formal rating system for accommodations. As a result, many travelers found their AAA guidebook a helpful tool for locating a clean, safe hotel on family road trips. The Michelin Guide started assigning stars for restaurant meals in 1926. Now there is increasing focus on establishing standards for sustainability initiatives.

Some standard programs cover a geographic region or state. Others address a tourism sector, such as hotels, conference facilities, or beaches. The Blue Flag program was started in Europe in 1987 to recognize municipalities that safeguarded beaches by meeting criteria for sewage treatment and the quality of bathing water.

It can be difficult to define and describe acceptable behavior across the different types of tourism sectors; for example, the sustainability behavior associated with tour operators would have little in common with the behavior of someone managing a large hotel. Some certification programs have avoided this problem by focusing on one sector, for example, the hotel industry, or developed different standards for different sectors. Australia is one of the few places where industry standards have been developed across a broader framework at a national level. Ecotourism Australia, a nonprofit organization, with support from industry and government has built a brand around sustainable tourism. Started in 1996, its ECO certification program allows tourism businesses offering the following products to be certified:

Travelers for many years have relied on certification programs such as the American Automobile Association's program to assess accommodations.

- Tours
- Skippered cruises and bareboat charters
- Attractions
- Accommodations

The program offers three levels of certification: nature tourism, ecotourism, and advanced ecotourism. The different standards reflect the sustainability practices employed. The program has certified more than 1,000 tourism products, and 66 companies have been certified for a decade or more. This level of participation and long-term support are evidence that going green is a good business decision.

Australia's example demonstrates that when a program receives enough support to certify a substantial number of businesses and to make travelers aware of the certification, something important happens. At this point, it is possible to create a sustainable tourism **brand**, the result of a marketing process to distinguish a name or product from its competitor's products. In 2013-2014 Ecotourism Australia (EA) estimated "the combined annual turnover of all EA certified operators exceeded $1 billion (Australian) demonstrating how ecotourism is no longer a niche but has become the mainstream" (Ecotourism Australia 2014a). It is possible that certification and the marketing partnerships created by Ecotourism Australia have contributed to this growth, but without research it cannot be proven.

Regardless, Ecotourism Australia has succeeded where others have not. A committed group of tourism professionals worked hard on the program, and the Australian federal government initiated and supported the development of a national ecotourism strategy and supported the program with funding for research and setup (Black and Crabtree 2007). By having the resources to create awareness of the program and a long-term strategy, Ecotourism Australia was able to develop detailed standards and provide training for business owners to adapt them. EA also uses external independent assessors to verify business claims before certification is awarded (Ecotourism Australia 2014b).

Few standards programs have been able to create a recognizable brand. Since the Blue Flag program was created in 1987, the number of tourism standard programs has exploded. It was estimated in 2007 that approximately 80 tourism standard programs existed (CESD 2007). Many of these programs are in Europe or developing nations, but approximately 20 programs operate in the United States. Many of them are state-level programs focused on the hospitality sector (Poser 2009).

There are too many tourism standard programs in the United States and Canada to list them all, so table 4.1 provides a sample of programs for lodging, tour operators, restaurants, and conference centers. Even golf courses have a certification program through the Audubon Cooperative Sanctuary Program. Many of the programs, such as Green Seal GS-33 or Florida Green Lodging, focus on accommodation. Given the large number of hotels in the tourism industry and the potential for cost savings through energy or waste conservation, it is understandable that this type of business would be well served. Tour compa-

Table 4.1 Tourism-Related Certification Programs

Program	Operator	Launch date	Type of business certified	Number of participants
Green Seal Standard for Lodging Properties, GS-33	Green Seal	1999	Lodging	90 in the United States (Feb. 2013)
Audubon Cooperative Sanctuary Program for Golf	Cooperative effort between U.S. Golf Association and Audubon International		Golf courses	500 in United States, 65 in Canada (Feb. 2013)
Florida Green Lodging	Florida Dept. of Environmental Protection	2004	Lodging	689 (Dec. 5, 2012)
STEP Eco-Certification Program	Sustainable Travel International	2006	Accommodations, attractions, tour operators, transportation providers, destination managers	More than 200 globally (March 2011)
Leadership in Energy and Environmental Design (LEED)	U.S. Green Building Council	2009	Hotels, conference facilities, visitor centers	141 certified globally, 1,200 registered (June 2012)

nies are fewer in number than hotels and have diverse characteristics; often they need to turn to a national or international program such as the Sustainable Tourism Education Program (STEP) Eco-Certification Program.

Take the following ecochallenge to see how many organizations you can find in your state or province that have established sustainability standards. Consider whether you would consider such a search before taking a vacation.

CONFUSION IN THE MARKETPLACE

If when you were completing the ecochallenge it seemed like it took too much work to determine which organizations had been certified for their conformity to sustainable tourism standards or that the certification benefits were unclear to you, you are not alone. The fast growth in tourism industry standards and the green marketing claims made by businesses have created confusion in the marketplace.

Many travelers realize there is a big difference between recycling pop bottles and setting up alternative energy sources, but they cannot easily determine which tourism businesses are sustainable. One study found that 75 percent of travelers were "skeptical, to some degree, of the environmentally responsible claims of hotel operators" (Roth 2010, p. xx). The same study found "there are presently over 350 'green' travel or hospitality certifications, and 97 percent of respondents could not name any" (2010).

The proliferation of tourism standards caused some tourism professionals to believe there was duplication of efforts and that no international brand for sustainable tourism could emerge. Representatives from many of the most important certification programs met at the Mohonk Mountain House in New Paltz, New York, in 2000 to craft the Mohonk Agreement, an informal consensus on the minimum standards for certifying sustainable tourism (CESD 2007).

This meeting planted the seeds for the Global Sustainable Tourism Council (GSTC). In the years following the Mohonk meeting, a Sustainable Tourism Stewardship Council feasibility study was undertaken and support for minimum standards solidified (CESD 2007). In 2009, the Global Sustainable Tourism Council was established. As described in chapter 1, its main focus is to develop a set of international standards for sustainable tourism.

GLOBAL TOURISM STANDARDS

Establishing global industry standards is a large undertaking, but the Global Sustainable Tourism Council is making progress. Industry stakeholders have reached consensus on sustainable tourism practices for hotels and tourism operators, and input is being solicited for the practices at tourism destinations. Because the range of businesses and environments involved is diverse, the process of reaching standards that satisfy everyone is complex and requires considerable effort.

Ecochallenge
Looking for Tourism Standards

After looking at the examples of tourism standard programs in table 4.1, see whether you can find similar programs in your state or province. If you cannot find one specifically for your region, look to see whether international programs such as Sustainable Tourism Eco-Certification have certified tourism businesses in your area.

What benefits did the standards programs you looked at offer to businesses? Were you aware of the program before your read this book? Do not be embarrassed if you were not aware, many programs spend money on setting up standards, training, and recruiting new participants. Building a brand and telling consumers about the program sometimes gets overlooked in the process.

Think about whether you will search for an organization that has been certified for sustainable tourism standards for your next vacation. If you will not, make a note of your reasons. This will give you insight into the marketing challenges discussed in later chapters.

One problem the GSTC wants to address through its international standards is compliance. Although the standards programs provide guidelines, following them is voluntary because it makes it easier to attract participants and reduces the cost to tourism businesses. The downside is participants can demonstrate a range of sustainable tourism practices, from barely acceptable to exemplary. Therefore, consumers may not be buying from the type of business they think they are. To establish credibility in the mind of consumers, it is critical that external reviewers verify performance claims. The Global Sustainable Tourism Council includes an audit in its process.

The GSTC is looking for partner organizations to help monitor compliance of the standards. Ultimately, the GSTC will rely on the organizations currently operating sustainable tourism standards programs to certify that tourism businesses are operating in accordance with the GSTC Criteria.

As shown in table 4.2, parties move through three phases—recognition, approval, and accreditation—to become a GSTC-accredited organization. Once the organization has received accreditation, it can certify tourism businesses that meet the GSTC standard. For example, the organization Biosphere Responsible Tourism is accredited to certify that businesses meet the standards of the GSTC. Businesses that successfully complete the certification process with Biosphere Responsible Tourism can tell customers they are certified and meet Global Sustainable Tourism Council Criteria.

In the first few months of the process, only one organization reached approved status, but several completed the first stage of GSTC standards. With time, more organizations will move through the process, and as certification starts, tourism businesses will be able to advertise a global standard. It will take years for consumers to recognize the GSTC brand, but hopefully the public's interest in sustainability will lead them to the GSTC's program.

As the Global Sustainable Tourism Council gains momentum in its accreditation program, you may want to align yourself with an organization that has GSTC certification and gain the benefit of being associated with a global sustainability brand.

CERTIFICATION AND YOUR BOTTOM LINE

Meeting sustainability targets will cost you money in the short term. In addition to formulating your processes around waste management, energy efficiency, and community partnerships, you will incur membership and certification fees with accreditation organizations. Many businesses wonder whether they will recoup their costs through cost savings or increased sales.

You will likely see operating cost savings, but you might find your customers reluctant to pay more for a green product. YPartnership, a U.S. marketing firm (now part of MMGY Global), says 85 percent of Americans consider themselves to be "environmentally conscious. Most, however, are not willing to pay a premium fare or rate to green suppliers as they expect them to be good stewards" (Hotel News Now 2008).

These findings are supported by the research reported in the CMIGreen Traveler Study. The study found that even people sympathetic to the sustainability philosophy were unwilling to open their wallets. Approximately 36 percent said they would be willing to pay a premium of 6 percent to 10 percent to decrease their ecological footprint while traveling. And 42.9 percent would only spend 1 to 5 percent. Almost 16 percent would pay nothing extra (Roth 2010).

If consumers are unwilling to pay a premium for sustainability, you may wonder whether there is a way to recoup your cost to establish green practices. Consumers may not pay for the concept of sustainability, but there is a good chance they will pay for its benefits. For example, if you sell the advantages of sustainable practices, like small group sizes, chances to engage in meaningful ways with residents, and breathing easier because of a

Table 4.2   Global Sustainable Tourism Council Approval Process for Standards and Certification Programs

Stage	Outcome
GSTC Recognized	Organization's standards are considered equivalent to GSTC's
GSTC Approved	Organizations can begin certifying businesses.
GSTC Accredited	Organization must start certifying businesses within two years of GSTC approval.

GSTC 2014

Consumers might be willing to pay for the benefits of sustainability practices, such as traveling in small groups.

Dob's Farm/fotolia.co

lack of cleaning chemicals, you can create extra value in the traveler's mind and price accordingly. This will be discussed in more detail in the next chapter on how to market your sustainable business.

SUMMARY

The tourism industry recognizes the need for sustainability, but work remains to define and implement global performance standards. The diversity and size of the tourism industry makes it difficult to develop a standard that fits all situations. The Global Sustainable Tourism Council has developed criteria for hotels, tour operators, and destinations and is building partnerships that will allow significant numbers of tourism businesses to be certified and to build a sustainable tourism brand that consumers will recognize. Travelers have shown themselves supportive of principles of sustainable tourism, but it can be difficult to translate that support into sales. The next chapter discusses how to market to tourists seeking sustainable travel.

GLOSSARY

accreditation—Verification that an organization's standards, testing, and certification process are acceptable to the governing body.

brand—The result of a marketing process to distinguish a name or product from its competitor's products.

certification—A process of assessment to confirm that standards are met.

sustainability standards—Benchmarks of or targets for minimum performance that a tour operator, transportation provider, hotel, attraction, or other tourism organization must meet to be considered sustainable or environmentally responsible.

|||||||||||||||| REVIEW QUESTIONS ||||||||||||||||

1. What are the benefits of sustainable tourism standards for consumers? For tourism business owners?

2. Explain the differences between certification and accreditation. How are standards used in the certification process?

3. Identify three tourism sustainability standards programs. Comment on the advantages and disadvantages of having a multitude of certifications for businesses in Canada and the United States.

4. What steps is the Global Sustainable Tourism Council taking to develop worldwide standards for sustainable tourism organizations?

5. Do you think travelers should pay more for a tourism experience or service provided by an organization certified as sustainable? Explain your reasoning.

|||||||||||||||| VIDEO CASE STUDY ||||||||||||||||

Visit the web resource to watch the video "Whale Watching Standards." After watching the video, answer the following questions.

1. Before you watched the video, were you aware there was a minimum distance required between whale-watching boats and whales?

2. Have you taken a whale-watching trip? What evidence did you observe that the business operating the tour was following standards of sustainable tourism?

3. Explain how the popularity of whale watching might help support conservation efforts and how it might have negative impacts on whales or marine environments.

4. Can you envision a situation in which a tourism business might be tempted to engage in behavior that could have a negative impact on whales?

5. Whale watching standards described in the video were started as voluntary guidelines. Do you think appropriate wildlife-viewing behavior will occur with voluntary standards or do you think legislation and mandatory compliance is needed in all cases?

6. How do you think standards of behavior contribute to sustainable tourism?

|||||||||||||||| YOUR BUSINESS PLAN ||||||||||||||||

As you create your business plan, think about what certifications might help you establish or market your business. Visit the websites of some of the organizations mentioned in this chapter or search for ones in your geographic region. Ask for information on their standards and determine whether they have training or educational materials. Often this knowledge can help you make the right choice in your business construction, operation, and types of products you offer. Some hotel certification programs will include cost savings on energy or waste management strategies; adopting their techniques can stretch your operating budget.

Compare how well known the brands are for each certification program. You want to determine whether the certifying organization will list your organization on its website when you are certified and whether consumers are aware of the certification. It is frustrating to put considerable effort into certification and then gain no recognition from travelers. Align yourself with organizations that promote their stakeholders and the benefits will help in your next step, planning your marketing efforts.

1. How did your opinion of certification programs change as you undertook research for your business plan? Explain why you are more or less convinced certification could help your business.

2. Were you able to find a certification program that matched your business objectives? Describe unique circumstances your business might face that are not adequately addressed in global certification programs.

3. Summarize the cost of registration in a certification program and the annual cost to maintain certification. Note your reaction as you complete this step. Do you think certification provides your business a good value? Are you worried your prices might not be high enough to cover these costs?

|||||||||||||||||||||||||||| REFERENCES ||||||||||||||||||||||||||||

Black, R., and A. Crabtree, A., editors. 2007. Quality assurance and certification in ecotourism. CABI. Oxfordshire, U.K.

Center for Ecotourism and Sustainable Development. 2007. A simple user's guide to certification for sustainable tourism and ecotourism. www.ecotourism.org/sites/ecotourism.org/files/document/Certification/Ecotourism%20Handbook%20I%20-%20A%20Simple%20User%27s%20Guide%20to%20Certification%20for%20SustainableTourism%20and%20Ecotou.pdf.

Ecotourism Australia. 2014a. A brief history of Ecotourism Australia. www.ecotourism.org.au/about/history.

Ecotourism Australia. 2014b. Certification process: How does it work? www.ecotourism.org.au/our-certification-programs/eco-certification-5/certification-process-2.

Global Sustainable Tourism Council. 2014. GSTC approval process for standards and certification programs. www.gstcouncil.org/resource-center/gstc-approval-process-for-standards-and-certification-programs.html.

Hotel News Now. 2008, Y Partnership predicts 2009 travel trends. Dec. 23. www.hotelnewsnow.com/Articles.aspx/439/Ypartnership-predicts-2009-travel-trends.

Poser, E.A. 2009. Setting standards for sustainable tourism: An analysis of US tourism certification programs. Master's project submitted to Nicholas School of the Environment of Duke University. http://dukespace.lib.duke.edu/dspace/bitstream/handle/10161/997/L.Poser%20final%20MP.pdf.

Roth, T. 2010. CMIGreen Traveler Study Report 2010. Vol. 1. San Francisco: CMIGreen Marketing. www.greenlodgingnews.com/downloads/cmigreentraveler2010v1.pdf.

MARKETING YOUR PRODUCT

|||||||||||| LEARNING OUTCOMES ||||||||||||

After reading this chapter, you will be able to do the following:

- Describe the four Ps of marketing

- Develop a marketing plan

- Complete a budget for marketing expenditures

- Understand the importance of monitoring and evaluating marketing expenditures

- Explain why a marketing plan is the cornerstone of a business plan

What happens after a tourism professional has created a tourism experience that engages customers, features unique aspects of a community's environment and culture, and is distinguishable from the competition? As good as the product is, the owner cannot sit back and wait for customers to arrive. They might not have heard of the town nor be aware of the attractions it offers, or they may be considering a similar product from another business. As a future tourism professional, you need to understand marketing and prepare an effective marketing plan that puts the product in front of customers and convinces them to buy.

Many people starting a tourism business confuse sales and marketing, but they are not the same. **Marketing** is the process by which you determine the potential buyers of your product, what their needs are, and how you can respond to those needs in a way that will encourage them to visit your business. It is a critical component and requires looking at the big picture. **Selling** is part of the promotional activities in the marketing process and occurs when you contact people to persuade them to buy.

As you read this chapter, you will learn about the critical elements of marketing and how this information is used to create a marketing plan that adds financial strength to a business plan. You will also learn to deal with special challenges as the owner or employee of a sustainable tourism business. Consumers may not respond to your advertising messages as expected or competitors might imply a level of sustainable tourism practice that does not exist. If you are one of the many people who do not like the idea of selling, remember that while you might be able to hire someone to help you sell, you can never remove yourself totally from marketing. After all, who is better equipped to convey the uniqueness and attractiveness of your tour or destination than the person who had the enthusiasm to create the company and the product?

FOUR Ps OF MARKETING

Marketing is a complex process that requires you to look at what you are selling, what you are charging your customers, where you are finding your customers, and how you are attracting attention to your wares. Marketing experts describe these core elements of the marketing process as the four Ps of marketing: product, price, place, and promotion (YP Advertising Solutions 2012).

- **Product** might involve a physical good, for example, baskets crafted

- by an indigenous tribe, or a service or experience, for example, offering nature-viewing tours in a unique setting.
- **Price** is what you charge your customer for a product.
- **Place** is where you distribute your product. Unlike other industries, tourism products must be consumed on-site. They cannot be shipped around the world like a package of coffee.
- **Promotion** is telling the target market about your product. It includes the selling activities often associated with marketing such as **advertising**, communication that calls attention to your organization to influence or convince the audience to take action, usually to purchase something.

The **marketing mix** refers to how the four Ps of product, price, place, and promotion are used. A manager will adjust the controllable elements of the four Ps until a mix is found that meets the needs of the markets and produces the desired income. Strategies for developing the optimum marketing mix are discussed later in the chapter.

DEVELOPING A MARKETING PLAN

Successful marketing requires you to develop the right product, put it in the right place, and sell it to the right people for the right price. A **marketing plan** outlines strategies for achieving your marketing objectives using product, price, place, and placement.

Your marketing plan builds on the work done in your strategic plan by adding detail to the **market analysis** and matching products to market segments. It helps you set specific marketing objectives and develop strategies and activities to sell your product. The marketing plan allows you to budget for marketing activities and to evaluate the effectiveness of those activities. While a strategic plan is usually developed every few years, a marketing plan is usually completed each year because marketing is critical to a tourism business's success.

As shown in figure 5.1, a marketing plan contains the following elements:

- Objectives
- Situation analysis
- Market analysis
- Competitive analysis
- Product–market match
- Marketing objectives
- Marketing strategies
- Marketing activities
- Marketing forecasts

Each of the marketing planning components is explained in the following pages. The marketing process is complex and time consuming, so you might need to refer to these sections as you refine your marketing plan.

Objectives

With any marketing plan, you need to know what you are trying to accomplish. Just wanting to sell more "stuff" is not specific enough to develop a good marketing plan. In the strategic plan, you defined objectives for your business. Revisit these objectives and your mission statement as you develop your marketing plan. Review your business values, the way you describe target customers, and how you want to accomplish your goals. If your mission statement calls for you to provide visitors with lifetime memories through sensory experiences in nature, you will market your tours differently than if you provide mountaineering activities for the extreme thrill seeker. As you proceed through the steps of the marketing plan, you will encounter many alternatives. By referring

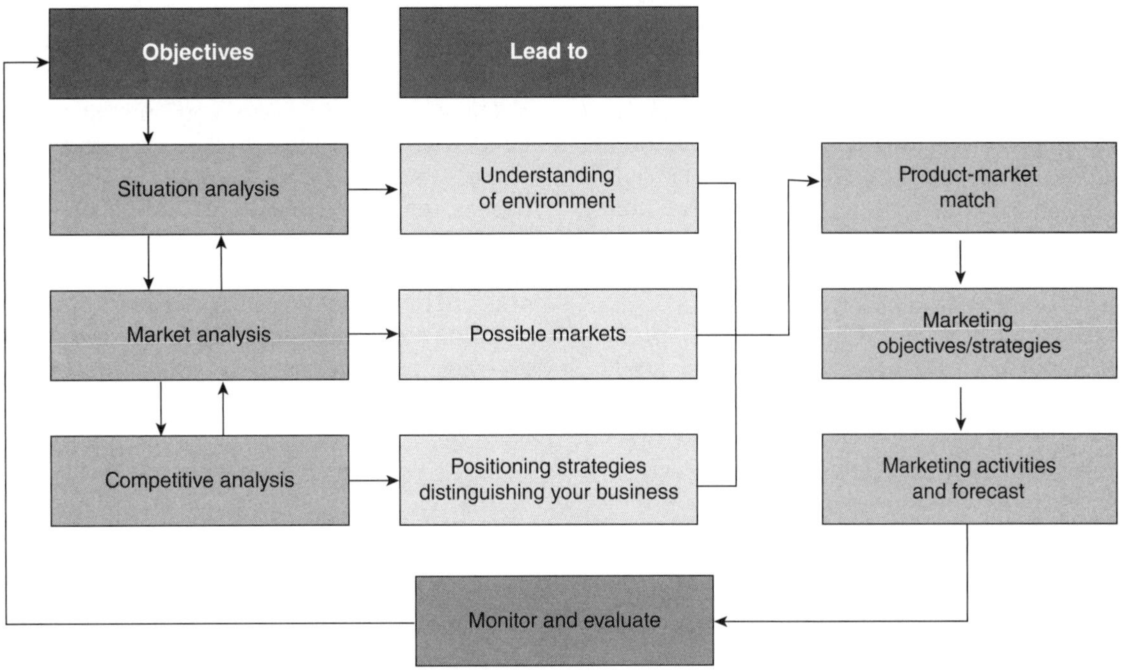

Figure 5.1 Overview of the marketing planning process.

to your mission statement and high-level objectives, you can make choices that are consistent with your values and vision.

Identify the goals and objectives from your strategic plan that need action in the next year and use them as a starting point for your marketing plan. For example, if one of the objectives of your strategic plan is to generate a profit of 10 percent, you need to concentrate your marketing activities on tours that have a healthy profit margin. You may also choose to target upscale customers who will pay a higher price for your product. In the next steps, analyze the situation, market, and competition to determine which marketing strategies and activities are likely to be successful.

Situation Analysis

As you developed your strategic plan, you completed part of the **situation analysis** by taking an inventory of local tourism resources. If you skipped this step or some time has elapsed since you completed a resource inventory, update your inventory. Perhaps a new orchid species has been discovered in your region or new roads have been built or an existing one closed, allowing more or less access to remote areas. Maybe a new festival in your community with a cultural or nature component would offer opportunities to share marketing costs. Reviewing the situation in your community will ensure you are familiar with the natural, cultural, and man-made features you can use to meet tourist needs.

You also want to consider negative influences that have arisen in your area lately. A limit on the number of tours that can occur on a certain trail can restrict the number or variety of tour products you can offer.

Another area to consider is the economic climate. Travel for most people is a discretionary expense. A downturn in the economy can reduce the number of international or national tourists who will purchase tour products, although regional visitation might increase because people will vacation closer to home.

Although you have completed much of this review when you undertook the SWOT analysis during the strategic planning process, you need additional detail to develop your marketing plan. You will also find that updating the information each year is important because conditions change rapidly in tourism.

Market Analysis

It has been a year or more since the organization has completed a strategic plan or previous marketing plans, and it's time to look again at the market. New tourism products will lure travelers to different destinations and activities. People's preferences and travel patterns change. Economic and political shifts can have dramatic effects on tourism. In September 2008 when the economic recession deepened dramatically, consumers changed their travel patterns. In 2009 travelers were looking for vacations close to home or short in duration and tourism businesses scrambled to respond with ideas for staycations—vacations where people stay at home overnight and participate in leisure and tourism activities during the day—and daycations, daylong holidays. When terrorism threats or fears of disease are high, many North American tourists choose not to fly overseas, possibly creating opportunities for tourism businesses located in Canada, the United States, and Mexico.

As you did when developing a strategic plan, look to many sources of market research to gain an understanding of tourism trends and prospective customers. In addition to knowing what type of activities customers are looking for, it is important to understand their motivations and trip decisions. As you develop your marketing plan, it will be helpful to know whether people are being lured to destinations because of the attractions, or whether they are escaping something, such as a cold North American winter. Other things that you would like to know are the time of year people prefer to travel and the factors that influence their choice of destination, accommodation, and activities. In North America, families with children have traditionally favored summer vacations. As some regions move to year-round schooling, people might begin traveling at different times of the year. With more two-career households and fear over job losses, some people look for short-term escapes, rather than extended travel. These trends will give way to others. You need to continually monitor them to develop the best marketing plan possible.

Reading market research while you develop your marketing plan will help you avoid the tendency to project your likes, dislikes, and habits onto other people whose backgrounds and preferences might be much different. Although you gain valuable information talking to friends and neighbors, you need to know what is going on with the traveling public nationally and internationally. Look at information gathered in large studies whenever possible.

A thorough market analysis also will show you which advertisers and advertising media are best suited to reach your clients. When you open for business, you will be deluged with offers to advertise and you want to make sure you select the best opportunities for your marketing plan. If you sell white-water rafting trips on class V rivers,

you would likely generate more inquiries from an adventure magazine that has a young, active readership than a publication aimed at a family market.

One of the outcomes of your market analysis is an identification of the market segments, or types of customers, you want to target. By studying your market research, you will learn their preferences, lifestyles, and locations. You will have done some of this in your strategic plan, but now you will update and add more detail to your analysis.

Using the market segments you selected in your strategic plan, describe the following about your potential customers:

- Their common interests, the geographic area where they live, and demographic information you have.

- Evidence that you can reach them by marketing to the segment. For example, if you have selected families within a one-hour drive as a market segment, you can probably reach them by advertising in magazines aimed at families or young mothers. Conversely, you will find a market segment of people who like nature to be too broad; reaching all these people with advertising will be expensive because you will need to advertise in many places. Narrowing your market segment to bird-watchers who have a life list and who travel to pursue their hobby will allow you to advertise in publications and websites catering to bird-watchers.

- Estimates of the size of your target market segment. With the reach of the Internet you can find people with a wide range of interests, but you need to determine whether there are enough people to make it worthwhile to focus your marketing on them.

If you have picked market segments that are cohesive yet narrow enough to market to effectively, your marketing plan will be more successful because you will know where to find the people who are interested in your product or experience. If you think people over 45 years old who are generally interested in nature, live in the Pacific Northwest, and enjoy organized club tours would like your tours, you can target these people through regional publications. You could aim advertising efforts at social clubs and conservation groups with large numbers of members over 45 years old.

Grouping your customers by common interests makes marketing easier because you limit your advertising messages and mediums.

You will find that most of the information you gain during your market analysis describes the demographics of your market segments or the activities they pursue while on vacation, but you may also want to look for information on the psychographics of travelers. **Psychographic information** helps marketers understand a traveler's view of the world and their values, travel behaviors, and motivations. Researcher Stanley Plog's model of psychographics was the first to segment travelers into five types ranging from psychocentric—nervous, not adventurous, and having an affinity for the familiar—to allocentric, self-confident and adventurous searchers of new experiences (Plog 1974). His premise that travelers' psychographics determine their behaviors has implications for your business. If your customers are psychocentric, your marketing materials might need to stress safety or the familiar. Conversely, customers who are highly allocentric will respond better to marketing that offers new experiences or activities that offer a higher risk. It is possible that people can shift from one category to another over their lifetime. A person might exhibit psychocentric tendencies until positive travel experiences make them willing to travel farther from home, which is more allocentric.

An innovative approach to market segmentation has been taken by the Canadian Tourism Commission. As described in the sidebar EQ Profiles, market segmentation that is expanded beyond age, income, and geographical origin to examine travelers' beliefs and social values offers a better understanding of the experiences they seek.

Information on your customer's preferences will be used in the product–market match. However, before we start that step, you need to know what competition your marketing plan will face.

Compevtitive Analysis

An old expression says if you build a better mousetrap, the world will beat a path to your door, but, unfortunately, that is not usually the case. You have to let people know you have a better mousetrap and you have to see who else is building mousetraps and how they might use your weaknesses to their advantage. In business, this process is called a **competitive analysis**, a review of other organizations offering similar products and the ways they distinguish their company or services.

A review of competitors lets you determine who is also selling sustainable tourism products and what they are selling. This analysis will also tell you the following:

- Whether the market is too crowded
- Your competitors' strengths and weaknesses
- What benefits they highlight in their marketing messages

In your strategic plan, you identified direct and indirect competitors. Take time now to look at the

---

EQ Profiles: Market Segments by Psychographic Characteristics

Explorers quotient, or EQ, is a process the Canadian Tourism Commission (CTC) uses to identify market segments. It focuses on psychographics, or people's view of the world and their values. The result is a breakdown by geographic market into market segments or psychographic groups called explorer types.

The CTC provides a quiz for travelers to determine their style of travel. Tourism organizations can offer different products for different traveler types. Matching the types of experiences to a traveler's motivations and behaviors offers a greater chance for marketing success.

The CTC evaluated the market segments determined by the EQ process and the likeliness of each to appreciate the CTC's brand Canada: Keep Exploring. The CTC determined that three explorer types (or segments)—free spirits, cultural explorers, and authentic experiencers—were the best targets, and the CTC now focuses its marketing efforts on these customers.

Canadian Tourism Commission 2012

---

marketing materials of your direct competitors in detail. By examining the images they use and the slogans or words prominently displayed on their website or brochure, you get an idea of which market segments they are targeting and the benefits they are highlighting. Their strategy for **positioning**, creating an identity in the minds of consumers, should also become apparent. A white-water rafting company that displays many pictures of young children and families in rafts on their website and words that stress safety and fun, could be targeting market segments that include families and positioning itself as a safe place for a fun experience or a place to build family memories. You might think environmentally friendly practices are a competitive advantage and should be featured prominently in advertising, but this might not be the case. If travelers do not consider that information when making their travel decisions, putting it on brochures or the front page of a brochure does not make sense. Look at where your competitors place information on sustainability; it will provide hints on how much, or little, travelers value sustainability.

Do not overlook the fact that while you are completing your competitive analysis, your competitors are analyzing you. They will look at the markets you target and the strategies you use to distinguish your product. If you are successful, they might copy what you do and create more competition. Updating your marketing plan each year will give you a chance to adjust your strategies to stay ahead of the competition.

Although you will be busy identifying your competitors' weaknesses and ways that you can take advantage of these, think about your own weaknesses. It is difficult to admit your business is less than perfect or destined for anything other than financial success. Take a minute or two and look at your venture from an outsider's perspective. Perhaps you depend on only one or two talented people for your guiding or you have enough cash in the bank to carry you through only two or three bad months. Maybe your targeted market segment is a very small niche and too small to generate sufficient sales. If you are successful or perceived as a threat, your competitors will analyze your strengths and weaknesses.

The Williamsburg Marketing Research Task Force in Virginia used this approach when it took time to compare its destination's performance against competing destinations. The group discovered that while it was successful at attracting high-income travelers, a higher use of time-shares was contributing to lower room demand than in Savannah, Georgia, and Virginia Beach, Virginia (Hess 2010). Further analysis revealed that these destinations, while similar, were using strategies such as marketing partnerships and social media marketing to increase business (Hess 2010). Knowing what their competition was doing and where they were succeeding, allowed Williamsburg to adjust its marketing plan.

Make sure you acknowledge your deficiencies and identify ways to try to correct them, and be prepared if others replicate your ideas where you are strong. Staying informed about what your competition is doing makes it easier to choose the right marketing strategies and activities.

One of the most important results of your competitive analysis will be positioning strategies for your business. The next section helps you decide which positioning strategies are best for your organization.

Positioning Strategies

Creating an identity for your tourism business in the minds of your customers is positioning. A successful positioning strategy communicates the unique features, or the perceived unique features, of your product and distinguishes your business from the competition. Disneyland uses the slogan "the happiest place on earth" in its marketing materials. This slogan reflects the positioning strategy to distinguish Disneyland from other theme parks that have similar elements and is likely to be seen positively by families looking for a vacation destination. Lindblad Expeditions has positioned itself as a leader in expedition travel, being the first company to take travelers to remote locations originally visited only by scientists, and now partners with National Geographic, one of the best-known brands in the world, with a fleet of expedition ships that carry the National Geographic image.

When considering how to position your sustainable tourism products, look for areas where you can develop a unique advantage and compete effectively. The following are areas you might consider when positioning your business:

- Price
- Quality
- Service
- Location and access
- Ability to customize
- Sustainability

Of these, price is probably the least desirable area in which to compete. If you decide to position yourself by offering the lowest price, chances are others will be able to offer an even lower price. They might also be using price as a competitive strategy and have the resources to sell a tourism experience similar to yours at a loss. If your customers are price sensitive and feel little loyalty to your brand, they might switch to another tourism business for a lower price. A better approach is to position yourself through quality or service and promote your company as offering the best value for the price versus the lowest price.

To position your sustainable tourism business as a leader in the quality of the product or experience requires tremendous effort to ensure all areas of your operation meet established standards. You will likely incur additional start-up and operating costs. These costs may be recovered through higher prices if you offer superior quality. Abercrombie and Kent is a tour company that has chosen quality and service as the basis for its position in the marketplace. The marketing message on the website lets prospective customers know that a traveler who selects one of its wildlife-viewing safaris to east Africa will stay at resorts of exceptional quality, travel in small groups, and be led by some of the most knowledgeable guides in the country.

Closely related to product quality is customer service, and using it as a position strategy makes sense. You do not need to invest in fancy buildings or upgrade older facilities. Employing guides and support staff who are consistently courteous, friendly, and attentive to the tourists' needs, will distinguish your company as one that delivers great customer service.

Sustainable tourism businesses offer an additional advantage in that interpretation can be considered part of customer service and when done well, can distinguish you in a way nothing else can. As you can see in the sidebar The Guide's the Thing, providing interpretation of an environment adds value to the tourism experience; for many travelers, visiting a natural area without interpretation is like watching television with the sound off.

Another area where you might position your sustainable tourism business is your location or access. If you are located in or have access to a unique setting, use this fact as a way to set yourself apart from other destinations or tours. Tourists interested in sustainable tourism often seek unique or remote locations. Although not consumptive users of wildlife, nature-seeking tourists like to have "trophy experiences," something they can brag about to their friends. Being able to offer them the chance to be the first to visit a destination or undertake a unique activity such as sea kayaking in the high Arctic will give them status and satisfy their need for variety.

The ability to customize a trip is another way to position your business. Many tourists like variety, unique experiences, and flexibility. If your clients can choose from several activities or locations to customize their own package, it will be more attractive to them. The flexibility to offer unique customized packages for each client will distinguish your business from others.

If you have invested a lot of money and time into your sustainable tourism practices, you may want to use your leadership in sustainability as a positioning strategy. Many travelers think first about the destination or activity when selecting a tourism business, worrying about sustainable tourism practices only after they have narrowed their search. Using green travel practices as your competitive strategy works

The Guide's the Thing

Ask your friends whether a traveler needs a tour guide and the answer is often a resounding no! Many travelers are fiercely independent, and do not think they need an expert to show them around, especially in their own country. But I beg to differ. I think visiting a destination without spending time with a local expert is like watching TV with the sound off. Everything looks great, but you are not sure what you are looking at.

When my husband and I took a trip to Vancouver Island, a place I have visited dozens of times, I wanted to see something different, and I thought a guided trip might offer new sights and new insights. Searching a Vancouver Island travel app, I found a half-day tour of fish watching amid old-growth rainforests. I thought watching a creature fight its way up a rushing river, while avoiding hungry bears, sounded like reality TV, Mother Nature style, and a great holiday experience.

Sandy McRuer of Rainbird Excursions agreed to meet us, and when his van sporting a bird logo pulled up in the rugged forest community of Port Alberni, I figured we were in for some local color. I was not disappointed. Sandy had worked for years in forestry before starting a guiding service. "I've been guiding for six years," he explained good naturedly, "and I don't make any money from it. People think they can explore an area by themselves." And then he proceeded to prove them wrong.

Sandy led us to trees several hundred years old. "It's like Cathedral Grove (a popular Vancouver Island park)," Sandy said, "except there are no other people around." But we weren't alone in the old-growth forest. The smell was the first hint. Usually, I like to breathe deeply while walking in the woods. This time, not so much. It smelled like rotten flesh, and when I almost stepped on my first fish, I knew why.

Judging by the 10-kilogram (22 lbs) fish lying at my feet, I knew this was no flying fish. Something fairly large had dragged this fish into the forest and I was pretty sure it was not a raccoon. "Bears," Sandy explained, "but it might have been left because it was rotten and didn't taste good." Without looking too hard, we found a dozen large fish along the trail. Suddenly, the forest that had seemed so deserted only a few minutes earlier now looked like a busier place as I saw evidence of bear movement all around us.

Sandy explained that forests near salmon rivers have larger trees. Scientists discovered that vegetation gains valuable nutrients from the fish left by the bears, something I would not have learned without a guide! We then visited the popular Stamp Falls fish ladders, jostling with other tourists for photographs until Sandy led us to a lesser-known pool where the fish rested before assaulting the falls.

Our trip ended all too quickly, but Sandy suggested other stops and tips on where to spot the fishing bears. He was not able to answer my questions on where to spot a lake monster (apparently, British Columbia has more lake monsters than anywhere in the world), but his guiding skills added immeasurably to this trip. So for less than a round of golf would cost, I was far wiser about one of Canada's natural phenomena and I had some great video. Next time, maybe I'll find a cryptozoological guide to track one of those lake monsters.

Courtesy of the *Red Deer Advocate*.

best if done in conjunction with other positioning strategies, such as location or service. Sustainability may be a successful positioning strategy if you operate in a location where negative tourism impacts have created consumer backlash. Ecuador's Galapagos Islands were listed as an endangered World Heritage Site in 2007, but were removed from the list after government and businesses put more emphasis on environmental preservation. Ecoventura, an expedition cruising company in the Galapagos Islands, was one of the first to seek Smart Voyager certification, a program recognized by the United Nations that encourages ecologically sound practices (BBCTravel 2011).

Your marketing plan should describe in detail (usually a paragraph or two) three or four businesses that are your main competitors. Describe how you are the same, how your business is different, and the positioning strategy you will use to compete in the market. You should include this information in your business plan as well, especially if you are seeking outside funding. Because tourism businesses often lack credibility with banks, you must work hard to illustrate the unique aspects of your business compared to other tourism operations and ways you will take advantage of this.

PRODUCT–MARKET MATCH

Looking at all the possible products you can offer gives you a better chance of matching these products with the markets identified in the market analysis. One of the most important steps in the marketing plan is the **product–market match**, a marketing process that matches the possible products you can sell to the market segments most likely to purchase them. For an example of a successful product–market match, watch the video "Marketing to Photographers" in the web resource.

In your strategic plan you identified the products you are capable of offering to the traveling public. You also identified the market segments you would like to target. Now you bring this information into your marketing plan to find the best matches between your capabilities and your prospective customers. If your research indicates that most tourists coming to your area are couples looking for a relaxing weekend retreat, you would not want to offer a weeklong tour filled with scheduled activities. Instead you would focus your efforts on weekend packages that might include fine dining, bird-watching, and sampling homemade jams from local farmers at afternoon tea. Or you might have an abundance

of bird life but no accommodations for large groups. This could mean you develop a product for one-day bird-watching trips or multiday trips with stays at small inns or bed and breakfasts. An example of a product–market match is shown in figure 5.2.

One product might appeal to more than one market segment, as you can see in figure 5.2. If you are short of money, you might decide to focus your marketing on the products that reach the most market segments. The two-day birding package in figure 5.2 would appeal to couples who want to relax, nature photographers, and casual bird-watchers. You could promote this product to three market segments in your early years and expand your marketing to the other product–market matches as your bank account increases.

By organizing your market segments and the products you are able to deliver into product–market matches, you can see what you can sell and to whom and the best marketing strategy for reaching your target market. Your marketing strategies and activities will likely be different for each market segment, although there is often overlap. Your market segments may also be other businesses, for example, companies offering tourism experiences to their employees for team building or as a reward. Market segments consisting of businesses require different marketing strategies; for example, you would only approach the organizer, instead of every person taking the tour. This can make marketing more cost effective, and for this reason, many tourism

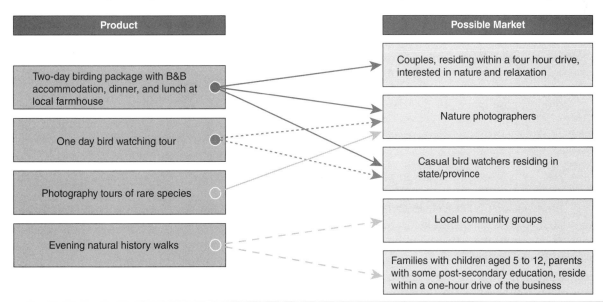

Figure 5.2 Product–market match.

Based on information from Canadian Tourism Commission 2012.

businesses find corporations, social clubs, and associations to be attractive market segments.

Sometimes people get confused while determining their product–market matches and label everyone as a potential customer. As described in the strategic planning process, you group customers into market segments so you can focus your business activities. This does not mean you will not be thrilled to see a customer from the other side of the globe if you are focused on school groups within a two-hour drive, but that person is the gravy, as opposed to the targeted market segments that form the meat and potatoes of your business. If you find you are getting a lot of clients from outside your targeted market segments, you might have overlooked a segment in your market analysis or are filling a travel need you were not aware of. In either case, revisit your product–market match to see whether you can include this new market in your plans.

To bring the concept of product–market match to life, take the Ecochallenge "What Kind of Traveler Are You?" The Canadian Tourism Commission (CTC) uses the explorers quotient (EQ) quiz to identify market segments. You, too, can take the quiz to determine how you would be classified. Think about what types of tourism experiences or products you prefer. The CTC uses the EQ quiz to

match travelers' needs to the products Canadian tourism businesses offer. Once travelers have taken the quiz, they can follow links on the CTC website to products that might suit them. Although this is a highly sophisticated version of a product–market match, you should apply the same concept as you develop your marketing plan.

Marketing Objectives

As with all business activities, setting objectives provides direction and measures success. Marketing is no different. You need goals and objectives that are measurable, time bound, and realistic. Of these, measurability is the one that causes the most problems for tourism businesses. By looking at the process of setting goals and objectives in detail, you can learn how to better define objectives for success.

As with the strategic plan, goals for marketing state your general intentions on the direction you are taking your business. An example of a marketing goal might be to increase sales revenues by 10 percent in one year. The goal does not say how you will increase revenues, but it does set a measurable, time-bound, and realistic goal. If the goal had been only to increase sales, it would not tell you how much of an increase or by what date.

Ecochallenge
What Kind of Traveler Are You?

Take the explorers quotient (EQ) quiz developed by the Canadian Tourism Commission to identify market segments at http://caen.canada.travel/traveller-types. The questions will help you determine what market segment you might belong to.

Although nine types of travelers exist, based on the CTC's product–market match, CTC describes its target market segments as these three types:

- Free spirits are highly social and open minded. Their enthusiasm for life extends to their outlook on travel. Experimental and adventurous, they indulge in high-end experiences that are shared with others (13% of global market).
- Cultural explorers are defined by their love of constant travel and continuous opportunities to embrace, discover, and immerse

themselves in the culture, people, and settings of the places they visit (12% of global market).

- Authentic experiencers are typically understated travelers looking for authentic, tangible engagement with the destinations they seek and they have a particular interest in understanding the history of the places they visit (9% of global market) (CTC 2012).

Are you one of the traveler segments targeted by the Canadian Tourism Commission? Based on your knowledge of Canada and the types of tourism products offered in that country, would you agree with the CTC's focus on free spirits, cultural explorers, and authentic experiencers? What market segments do you think marketing organizations in your state or province focus on?

If you sold only one extra dollar's worth of tours over previous years or months, you would have met your goal.

Marketing objectives are specific, measurable, and time-specific targets that help you reach your goals. A goal to increase sales revenues may require objectives that increase prices, sell more products, or change the mix of your products to book more-expensive tours. If the marketing goal is to increase sales revenues by 10 percent in one year, the marketing objectives might be as follows:

- Increase sales of winter packages by 5 percent for the coming winter
- Increase sales of weekend hiking trips to social clubs by 20 percent in each of the next three years
- Increase the number of evening interpretative talks from one to two each week from July 1 to September 1

For each of your goals, write three or four marketing objectives.

Marketing Strategies

Once your marketing goals and objectives are in place, you can finalize your **marketing strategies**, plans you make to achieve your marketing goals. You will establish marketing strategies for product, price, place, and promotion. Each of these will be discussed in the following sections. As you work through each section, you will see that they are interrelated and a change to one will affect the others. Even though the four Ps are presented sequentially, you will often need to work on them simultaneously.

Product

Marketing strategies related to product can include the following:

- What experiences are included in the product
- What the product is called
- How the product will be differentiated from others offered by competitors

In earlier chapters, you gained background information on sustainable tourism and learned how to identify possible products through the strategic planning process. You completed a resource inventory and identified the products that your business could offer. In the product–market match you selected the products that were most likely to be favored by consumers. These steps help you create marketing strategies related to the product by helping you develop a clear idea of what your customers want from your product and the features or benefits that you will highlight during the promotion of the marketing mix. Your competitive analysis will have yielded a positioning strategy to help you develop marketing messages in your promotion and select venues that will put your marketing activities in the right place.

Price

Marketing strategies related to price can include the following:

- Determining the price customers will be willing to pay for your product
- Determining the compensation you will offer to organizations that sell your product
- Assessing what pricing level or discounts are necessary to compete with competitors
- Calculating your costs and the price you can afford to offer

When determining your price-related marketing strategies, you need to look at what other businesses are doing. As discussed earlier, if your competitors seem to be trying to underbid each other, then perhaps the best strategy is to offer a product of higher quality and with better service. You would then focus on upgrading your product, and the price and higher revenue might make it worth the effort. Or you might consider the use of coupons or discounts. Many consumers like to believe they are getting a deal. One of your pricing strategies might be to offer frequent discounts or specials to encourage people to buy. If you choose this method, you need to set a price high enough that you can afford to offer discounts.

You may also have a strategy related to the third P, place, that encourages other people to sell your product. This requires a price high enough to pay **commissions**, the compensation that people or organizations charge for selling your product or service. You also need to set a price that covers your operating costs. Although you are likely to encounter higher costs with sustainable tourism practices, it is unlikely you can charge a premium just because your business is green. Consumers have shown themselves reluctant to pay more to decrease their ecological footprint (Roth 2010).

Instead, you might need to stress other advantages such as small group size or unique location to justify a higher price. Before moving onto the remaining Ps of place and promotion, it is worth looking at how to set a price that supports all of your marketing strategies.

Setting the price for your experience or service is a difficult step in the marketing process and can be approached in different ways. You can determine what other companies are charging for the same product and see whether you can make money at that price, or alternatively, you can determine your costs and add extra for profit and commissions. The second method provides better assurances that you will be able to cover your costs, so that method is described here.

To calculate a price for a product you will need to know the following:

• **Variable costs** are expenditures that vary based on the number of people who take your tour, stay in your hotel, eat at your restaurant, or visit your attraction. Examples of variable costs are food for meals, equipment rental, electricity for lights in an occupied hotel room, and housekeeping labor to clean rooms.

• **Fixed costs** fluctuate but do not vary directly with the number of participants. For example, if you rent a van to shuttle guests, the cost will be the same whether you have one guest or twenty.

• **Overhead** is a type of fixed cost that does not vary directly with the number of tours or guests and includes expenditures needed to run your business. Insurance, management salaries, rent, licenses, and taxes are common examples of overhead costs.

• **Contingency** is an amount of money set aside to cover unexpected problems, such as changes in foreign exchange rates, unexpected cost increases, or last-minute opportunities.

A plan is your best guess. Because conditions will be different when you are in the middle of the operating season, having built a contingency into your prices will allow you to survive bumps and take advantage of unexpected opportunities.

To incorporate these elements into a pricing calculation, start by gathering your financial information. An existing business will have financial statements from previous years. A person starting a new business should talk to experienced tourism operators and call suppliers to estimate what the costs might be.

A pricing worksheet, like the one shown in table 5.1, makes calculating the price easier. A blank version of the pricing worksheet is provided in the web resource. To complete the worksheet, perform the following steps:

Table 5.1
Sample Pricing Worksheet

Item	Amount ($)
VARIABLE COSTS (PER PERSON)	
Box lunch	15.00
Total variable costs	15.00
FIXED COSTS (PER PERSON)	
Van rental	66.67
Guide	25.00
Total fixed costs	91.67
Overhead costs (assumed to be 125% of variable and fixed costs)	133.34
Total cost	225.01
10% contingency	22.50
Subtotal	247.51
Profit (assumed to be 5%)	12.38
Net cost	259.89
Commission (assumed to be 10%)	25.99
Retail cost (per person)	285.88

1. **Calculate variable costs.** List all costs that vary with the number of participants. For example, if you are providing a lunch on your tour, your cost of the meal is listed as a variable cost.

2. **Calculate fixed costs.** To calculate your fixed costs for a tour or program, first identify the cost, then determine an average cost if fully used. Then you apply a **load factor**, the percentage of average participation, to the maximum participation to take into account that you will likely operate below capacity. For example, if you rent a 20-passenger van to take a group on a tour, and the van costs $1,000 for the day, the cost per participant is $50 ($1,000 ÷ 20). It is unlikely that you would fill every trip, so you need to apply an estimated load factor. If you assume you will fill 75 percent of your tours for this example, your fixed cost per person is $66.67 ($50 ÷ 75%). Similarly, if you hire a contract guide for the day, you follow the same calculation to arrive at a cost per person.

3. **Determine overhead.** Your business needs to cover all your costs, not just your trip costs. You need to ensure each trip is making enough to cover your overhead costs. To include this in your calculation, look at your organization's operating budget (or last year's financial statement), and determine what percentage of the total budget your overhead costs are. For example, if you determine $50,000 of your total budget is overhead costs, and your variable and fixed costs for tours are $40,000, you could assume that for every dollar spent on variable and fixed costs for a tour, you will have 1.25 times (or 125%) as much for overhead ($50,000 ÷ $40,000 = 125%).

4. **Set a contingency reserve.** If you are facing moderate risk, you might use a 10 percent contingency. This is calculated by taking the estimated cost of the product and then calculating an additional amount, usually as a percentage of the total fixed and variable costs, to cover unexpected expenses. The percent varies with the risk, perhaps as low as 5 percent in situations with low risk to 30 or 40 percent if there are many unknown variables or higher risks. If you are operating in very remote locations or politically unstable environments, you should use a higher percentage. As you gain experience in your business, you will have a better idea of the level of contingency needed for unexpected costs.

5. **Add a profit.** You need to make money over the long term to buy new equipment or repay investors and lenders, so when you have covered all your costs of operating each year, add an allowance for profit. Once you have done this, you have calculated your **net rate**, the amount of money you keep if you sell your product through a travel intermediary such as a travel agent.

6. **Determine commissions.** Many people start a tourism business and make the mistake of omitting commissions in their pricing calculations. They run into trouble when other people offer to sell their product. Some people will refer your business products out of courtesy, but if you want to expand your sales, you must offer a commission to the people who sell your product. Make sure you set your price high enough to pay commissions. Table 5.2 offers guidelines for the com-

missions you might expect depending on the organizations you ask to sell your product. In the example in table 5.1, it was assumed that a 10 percent commission would be needed for possible marketing partners. Do not try to charge two prices, one for customers who book directly with you and another to people who book through a travel agent. With the almost instant nature of the Internet, people will quickly realize they can book cheaper with you and the travel agent will not appreciate being undercut.

Table 5.2   Tour Commission Guide

Travel intermediary	Average percent commission on retail rate*
Travel agents	10
Wholesalers who sell directly to customers or to retailers	20
Inbound tourism operators who sell to wholesalers (who then sell to customers or retailers)	30

*Commissions can vary by company and situation.
Data from State of New South Wales 2010.

7. **Set retail price.** Once you have determined your commissions, add this to your net rate. This is your **retail price**, the price the consumer will see on your brochure or website. This is sometimes called the rack, gross, or sell rate.

Once you have calculated your retail price, give it a reality check by comparing it to the prices charged for similar products. Is it much higher or lower? If you are lower, you may not have included all the costs. Check your figures and if you are still lower, decide whether you want to compete on price. If customers choose you only because of your low prices, you will lose them if other companies offer even cheaper prices.

If your price is higher than the competition, how will you convince people to buy your product? If you have access to a location that few can offer, make sure to mention that in your advertising. Or if you have a retired park warden as your guide, stress the behind-the-scenes feel of your trips and include expert interviews in your marketing.

If you are not sure whether your price is too high or low, consider setting it slightly higher. You can use the cushion to offer discounts, sales, or limited-time offers. If you start with your lowest price, you cannot offer sales and many travelers like to believe they have gotten a deal. It is also difficult to raise prices, so pick a price you can live with for a year or two.

Place

Marketing strategies related to place can include the following:

- Where will buyers look to buy your product?
- Will you sell the product directly to travelers or will you use other tourism organizations?
- If you use other organizations to sell your product, how will you find them?

Tourism requires fewer decisions about place than many other industries. A business selling a manufactured product, shoes for example, must decide whether it will set up a store, sell in other stores, or sell online. A traveler cannot send someone else to experience a trip, although someone can buy the ticket or book the tour. You must decide where you will place your promotion to generate sufficient business at a cost you can afford.

Many tourism businesses sell their products or services directly to the traveler. The advantages of direct selling include saving money on commissions and a fairly simple starting process. You will need to invest significant time and money in the last P, promotion, but you will control how you place your product in front of potential customers.

Relying strictly on direct selling to reach all your market segments may limit your business growth. As tour operators expand, they can find direct sales too time consuming and turn to specialized businesses, or intermediaries, to help sell tourism products. Intermediaries can be an effective way to supplement your own direct marketing efforts. You might even choose to rely solely on them to sell your product.

Using travel trade intermediaries also has disadvantages. These businesses expect a fee or commission for selling your product. They require long lead times to promote your tours or facility. It can be difficult to find an intermediary to sell your product. Many companies have established suppliers in your region or are not interested in adding another tourism product. You will often need to attend trade shows to establish connections with these companies, and once you do, it may take 18 to 24 months to establish the relationship and

create and sell the product. This topic will be explored in detail in chapter 7.

Promotion

Marketing strategies related to promotion can include the following:

- Where you will place your marketing messages
- What types of advertising you will engage in
- The best time of year to advertise

Promotion includes many of the most visible parts of the marketing process, such as advertising, direct sales, and publicity. These activities are expensive and will consume a significant part of the budget each year. It is critical to complete market research and set marketing objectives before committing to promotional strategies. You do not want to place an advertisement—a paid notice of your tourism product or service in a media outlet—in a bed and breakfast directory if your customers rely solely on word-of-mouth recommendations or travel stories when selecting accommodation. It might be better to invite a travel writer and get a mention in a publication your target market reads.

You will also need to know when your customers make their travel purchasing decisions. If they like to decide at the last minute on a trip, you want to use a promotion method that puts your product in front of the customer at the right time. You also need to make sure your other P, product, is flexible enough to accommodate last-minute bookings. The next section explores promotion and the marketing activities to promote a business.

MARKETING ACTIVITIES

A lot of the time you spend developing a marketing plan will be spent on selecting and implementing marketing activities, such as advertising in newspapers or developing a social media strategy. You will not have enough money to undertake every marketing activity you can envision, so you will need to select the ones that fit your marketing goals and objectives and your promotional strategies.

The following are some of the marketing activities you might include in your marketing plan:

- Internet
- Direct sales

- Brochures
- Video
- Signage
- Print media
- Trade shows
- Tourism conferences
- Television and radio
- Publicity

A good marketing plan includes a combination of these marketing activities, although small or medium-size businesses often find they cannot afford all the activities they would like. Each of these activities will be discussed in the following pages, but regardless of which activities you select, be consistent in the messages you convey in your promotional materials. One technique that might be helpful is to focus on a theme.

Creating a Theme

A **marketing theme** is the main image or message you leave with potential customers. Identifying a theme early will keep your marketing activities focused and help a tourist form a clear picture of your company. Your theme can also form the basis for slogans used in promotions.

Pick a theme that highlights the areas where you have a competitive position. If you offer friendly service, you might emphasize the tips your helpful staff share with guests trying new activities. If you take people to undiscovered and out-of-the-way places, use that as your theme. A company that prides itself on low-impact travel practices would emphasize its compatibility with nature.

Once you have picked a theme, draft marketing materials such as a brochure or website page. Provide copies to customers or people with interests similar to those of your customers and ask for feedback. Have them describe the images that come to mind when they look at your materials. If you view yourself as the company with the best access to remote hiking sites, and people think your trips are a great way to meet people with similar interests, you might need to use different words and pictures to get your theme across. Do not use images or words that encourage unsustainable behavior. For example, photographs showing a whale breeching close to a boat can create expectations that each person taking a whale-watching tour will see a whale up close. Take the time to clarify your theme before you invest your marketing dollars and you will be happier with the results.

Pick images and messages for marketing materials that resonate with your customers.

Once you have your theme, it's time to select your marketing activities. A variety of marketing activities are described briefly in this book. You might find you need more detailed information to hire business consultants to help you before you can implement some of these activities in your business.

Using the Internet

Internet marketing is critical to every tourism business. WWW Metrics, which provides Internet business statistics, describes an amazing growth rate in online travel booking. The Travel Industry Association of America data in 1999 showed 15.1 million consumers booking online; by 2011 a research study by Jupiter Research showed it had grown to nearly 70 million people (WWW Metrics 2014). Your customers are shopping online and to get their business, you need a good website and increasingly, a presence on Web 2.0. (Web 2.0 and social media are covered in more detail in the next chapter.)

The Internet has leveled the field of tourism marketing. Small and medium-size tourism businesses through their websites can offer professional images to rival large companies, and they can reach customers directly. The advantages are offset by the fact that people must find your website in a crowded marketplace and will spend time on it only if they find something interesting. Unlike a bad radio ad sandwiched between good programming and heard by a captive audience, a poorly executed website gets no attention. If your site is difficult to access, slow to upload, lacks information, or is poorly organized, your potential customer is gone in a matter of seconds and may never return.

Marketing on the Internet is an environmentally friendly way to disseminate information. People can learn about your product without the paper required for brochures or fuel used to transport mail.

If you decide to use the Internet as a promotional tool, remember your website is part of the marketing mix and should support other promotional activities. When developing a site, consider the following:

• *Purpose.* Determine how Internet technology will support your marketing objectives. If you want to make people aware of your tour and book online, your website needs a shopping cart. A tourism attraction that wants to make customers aware of its current events and operating hours may focus more on information and leave purchasing to when customers arrive onsite. If you are including Web 2.0 techniques, such as blogging, you might want a website you can easily update yourself.

• *Content.* Use pictures, text, and video to get your message across. People respond well to images. As evidenced by the rapid growth of websites like Pinterest and Instagram, people love to look at and share images. Leave lots of room for images and video and make sure the space allo-

cated for text is well used. Focus on content that shares information and uses key words (more on that later). Consumers are leery of a heavy sales pitch. As described in the sidebar How to Write Copy, make sure you emphasize the benefits of your tourism experience to the consumer, not the technical specifications of your trip. Customers can ask for more details once you have captured their attention. Or you can provide the details on supporting pages and leave the home page for your main marketing messages. Once you have developed your content, update it frequently. This will give people a reason to return to your site.

• *Design.* Your website needs to be well organized and stay true to your marketing objectives. Use formatting, a variety of fonts, and graphics to make your site visually appealing. Links to other websites add depth to your site and provide more useful information. These links could include destinations, equipment manufacturers, or conservation websites. Swapping links also helps direct people to your site. Consider other ways to make your page unique. Monterey Bay Whale Watch in California provides a summary of marine life seen in the area and links to media talking about Monterey Bay marine life. Adding updates to wildlife research can attract frequent visits from potential customers. It can also provide exposure for wildlife researchers, who are often looking for financial support for projects, a good example of a partnership between business and conservation groups.

• *Access.* Once you have developed a website, you must help people find it on the Internet. For many organizations this means ranking high in search engine ratings. **Search engine optimization (SEO)** is a process of identifying the key words your customers use to search the Internet and prominently using those words on your website to move your site up the search engine ratings. It may also require purchasing ads linked to those key words. The field of SEO is complex and requires more explanation than we can cover in this book. Check with SEO firms or local tourism organizations for recommendations for your business.

• *Promotion.* You will need to cross-market your website. When you attend a trade show or meet with a travel intermediary, you will send them to your website for detailed information. You may want to purchase banner ads on other organization's websites to drive travelers to your website. You may find social media a good way to cultivate interest in your website and get people to ultimately book at tour. Other strategies might include swapping links with other organizations or providing guest blogs for an organization's website that potential customers visit. These strategies will be discussed in more detail in the next chapter.

Direct Sales

Direct sales are made directly to the customer via Internet, telephone, fax, or mail or in person. This could include mailing your brochure to prospective customers or calling customers. It could take the form of an electronic magazine, or e-zine, to past customers, letting them know about upcoming tours. If you sell to corporations, you might visit prospective customers in person. All of these methods are relevant for sustainable tourism businesses. Direct sales can be even more powerful if you are able to access contact lists of conservation groups, perhaps by offering a special trip or program for their members led by a celebrity guide or offering access during a special time.

When using direct sales, stay focused. You must target your most important market segments. When sending a direct mailing, use a qualified mailing list that is based on a characteristic meaningful to your target market, perhaps residence in a certain geographic area or past consumption of

certain trips, and thus containing a lot of potential customers. A mailing list from a conservation group could be good for direct sales for a sustainable tourism organization because everyone on the list has an interest in conservation. However, a list obtained from an organization in Omaha, Nebraska, could have little benefit unless you have determined that proximity to Omaha is a key characteristic of your market segment or that the people on the list are known to favor trips of greater distance.

Once a potential list is identified, you will test it by sending a mailing to a portion of the list, perhaps 10 percent. Monitor the response from this mailing. If you achieve a response rate greater than 7 percent, then increase the mailing to everyone on the list. Qualified mailing lists can generate business, but you will pay for them. Remember to include this cost in your marketing budget.

Direct sales by telephone and in person are more relevant for tourism businesses when selling to groups or to travel organizations selling other tourism products. Mailing to these groups without follow-up is not effective, so phone calls or personal visits are needed. Because of the labor and travel costs, direct sales calls and visits are relatively expensive, although you can save money by making direct sales at conferences and **tourism marketplaces**, gatherings of tourism suppliers and

How to Write Copy

When advertising, take the time to develop a message, or "copy," that sells. One of the ways to accomplish this is to sell to a feeling. People want to hear about the personal benefits of a tour, not necessarily the specific features. The decision to take a particular trip is often based on emotion. If you can attract the customer's eye (or ear) with an emotional appeal while providing the reasons they would benefit from your trip, you have a better chance of making a sale.

People buy trips for a variety of reasons: to escape from something, to satisfy curiosity, to spend time with family, to meet new friends. The list is long. Focus on the personal reasons people have for taking a trip and explain how your tourism experience will satisfy their needs.

When describing the benefits your customers will enjoy, include information to help them overcome the following objections:

- Lack of time or money
- A belief they do not need your trip
- A fear it might not be the right experience for them
- Skepticism about your claims

Think about including a guarantee in your advertisement. You can remove some of the apprehension by offering a refund or a chance to travel again. Eagle Wings Tours, a whale-watching company in Victoria, British Columbia, guarantees that customers will see a whale on its tours. If customers do not see a whale on their first trip, Eagle Wings offers free additional trips until they see a whale.

marketing organizations with the intent to create marketing partnerships. If your direct sales at tourism marketplaces are successful, you will find that the opportunity to sell a significant number of tours to one organization is a great way to grow your business. Before you attend, be sure to research prospective clients thoroughly, ensuring that their customers fit your market segment profile.

When using direct sales, keep track of your past and prospective customers through a database. The customer base built through direct sales will often provide you with personal referrals. By staying in touch with your past clients, you can share your latest news and products; hopefully, they will book again with you or remember to recommend your company to their friends.

Brochures

Brochures are pamphlets used to inform visitors about your tourism product and region. They are sometimes called lure brochures. They make good handouts and can be used to respond to inquiries and to support promotional displays and presentations.

When developing a brochure, use the same guidelines for developing a website. Incorporate your themes and write copy that sells. Many resources on how to create a brochure can be found on the Internet and at the library. Also consult with people who have experience with writing copy and desktop design for tips on designing printed material.

Before you create your own brochure, look at brochures of other businesses. Look for things that work and do not work. Incorporate the elements into your brochure that help sell your product. Resist the temptation to cover every square centimeter with text and graphics. Leave plenty of white space so it is easy to read and pleasing to the eye, not jumbled and confusing.

A savvy sustainable tourist looks for information, not fluff, and wants to be convinced you offer a quality nature or cultural experience. Include photographs and descriptions of the area visited and key elements of the trip. As a sustainable tourism operator, you may want to include information

Brochure racks can generate sales from travelers wanting adventure or cultural activities.

on the interpretation component, guide qualifications, or tourism certifications. You should mention partnerships or alliances with conservation groups. You may want to print your brochure on recycled paper or paper harvested from sustainably managed forests. By the time people are looking at your brochure, they have already shown an interest in your region and business. To complete the sale, you need to convince them you have the key elements they are looking for in a sustainable tourism experience.

When developing your brochure you will go through the following steps:

1. **Identify your objectives.** Decide on the action you want people reading the brochure to take. You might want to generate sufficient interest for people to call or e-mail for details, or you might want them to make a booking. Consider who will receive the brochure and how they will get it. Some people might receive it in the mail; other people might pick it up at a visitor center or at a hotel.

2. **Select text and visual images.** Determine what combination of text, illustrations, and photographs is best to convey your product information. If your brochure will be displayed in a brochure rack, remember that only a few inches of the brochure will be visible. This part of the brochure needs to be eye catching so that people pick it up. Be sure to use images that convey the experience you are selling and that the people in the images resemble your market segments. It is important to use high-quality photographs in your marketing material. Nothing ruins a customer's impressions of a tourism business faster than photographs that are out of focus, shot in poor light, or low resolution. If you are not a great photographer, hire a professional photographer and invest in images that attract attention and showcase your business and its unique features.

3. **Write the copy for the brochure.** Just as it's important that your website design promotes sales, write copy that sells. If you are not familiar with this skill, consider hiring a copywriter.

4. **Create a mock-up.** Before you pay for a full print order, create a sample brochure to see how your ideas look in print.

5. **Get feedback on the mock-up.** Show the brochure to people from your target market and get their response. If they suggest changes or are confused by some of your messages, adjust as needed. If the changes are significant, create a second mock-up and test it again.

6. **Obtain camera-ready artwork.** This is the final step before printing and involves many technical details best handled by an expert. Get the help of an expert to make sure your photos are the correct resolution and that all elements are correctly placed.

7. **Print.** Print enough brochures to meet your marketing needs. Most organizations update their brochures each year if they operate seasonally. Companies operating year-round might have a brochure for each season. Order enough brochures to last until your next revision.

Once your brochures are produced, put them into the hands of potential customers. You can mail brochures to customers as part of your direct sales or you can distribute brochures at the following places:

- Consumer travel shows, events aimed at the public that include tourism destinations and business displays promoting travel to their locations
- Tourism marketplaces, tourism industry events that allow tourism businesses supplying products to sell to tourism organizations promoting tourism experiences
- Visitor bureaus and tourist information centers
- Hotels and motels
- Shopping malls

Brochures distributed through these channels are most effective if the product is suitable for people once they have arrived at a destination and who do not have Internet connectivity. For example, if a family has chosen to visit southern Arizona, and you operate a museum, a brochure displayed at a visitor center or hotel might convince them to spend a day at your attraction. However, with greater access to Wi-Fi, consumers are increasingly turning to the Internet to research travel options. If you are unsure whether a brochure will be an effective marketing tool for your business, you may want to forgo a print brochure and invest your marketing dollars into your website or a smart phone application.

Video

Video is becoming more important as a marketing tool for sustainable tourism businesses. Relatively inexpensive video cameras allow almost anyone to become a videographer through training and practice. Video can often convey experiences quicker than words or a picture can. Allowing customers to share their videos on your website can help prospective customers picture themselves on one of your tours and help you save money.

If you decide to record your own promotional video, use the same guidelines discussed earlier for developing printed material. Again the key to success is to determine the objectives of the video and how they relate to the target market. Determine which scenes will best convey your message and make sure you capture them in your videos. You may want footage of visitors enjoying your tours. As the operator of a sustainable tourism business, you might want to show employees undertaking activities that make your business environmentally friendly. Or you might highlight a design element of your lodge that lessens its environmental footprint and impacts.

Signage

Signage refers to the signs that identify your business and direct people to it. Signs can attract tourists to your tourism property and provide interpretation once they arrive. A tourism businesses with a lodge or attraction needs signs on highways, access roads, and entrances. Signs should tell people what services are offered and direct them to your business. At your site, you might need interpretive signs to create interest in unique natural or cultural history features.

Signs are an extension of your corporate image, so create signage that fits within the overall framework of your marketing plan. A large plastic sign with flashing lights may not be consistent with the image of an elegant log structure in a wooded setting. Also, wood used in your sign should be from sustainable sources; a beautiful sign from a rare tree may offend sustainable tourism customers. If your visitors arrive by air and are shuttled to your remote lodge by employees, you will not need extensive or elaborate signs.

You may need to obtain approval for your signs from various government agencies. Check with your municipality and state or province to determine signage regulations. Your design ideas and their requirements may require compromise on your part. Once your sign design has been approved, construct, install, and maintain it. A broken, dirty, or poorly maintained sign does not give a favorable impression of your facility.

Print Media

Print media refers to publications printed on paper such as newspapers, magazines, or directories. Traditionally, tourism businesses placed ads in newspapers and magazines, but the use of print media is declining as travelers turn to the Internet to make their travel decisions. Placing an advertisement in the local paper will only work if you pick a publication your market segments read. As seen in table 5.3, some publications, like *National Geographic*, are popular with people who have shown an affinity for sustainable travel.

Price varies with the format and publication. An ad in *National Geographic* will be out of reach for many organizations, but local publications could be cost effective and will generate sales for tourism businesses if the message, type, and timing are well planned.

The best way to select the appropriate media is to compare target markets with the types of people who read a publication. The advertising department of print media companies can provide a description of their readers. Compare this to your targeted market segments and if they are similar, you might choose to place an advertisement. Tips for getting

Table 5.3   Use of Environmental Media

Media	Percentage (%) of respondents subscribing to or regularly reading
National Geographic	39.9
Other	19.1
Mother Jones	10.3
Audubon Magazine	10.1
Mother Earth News	10.0
Utne Reader	7.4
Friends of the Earth Newsmagazine	6.1
Grist	5.2
E–The Environmental Magazine	4.9

Adapted, by permission, from *CMI green traveler study report 2010: v1.*

the most out of print media, such as directories, newspapers, and magazines are provided in the following sections.

Directories

A **directory** is a listing of businesses that have something in common. Often tourism directories are organized by geographic region or activity and are created to sell travel products to tourists. State or provincial tourism departments often create directories and list tourism businesses in their state or province. Some directories offer free listings, and others charge to be included. Many offer opportunities to advertise or highlight your listing. These directories often have a broad distribution, so this may be a good way to get your tourism product noticed. Some publications may require you to be in business a year or two before you can be listed. The publisher is looking for an indication that the companies listed are established and will be in business when customers arrive.

Some directories are created by businesses and focus on a specific sector, for example a directory of bed and breakfasts, and a listing can be expensive. Before you decide to list or advertise, determine how many directories are published and where they are distributed. If it appears they will reach your target markets, you may decide to include the publication in your marketing plan.

Newspapers

Fewer people are reading newspapers, but advertising in them may still be a good way to reach segments of your market if a large part of your business originates in the area where the newspaper is published.

An effective way to use newspaper advertisements is through consortium opportunities. If several tourism businesses from a region band together to create a special advertising feature on their travel products or services, they can create a larger, more noticeable presence in the newspaper while sharing the cost. If a travel writer is doing a story on your region or business, taking out an advertisement in that issue might be just what you need to sell trips. You do not need to plan as far in advance for newspaper advertising as you do for directories and magazines. This is an advantage when a special opportunity arises and you need to reach your customers quickly. If you are offering a series of summer hikes and need more bookings, you can quickly advertise in the spring when people are making vacation plans.

Newspaper advertising can be expensive. You might need to place several advertisements before people actually make a reservation, and advertising rates in major newspapers can be out of reach for many small businesses. One way to manage this is to look at smaller newspapers that have lower rates or partner with others to share the cost.

Magazines

Magazine advertising can be an important part of your marketing activities. Some well-known travel magazines are *Explore, National Geographic Traveler, Escape,* and *Outside.* They reach the type of travelers likely to book a sustainable tourism experience, but advertising in them is expensive. A single advertisement in a national or international publication can cost hundreds or thousands of dollars. To get results, you may need to run the advertisement more than once. One way to reduce costs is to purchase a listing instead of a display advertisement. Some publications list travel companies in the back pages; this placement is less expensive but still puts your company name in front of qualified customers. You may want to consider regional magazines. They normally have lower advertising rates and can provide better coverage with your target market, especially if most of your customers come from a local area.

Another approach that might save you money is to advertise in less-expensive women's or lifestyle magazines. Many women's magazines include sections on things to do with the family. If you have a unique activity that lets a busy woman spend time with her family, the magazine may publish information about it at no cost.

Look as well for seasonal or regional magazines for lower-priced advertising options. You might also find travel inserts in metropolitan magazines or newspapers a good place to promote your tourism attraction, lodging, or restaurant.

Instead of advertising, you could try to get your company mentioned in a travel story in a magazine. Getting a travel writer to mention you is more effective than paid advertising because the reader assumes the writer is unbiased, giving the recommendations more credence. Attracting a travel writer can be expensive. Usually, a tourism business would offer a writer a **familiarization tour**. Sometimes called fam tours, these trips offer complimentary accommodations and activities to showcase destinations and businesses to people in a position to help sell the experience. You can reduce your costs by convincing other businesses that will benefit from the story to contribute goods and services. If you decide hosting travel writers is something you want to include in your marketing plan, make sure to invite writers with proper credentials. You want someone who is published frequently and writes for publications read by your market segments.

Trade Shows

A **trade show** is a gathering of businesses to showcase their products and services. Often they are only open to people in the industry, although some are open to the public. Displaying at tourism trade shows can be an effective marketing activity because you will have the opportunity to connect with a lot of people in a short time. Select trade shows based on your target market and distribution methods and the show's ability to provide the best links to your target audiences. If you said you would use other businesses to help you sell your tourism experiences when developing your marketing strategies, you want to attend a trade show for people in the industry. If you are selling directly to the consumer, attend consumer trade shows that focus on leisure and travel for quick access to lots of interested people, such as The Philadelphia Inquirer Travel Show. As with all marketing activities, make sure the market segments you target are the ones using the medium.

Some of the largest and best-known trade shows are the ITB Berlin, the World Travel Market (London), or the American Bus Association Marketplace. Many states and provinces also hold trade shows to promote regional tourism. Contact your local tourism or economic development organizations for a list of upcoming trade shows and contact information. Many tourism bureaus or marketing boards attend trade shows and encourage local businesses to attend as part of a larger group. This is a good way to reduce your cost and generate attention and credibility for your product, especially at the large trade shows where a small operator can get lost in the shuffle. To cut costs dramatically, consider not attending at all and instead sending your material with a representative from your destination or industry type.

If you decide to attend trade shows, remember they can be an expensive undertaking. The cost of travel and display space are only the beginning. You might be required to pay workers to set up and take down your exhibits. There might be a fee for table coverings, tables, chairs, electricity, and backdrops, just to name a few possible expenditures. If you are going to another country, a cus-

toms broker might be needed to ship promotional material across borders. Include all of this in your marketing budget and think long term. You will need to attend a particular show for several years to develop name recognition and see the benefits of increased bookings.

Once committed to attending a trade show, give thought to your display. Because the goal of attending a trade show is to sell your product or to network with other industry people, your display should attract attendees and convey the selling points of your tour. Increase the odds of people stopping by incorporating a special point of interest into the display. Some displayers have found that offering candy or a prize drawing is the best way to get people to linger at their booth. Be creative. Remember, this is an extension of your business image, so make it a good one.

Selling at a trade show is different from many other marketing activities. As shown in the sidebar Making the Most of a Trade Show, you need to prepare. It is a significant investment and you want it to pay off with significant sales.

Tourism Conferences

Many conferences deal with tourism in general and several pertain specifically to sustainable tourism, such as the Ecotourism and Sustainable Tourism Conference, the Adventure Travel World Summit, the Educational Travel Conference, and the Responsible Tourism in Destinations (RDT) Conference.

Conferences are unlikely to generate new business unless a trade show is attached. Their main purpose is to keep you informed on industry developments, generate ideas for new products and marketing strategies, and help make new contacts. Partnerships are an effective way to stretch your marketing dollars. Conferences are the place to meet people with similar businesses or from the same geographic regions and can be a good place to form worthwhile partnerships.

Offer to speak at conferences you will attend. You will gain greater visibility for your business (all of it free promotion) and, in many cases, you will receive a break on conference fees.

Television and Radio

Advertising on television and radio may not be appropriate for many tourism businesses. The short message time, 30 to 60 seconds, does not lend itself easily to influencing a major vacation decision. How-

---

Making the Most of a Trade Show

Attending a trade show as an exhibitor is a big investment of time and money. If you decide to become an exhibitor, make sure you maximize the opportunity to sell your product.

Make sure you have an attractive display and that traffic flows well so people can see your display or talk to your staff. Have your best people working at your booth. They are both your ambassadors and welcome committee. They need to maintain a fresh, friendly, and professional appearance, so make sure you have enough staff to give people breaks to rest and eat and for other necessities, including seeing the show and the booths of your competitors.

As people come to your booth, provide them with your business card and other promotional material as necessary. Take the time to briefly explain your unique selling features and answer questions. Explain the great experience tourists will have if they take your tour or stay at your lodge. If people show an interest in your products, ask them to fill out a sign-up sheet so you can provide additional information by mail or phone. Then do the needed follow-up after the show. Asking for business cards or adding a prize drawing will help build your contact list. If possible, code the information you hand out so you can tell whether future sales came from contacts made at the trade show.

During the quiet times, talk to other exhibitors to find out what works for them and which trade shows have generated good returns in terms of new contacts and bookings. Exhibiting at a trade show will leave you tired, but with proper planning, you will have generated new leads and sales.

---

ever, they can be used to promote special events, rates, or season opening in the local area.

You might get free television coverage by approaching community, education, or science and nature channels with a story idea. These channels are always looking for stories and new programming ideas; your sustainable tourism product or service may appeal to them as a way to highlight nature discovery in the community.

Publicity

One of the best ways to make your marketing dollars go further is to seek **publicity**, which is the dissemination of information about your company to gain public interest. Although you will incur some cost for labor and letterhead for your business, if you have put careful thought into a publicity campaign, you can gain public attention and support for next to nothing. Obtaining free coverage through radio, television, magazines, fliers and newsletters from other businesses, and tourist bureaus can enhance the image of your business.

Obtaining maximum publicity takes time, research, and creativity. You need to determine which media are used by your target markets, obtain contact names and e-mail addresses or phone numbers, and convey what you are doing that is newsworthy through a written **media release**, a document sent to media outlets announcing something they might want to report on. The most critical element of writing a media release is offering a news angle. Without that, it is unlikely the media will consider your story. If you are a for-profit business, present your activities in a way that is news, not promotion. This can include information on new staff, awards, innovative policies and special activities or human interest stories about special clients. If you can showcase something unusual, invite the media to attend. Tourism organizations can offer great visual stories that editors will appreciate.

When writing a news release, include information about the unique features of your organization. For example, if you are the first tourism business to develop a comprehensive environmental education policy in your region, tell the media. Include a human interest element. This is an important criterion when editors determine which stories to cover. Your human interest element may be the school children that receive conservation talks from your company's guides or the charity that receives your used equipment. Sustainable tourism businesses are in a good position to generate publicity because of human interest elements and the sustainability benefits. One ecotourism company in Alberta, Canada, took a local news anchorman on a snowshoeing trip. The trip and the antics of the anchorman received significant coverage on the weekend news. It gave the television station a chance to show something new and interesting in a way that was entertaining to viewers and the ecotourism operator got exposure to a large audience.

Do not forget the five Ws (who, what, where, when, why) in your press release, but stick to one story idea. Adding too many ideas causes confusion and minimizes your chance for coverage. You may also want to convey a sense of immediacy so the media will respond quickly. Include background information on your organization in the latter parts of the press release or as a separate item.

If the thought of writing a media release leaves you a bit nervous, there are companies that can help businesses get free publicity. Some of these hire people from the news industry and have a good idea of what an editor looks for. For a flat fee, they will write your media releases and send them to appropriate people at newspapers, magazines, radio stations, and television stations. They will also assist in obtaining public service announcements.

Remember that publicity is advertising over which you have little control. You do not get to approve the story before it goes to the public. If the media have incorrect information or are following an angle that you had not counted on, there is little you can do. Preparing a media kit with background information on your tourism product can prevent errors arising from ignorance, but the slant that a news organization puts on your story can be a surprise, and in some cases, cast a negative light. In those situations, consider it a learning experience and vow to work more closely with the media so they have a clearer understanding of what you represent.

If you like writing or speaking, consider writing a regular column for a newspaper or becoming a regular contributor to a radio show as a way to get your name in front of people. If you write a column on local wildlife or recreational activities, you will establish yourself as an expert in the field. This will work best if you contribute regularly and write about topics that are of interest to local readers. Another approach is to establish relationships with reporters and editors as an expert source for background information and quotes. Become the area expert the media call with the question. Being able to comment on tourism trends and activities, or culture and natural history, may put your name in front of local audiences several times a year.

MARKETING FORECASTS

Marketing relies heavily on concepts, images, and words, but there is also a need for numbers.

Responsible business owners need to estimate the costs of their marketing to ensure their marketing plan is affordable, and they also need to estimate the sales they will realize when the plan has been completed to evaluate their success.

Marketing Budgets

After you select your marketing activities, you should complete a **marketing budget**, an estimate of the money you will spend on marketing for the coming year. In completing your budget, you will find it helpful to use a worksheet like the one shown in table 5.4.

Estimate the cost of the marketing activities you selected as being the best for your business. Add the expected costs for each of the next three years because you will find that some activities take many months or years to yield results. If you find that you do not have the funds to market your business as you would like, you can take a couple of approaches. First, consider marketing partnerships where you join with other businesses to promote your destination. Secondly, carefully evaluate past marketing efforts and put your money into the activities that generated the highest yield. If you have no history or have not monitored your marketing programs, make a calculated guess of which activities to select. Plan to collect this information for your current marketing activities so you can make better decisions in the future.

Forecasting Sales

It is a good idea to do a sales forecast as part of marketing plan. A **sales forecast** is an estimate of the amount of money your customers will pay for your tourism product over the next year. Sales are calculated by multiplying the estimated price by the units of product sold (a unit might be a tour or hotel night or admission ticket). It is important you understand how to complete a sales forecast because it is the starting point for other financial forecasts and analysis.

You might find it easier to complete your sales forecast by following a format similar to the one shown in table 5.5. A blank sales forecast spreadsheet is provided in the web resource. Modify it to match the uniqueness of your product. Add additional lines for each type of tour or to distinguish between different prices, such as low season and peak season. The forecast format refers to the number of tours or number of tour days. If your business offers accommodations or

Table 5.4   Marketing Budget Worksheet

Category	Year 1 Expenditures $	Year 2 Expenditures $	Year 3 Expenditures $
Direct sales			
Direct mail			
Direct sales: fax			
Direct sales: telephone			
Direct sales: in person			
Brochures			
Brochure development			
Brochure printing			
Internet			
Website development			
Search engine optimization			
Social media development			
Internet maintenance			
Video			
Signage			
Print media			
Directories			
Newspaper ads			
Magazines			
Trade shows			
Registration			
Travel costs			
Conferences			
Conference fees			
Travel costs			
Broadcast media			
Television			
Radio			
Publicity			
Press kits and releases			
Complimentary items			
Familiarization tours			
Travel writers			
Travel agents			
Wholesalers and packagers			
Market research			
Monitoring			
Total marketing costs			

Table 5.5   Sales Forecast

SALES FORECAST FOR YEAR ONE													
	J	F	M	A	M	J	J	A	S	O	N	D	Total
Sales volume: half-day tours					20	150	400	400	48				1,018
Price ($)					85	85	85	85	85				
Revenue ($)					1,700	12,750	34,000	34,000	4,080				86,530
Sales volume: rentals					30	80	120	120	20				370
Price ($)					30	30	30	30	30				
Revenue ($)					900	2,400	3,600	3,600	600				11,100
Total revenue ($)					2,600	15,150	37,600	37,600	4,680				97,630

is an attraction, use it to forecast the number of bed nights or number of visitors. Earlier in the chapter, you learned how to establish a price. To complete the forecast, estimate the volume you can sell; suggestions on how to do that follow.

To increase the accuracy of your volume forecasts, gather information from a variety of sources:

• *Historical sales information*—While the past is not a predictor of the future, looking at the historical level of sales both in terms of dollars and number of trips sold, can be helpful in identifying trends. You might notice that trips featuring aboriginal heritage have been popular and feel confident that the popularity will increase. This would lead you to forecast a larger number of trips than in past years.

• *Research studies*—If research studies provide estimates of the market size or the amount being sold by other companies, you can estimate how many tours, experiences, or room nights you might sell. Research can also identify trends so you can decide whether sales are likely to increase each year, remain constant, or decline.

• *Competitors and suppliers*—Competitors may be willing to provide you sales information in exchange for information about your operation. If a competitor is expecting a large increase in the number of fully independent travelers for natural history hikes, consider increasing your sales forecasts from last year's level for comparable tours. Suppliers also have helpful information about who is doing what in the industry, and some of it might affect your business. If you talk to the company that rents kayaks, they can give you an idea of how busy they expect their year to be, the anticipated

length of rental they anticipate, and the type of customers, such as independent travelers or tour packagers.

• *Destination marketing organization (DMO)*—These organizations market tourism destinations. They can include the regional chamber of commerce, division or department of tourism, or convention and visitors bureaus. They often conduct market studies or answer queries from travelers considering your destination. They can share information on estimated market size for travelers to your area, regions and countries that are growth markets, the products tourists are seeking, and ways to market to high-yield groups. Not all the markets targeted by DMOs will be of interest to you, but their activities have some relevance to your sales. If they are targeting large tour groups in the Japanese market, it could mean you will not benefit because the travel patterns of these groups (large numbers, highly structured itineraries, little time in one place) are not consistent with many small-scale tourism products. Conversely, a DMO marketing to the German market might bring people into the area who are interested in a nature-based tourism product, thus increasing your sales opportunities.

• *Customers*—By asking your customer base what its travel plans are and monitoring requests for brochures and trip itineraries, you will have an idea of how many past customers will travel with you in the upcoming year.

Once you have gathered information from these sources, make your best estimate of what you can sell. Although it is a guess, by gathering information from as many sources as possible and cross-checking your findings, you increase the probability that your sales targets are reasonable. You want to measure your actual sales against your forecast to help you improve your forecasting each year.

Once you have finished this step, you will have completed the main steps of your marketing plan. Document your work and keep the file nearby. You will add notes as you learn more about your customers or marketing opportunities, and it will help you decide whether you should take advantage of unexpected marketing opportunities.

MONITORING AND EVALUATING MARKETING ACTIVITIES

You will invest a lot of time and money in marketing; it is important you place it where it will generate the best results. After selecting your marketing activities and forecasting sales, consider how to monitor and evaluate your marketing effectiveness. Even if you have a successful year, you still want to know which parts of your marketing plan were most effective. Did your appearance at the ITB Berlin trade show generate sales? Did you advertise in a directory that was not distributed to your market segment? Was a special deal advertised on the Internet helpful in selling tours during the off season? You cannot answer these questions without monitoring and evaluating your marketing activities.

To successfully monitor, you need to track the number of inquiries and bookings resulting from each marketing activity. In its simplest form, ask each person who calls for information or makes a reservation how he or she heard about you. If you collect data in sufficient detail, for example, the name and issue of the magazine where people saw your advertisement, you will be well on the way to evaluating your marketing plan.

Staff may not always query callers in detail and customers do not always remember how they heard of you. Coding your marketing efforts can help. If you have an 800 number, you can have people ask for "operators" that correspond to specific advertisements. An advertisement in the *New York Times* might have operator 22 next to the telephone number. When a person calls asking for operator 22, you know he or she saw your advertisement in the *New York Times*. You can be even more specific and code the operator to advertisements placed on certain days.

Special prices or offers also can help track where people heard of your business. If you have a nature walk that costs $40 for three hours and you offer a special rate of $39.95 in a newspaper advertisement, you will know where people heard about you when they ask for the $39.95 rate.

Another component of tracking your marketing effectiveness is to make sure your costs are recorded in a manner that makes analysis possible. If you record all your marketing costs in one account called marketing, evaluating your marketing programs will be difficult. At the very least, separate marketing expenditures into the same categories as your budget. If you have a large outlay for a specific product or advertisement, set up a separate account for it. Discuss these needs with your accountant so he or she can create a reporting system that enables you to easily evaluate your marketing plan.

When evaluating marketing program effectiveness, look at some of the financial performance indicators you use to evaluate your business as a whole. Some of the most useful are cost per inquiry, cost per visitor, and return on investment. The formulas shown in figure 5.3 are simple to apply; the difficulty is in gathering the information. If you do not have detailed information, estimate where possible. For example, if you spent $4,000 to advertise in *Escape* magazine and you received 100 inquiries that led to 10 bookings, cost per inquiry is $40 ($4,000 ÷ 100) and cost per visitor is $400 ($4,000 ÷ 10).

When calculating return on investment for marketing activities, look at sales generated from

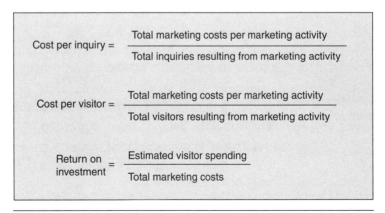

Figure 5.3 Formulas for evaluating marketing activities.

a specific marketing activity, for example, trips sold from a listing in your state's accommodation directory. The marketing costs are the cost of a listing in the tourism directory. Using the previous example, we assume each booked trip is worth $3,000. Your return on investment is $30,000 [(10 trips × $3,000) ÷ $4,000], or 750 percent.

Analyzing your marketing activities this way can give you concrete information on which marketing activities are worth spending money on. If activities are not performing, stop them and reallocate your funds to marketing activities generating better returns.

SUMMARY

Completing a marketing plan takes tremendous effort by tourism business owners and managers. They must pull together information from the strategic plan, market research, their past experiences, and their understanding of future trends. The process outlined in this chapter will help you understand the activities you must undertake to build or support a marketing plan. As you learn more about the financial management in future chapters, you will appreciate how important effective marketing plans are to an organization's long-term success.

GLOSSARY

advertising—Communication that calls attention to an organization to influence or convince the audience to take action, usually to purchase something.

brochures—Pamphlets used to inform visitors about a tourism product and region. They are sometimes called lure brochures.

commission—The compensation that people or organizations charge for selling a product or service.

competitive analysis—A review of other organizations offering similar products and the ways they distinguish their company or services.

contingency—An amount of money set aside to cover unexpected problems, such as changes in foreign exchange rates, unexpected cost increases, or last-minute opportunities.

destination marketing organization (DMO)—An organization that markets tourism destinations. It can be a regional chamber of commerce, division or department of tourism, or a convention and visitors bureau.

direct sales—Selling directly to the customer via Internet, telephone, fax, mail, or in person.

directory—A listing of businesses that have something in common. Often tourism directories are organized by geographic region or activity and are created to sell travel products to tourists.

familiarization tour—Sometimes called fam tours, these trips offer complimentary accommodations and activities to showcase destinations and businesses to people in a position to help sell the experience.

fixed costs—These are costs that fluctuate, but do not vary directly according to the number of participants. For example, if a company rents a van to shuttle guests, the cost will be the same whether it has one guest or twenty.

load factor—The percentage of average participation that a business applies to maximum participation on a tour to take into account that it will likely operate below capacity.

market analysis—A review of tourism market research and trends with the goal of identifying an organization's most profitable market segments in the next one to three years.

marketing—The process for determining the potential buyers of a product, what their needs are, and how to respond to those needs in a way that will encourage them to visit the business.

marketing budget—An estimate of the money a business will spend on marketing for the coming year.

marketing mix—How the four Ps of product, price, place, and promotion are used.

marketing plan—A plan that outlines strategies for achieving marketing objectives using product, price, place, and promotion.

marketing strategies—Plans made to achieve marketing goals.

marketing theme—The main image or message that marketing materials leave potential customers.

media release—A document sent to media outlets announcing something they might want to report on.

net rate—The amount of money kept when a product is sold through a travel intermediary such as a travel agent.

overhead—This fixed cost does not vary directly with the number of tours or guests, and includes expenditures needed to run a business.

place—One of the four Ps, this is where a product is distributed. Unlike other industries, tourism products must be consumed on-site. It cannot be shipped around the world like a package of coffee.

positioning—Creating an identity in the minds of consumers.

price—One of the four Ps, this is what a business charges a customer for a product.

print media—Publications printed on paper such as newspapers, magazines, and directories.

product—One of the four Ps. This can be a physical good, for example, baskets crafted by an indigenous tribe, or a service or experience, such as offering nature-viewing tours in a unique setting.

product–market match—A marketing process that matches the products to the market segments most likely to purchase them.

promotion—One of the four Ps, this is telling the target market about a product. It includes the selling activities often associated with marketing.

psychographic information—Information that helps marketers understand a traveler's view of the world and their values, travel behaviors, and motivations.

publicity—The dissemination of information about a company to gain public interest.

retail price—The price the consumer sees on a brochure or website. This is sometimes called the rack, gross, or sell rate.

sales forecast—An estimate of the amount of money customers will pay for a tourism product over the next year. Sales are calculated by multiplying the estimated price by the units of product sold.

search engine optimization (SEO)—A process for identifying the key words that customers use to search the Internet and ensuring prominent use of those words on a website to move the website up the search engine ratings. It may also require purchasing ads linked to those key words.

selling—Promotional activities in the marketing process that occur when a business contacts people to persuade them to buy.

signage—The signs that identify a business and direct people to it.

situation analysis—A review of the economic, political, environmental, and social climate an organization will face in the upcoming year.

tourism marketplace—Gatherings of tourism suppliers and marketing organizations with the intent to create marketing partnerships.

trade show—A gathering of businesses to showcase their products and services. Often they are only open to people in the industry, although some are open to the public.

variable costs—Expenditures that vary according to the number of people who use a service, for example, take a tour, stay in a hotel, eat at a restaurant, or visit an attraction.

|||||||||||||||||||||| REVIEW QUESTIONS |||||||||||||||||||||

1. What are the four Ps of marketing? Do you think this model works as well for service businesses as it does for those selling products? Explain your reasoning.

2. Why does an organization prepare a marketing plan? How can information from a strategic plan help in the preparation of a marketing plan?

3. Explain how market segments are created and the benefits market segmentation offers organizations.

4. Give an example of a marketing strategy related to pricing. Identify the steps required to calculate a price for a product.

5. List several marketing activities that could be used for promotion. Describe how to create a marketing theme and how it helps promotion activities.

6. How can an organization assess the effectiveness of its marketing plan? Give examples of possible measurements.

||||||||||||||||||||||| VIDEO CASE STUDY |||||||||||||||||||||

Visit the web resource to watch the video "Marketing to Photographers." After watching the video, answer the following questions:

1. What is the unique experience the Northern Lights Wildlife Wolf Centre offers tourists?

2. Describe which market segments are likely to purchase photography tours. Which market segments are more likely to be interested in the shorter and less-expensive tours of the Centre?

3. How successful do you think founders Casey and Shelley Black have been in matching products and markets? Explain your reasoning.

4. List and rank the marketing activities you think would be most effective for the Northern Lights Wildlife Centre, keeping in mind most organizations have limited funds for marketing.

5. What positioning strategies do you think an organization like the Northern Lights Wildlife Centre might use? Identify the competitive advantages a sustainable tourism organization might promote.

YOUR BUSINESS PLAN

The marketing plan is the cornerstone of your business plan. After reading this chapter, you will see how important it is to understand your customers and spend your marketing budget where you can reach the people most likely to buy. Complete the marketing sections of the Business Plan workbook. Leave room to add notes on using Web 2.0 for advertising and selling through the travel trade. These topics will be covered in more detail in upcoming chapters.

1. Explain your process for gathering information on potential market segments. Identify any information gaps you found. If you had the resources, what survey questions would you ask?

2. When reviewing your competitors, describe differences you noticed in the frequency of website updates, new product offerings, and social media posts. Provide possible explanations for the divergences.

3. List marketing activities that you like companies to use when they are selling to you. Select those that might be effective with your customers, remembering they might have different preferences. Pinpoint activities your targeted customers prefer that are unfamiliar to you, and describe ways you can gather more information.

REFERENCES

BBCTravel. 2011. Have the Galapagos been saved? www.bbc.com/travel/blog/20110203-travelwise-have-the-galapagos-been-saved.

Canadian Tourism Commission. 2012. EQ profiles. http://en-corporate.canada.travel/sites/default/files/pdf/Resources/1e-ctc_eq_profiles-2012_fnl-eng.pdf

Destination NSW. 2012. Pricing your tourism product. http://www.destinationnsw.com.au/wp-content/uploads/2014/03/Tourism-Business-Toolkit-VOL2-Chapter3.pdf.

Hess, Ronald L. 2010. Tourism competitive analysis study. Presentation on June 16 to Williamsburg Marketing Research Task Force. The Mason School of Business, College of William & Mary. www.hrp.org/Site/docs/ResourceLibrary/Hess%20Competitive%20Destination%20Study%202010_WM-MasonSchool.pdf.

Plog, S.C. 1974. Why destination areas rise and fall in popularity. *Cornell Hotel and Restaurant Administration Quarterly*, 42(3), pp. 13-24.

Roth, T. 2010. CMIGreen Traveler Study Report 2010. Vol. 1. San Francisco: CMIGreen Community Marketing. www.greenlodgingnews.com/downloads/cmigreentraveler2010v1.pdf.

WWW Metrics. 2014. Growth of the travel industry online. www.wwwmetrics.com/travel.htm.

YP Advertising Solutions. 2012. Perfecting your marketing plans with the 4 Ps. http://adsolutions.yp.com/articles/perfecting-your-marketing-plans-4-ps.

MAKING THE INTERNET WORK FOR YOU

After reading this chapter, you will be able to do the following:

- Describe how the Internet is evolving to include more user content and participation

- Understand what Web 2.0 is and how social media are changing business

- Identify the implications of the Internet for sustainable tourism organizations

- Maximize the time spent on Internet activities

The invention of the Internet revolutionized our lives and our businesses. E-mail makes it possible to stay in touch with friends and business contacts cheaply and frequently—no need to buy a stamp or wait weeks for a reply to a letter. Doctors can dispense medical advice to patients thousands of miles or kilometers away. Consumers do not need to wait for a catalogue to be left on their doorstep to shop at home, and if you do not know how to assemble what you bought online, a tutorial with pictures and video is a few clicks away.

Many people alive today have never lived in a world without the Internet. Now, the invention that started by sharing information among scientists and academics is shifting to one in which the content is generated by users and interaction is expected, not a bonus. This new technology is dramatically changing the way business is done; because the tourism industry is large and travel is based on sensory experiences, the tourism industry is experiencing large changes, much of it beneficial. This chapter describes how the Internet is evolving and what it means for tourism organizations.

WHAT IS WEB 2.0?

Web 2.0 is the second stage of development of the Internet. It is characterized by the change from static web pages to user-generated content and the growth of social media. So Web 2.0 is not a technology per se, but rather an evolution in how the technology is used. In the early days of the Internet, tourism businesses developed websites

Travelers expect to interact with tourism company websites and like to share their vacation images.

using the same information they would have put into a brochure. Travelers read the information and if they had questions or comments, they called or e-mailed the tourism company.

Today, travelers expect to interact with a website and create content for it. This phenomenon is referred to as **social media**: forms of electronic communication, such as websites for social networking and microblogging, through which users create online communities to share information, ideas, personal messages, and other content, such as videos. The following are some of the most well-known facets of social media:

• Facebook—A website where users can create profiles and share pictures, videos, and updates with family and friends through posts. Businesses are treated differently than individuals. A business creates a fan page (often called a page) and people "like" a business' page on Facebook to see their posts in the news feed.

• Blog—A website that allows a user to create on online diary quickly and cheaply. Inexperienced users can make their first blog entry within an hour on a free blogging website. People can set up a blog to share travel experiences and photos, and many blogs allow readers to leave comments.

• Twitter—A website that allows users to tweet a miniblog post of 140 characters or fewer. The tweet can include links to websites or photos

and video. People choose to follow other users but do not need permission to do so, as in Facebook. Because it can reach many people quickly, Twitter is often used to break news stories or announce promotional offers.

• LinkedIn—A website that facilitates networking among professionals. Users connect to other people they have worked with or known and start discussion groups on topics of interest. Users can also post updates on activities they have undertaken and show where they are traveling.

• Instagram—A photo-sharing application that allows smartphone users to apply filters and share photographs.

• YouTube—A website that allows users to watch and upload videos. Users can create their own channel for their videos.

• Flickr—A website where users can post their photos for others to view and comment on. Photos can be grouped into themes, for example, national parks, allowing people from around the world with similar interests to share information.

• Wiki—A collaboration among people to share information previously found in books such as encyclopedias. Wikipedia allows users to post information on topics they find of interest and allows the online community to add to and edit the content.

• Pinterest—A website that allows users to share and categorize images found online into themes. Although brief descriptions of material can be added, Pinterest is a visual experience.

• Podcast—An audio file that can be downloaded from a website. Users can create their own podcasts to share with others.

• Mash-up—The combination of two or more information sources to create a new user experience. An example is when a bike company uses Google maps to show its cycling tour route on a website.

One study found that people used the Internet more to plan vacations (80%) than for work (70%) (Cameron 2012). Other research indicates that 86 percent of online Americans engage in social media and that they spend more time on social media than volunteering, praying, e-mailing, talking on the phone, or exercising (Fleming 2012). Although some consumers are still reluctant to use the Internet (see sidebar Technology Use Among Older Adults), tourism professionals cannot ignore the amount of attention consumers give social media and how it is changing tourism.

HOW SOCIAL MEDIA IS CHANGING TOURISM

The Internet first became important to the tourism industry when consumers started using it to research their trips. Travelers no longer had to go to a travel agency or a visitor's center to get brochures or travel catalogues to find information for their next trip. Prices, itineraries, and trip features were delivered instantly with a few clicks. People still use the Internet to research their holidays, but social media and Web 2.0 are making the process more interactive. Now, consumers can easily get input from other travelers and customize their vacation experience so they get exactly what they want. Many travelers are turning away from the standard tours that might have appealed to their parents 30 years ago and seeking unique experiences, often with the intent of online sharing (or showing off) to their friends.

The following are some of the ways travelers are using social media and changing the travel landscape as a result:

• Rating experiences
• Seeking insider tips
• Sharing

• Complaining
• Group purchasing

Each of these is discussed in more detail in the following sections.

Rating Experiences

Everyone has an opinion on their last travel experience. Two decades ago, you might have shared those comments with coworkers around the coffee station or your neighbors over the fence. Now, you can share your opinions of your travel experiences with people around the world in an online discussion forum. TripAdvisor is one of the best-known websites for rating trip experiences, with over 100 million travel reviews and more than 60 contributions posted every minute.

Why has online rating become so popular? Probably because research suggests consumers trust the recommendations of people perceived to have similar interests more than they trust traditional advertising. A recent survey showed that people

People look to other travelers for trip recommendations and tips.

trust recommendations from people they know (92% trust completely or somewhat) or consumer opinions posted online (70% trust completely or somewhat) versus ads in magazines or on TV (47% trust completely or somewhat). This trust in recommendations is increasing; in the same study, an 18 percent increase in trust was seen in four years (Nielsen 2012).

It is challenging to market your business when consumers rely more on messages over which you have little control. Your best strategy may be to ensure your travelers have a great experience and when they do not, find them on social media so you can comment on negative ratings and hopefully mitigate some of the backlash.

Insider Tips

As mentioned earlier in the book, consumers are seeking unique and authentic experiences. For many people, this means avoiding standardized packages or at least looking for wow-factor activities to add to their vacation. Consumers may check travel-rating websites for tips from other travelers on which

rooms to book or which activities to undertake or what discounts to seek. Travelers are encouraged to share this information in their reviews, and the popularity of theses websites suggests consumers are finding benefit in these tips from fellow travelers.

The Canadian Tourism Commission (CTC) tapped into this desire for insider tips with its Locals Know campaign. Instead of presenting information in more traditional advertisements, vacation ideas were promoted as insider travel ideas that only Canadians would know about. The CTC launched the Locals Know campaign to inspire travelers to discover little-known tourism attractions and destinations. Images used to launch the campaign were those one would not associate with Canada, for example, desert dunes in the middle of the country or volcanoes near the Pacific Ocean. They were tagged with the question "Where is this?"

The campaign encouraged Canadians to upload their pictures and videos of favorite travel spots onto the campaign website. In less than three months, the website had over 3 million page views, and the campaign generated over C$1.1 million of media coverage. The social media campaign succeeded because it appealed to travelers who liked to explore, the market segment targeted by CTC (Wexler 2009).

Sharing

No longer do people put their vacation photos in albums to gather dust in their bookcases. They share their photos quickly and frequently with friends and strangers through social media websites such as Flickr or Instagram. Improved camera technology is turning everyone into amateur photographers, and making videos has never been easier. With a few clicks, travelers post their travel videos on websites like YouTube. The proliferation of smartphones and cameras means that no travel experience need go uncaptured. Some attractions now post notices at their entrance warning that visitors might be photographed while on the grounds and if they cannot agree to that happening, they should not enter!

Although many of these photos and videos are not great art, they fill a need in the psyche of travelers to share what they are seeing and experiencing, often while they are on the road. A recent study found that 31 percent of U.S. travelers who are active users of social media post comments

Looking at photo-sharing websites lets people form impressions of a destination through images taken by people like them.

or photos while traveling (Voyager's World 2012). This sharing, especially while on the road, can be expected to grow. In 2012, 64 percent of U.S. travelers active online owned smartphones, up from 52 percent a year earlier (Voyager's World 2012). This means that the travel experience your business is offering is likely to be displayed in real time to travelers around the world. You want to make sure the experience is positive, or you will feel the power of Web 2.0 when it comes to complaints.

Complaining

Travelers place extremely high expectations on their vacations. The images businesses use to advertise travel usually show blue skies, smiling people, clean hotel rooms, and close-up encounters with wildlife. Most travelers hope (expect) they will have those same experiences and if the reality is different, disappointment arises. If customers get a lukewarm cup of coffee from their local barista, they might shrug it off; when they get a subpar vacation experience, the reaction is more acute. People might have waited all year for their two-week vacation and saved for months, or added to their credit card debt, to pay for it. They want the trip of a lifetime and if they feel cheated, they can share their heartbreak or anger with other travelers quickly and effectively.

No longer does a disgruntled traveler need to fill out a customer feedback survey and then wait weeks for an impersonal reply. Unhappy travelers can share their thoughts in an online discussion group, tweet their annoyance, post a photo of a dirty room on Facebook, or give a negative rating on TripAdvisor. The tourism business that did not meet the traveler's expectation now has a consumer marketing against it. As mentioned earlier, travelers trust the recommendations and comments of friends and fellow travelers. When someone complains on social media, people listen, and future sales can be jeopardized. A tourism business manager must respond to these complaints quickly through social media to stem the damage and, optimally, turn the customer relationship around. Strategies for doing this will be discussed later in the chapter.

Group Purchasing

Large companies enjoy the benefits of **bulk purchasing power**, discounted prices negotiated with suppliers in exchange for large orders. Now travelers use social media to negotiate better prices for their trip experiences through bulk purchasing power. Websites like Groupon allow travel businesses to offer substantially discounted trips to travelers if a certain number of people take the deal. The trip does not go if the specified number of travelers do not sign up, so if a traveler really wants the deal, he or she will tell friends in an effort to convince them to take the deal. In effect, this social media mechanism turns customers into sales people for the travel company.

More businesses are taking advantage of this model to sell their travel product. One company, Jump On Flyaways, uses group purchasing to create a new travel experience. As seen in the sidebar Power of Social Media: A New Way to Travel, social media is the mechanism that makes this tourism business possible.

Power of Social Media: A New Way to Travel

What do you get when you cross an empty plane and the power of social media? How about the chance to fly weekends at a 30 percent discount and no connecting flights? Jump On Flyaway's founder, Roger Jewett, is taking a page from Groupon's playbook and asking travelers to use group purchasing power for weekend jaunts. The planes they use shuttle crews to the oil sands during the week, but sit idle all weekend. But if this business concept takes off, the planes will be idle no more. If at least 120 people take the deal, travelers spend a weekend in Las Vegas at a reduced price and with the convenience of a direct flight.

Social media is the main mechanism for marketing Jump On. Company executives use their social media networks to tell people about the concept and offer a C$50 insider credit if they book. By encouraging consumers to become insiders, the company hopes to build customer loyalty and a sense of belonging. Customers are encouraged to get involved in ways that go beyond buying a trip; Jump On passengers vote for preferred future destinations, so while initial flights go to Las Vegas, future flights might go to San Francisco or beyond.

In the next section, the implications of social media's rising popularity for tourism business managers will be examined. Savvy business owners will find social media is a powerful communication tool and familiarity with it is necessary for success.

IMPLICATIONS FOR SUSTAINABLE TOURISM BUSINESS MANAGERS

The full impact of the user-generated content of Web 2.0 has not been seen, but it could rival the Internet's introduction for the effect it has on our lives. People are increasingly connected to their online worlds and are building social relationships there that will affect all businesses. The video "Social Media and Travel" illustrates how managers of sustainable tourism businesses need to adapt their business processes for this new world. Some areas where adaptation is required are discussed in the following sections.

Product Launches

You can use social media to quickly announce a new product or publicize specials or discounts on tours. You do not need to plan advertising copy months in advance as you might to meet advertising deadlines found in magazines. If you have a database of client e-mails or a community of followers on Twitter or Facebook, you can announce new products at a lower cost than you would spend on other forms of marketing.

Website Enhancement

Social media can add visual appeal to your website by supplementing your professional photographs and video with trip images or videos your customers share. These photos can keep your company in front of potential clients and generate discussion. For example, Quark Expeditions asks travelers to share their vacation photos during their polar cruises. Dedicated computers are set up in common areas for customers to upload a few of their best photos each day. Quark provides customers with a disk of everyone's photos at the end of the trip. Some photos find their way onto the Quark Facebook page, which keeps people following Quark's social media. One passenger photo of a penguin leaping into the water generated almost 200 likes on Facebook in the five hours after it was posted to Quark's Facebook page.

Social media users expect to interact with your website, so you need to provide ways they can share or comment on content. This might include icons on your website directing them to your social media streams such as Twitter, Facebook, or Pinterest. If you have a blog on your website, you might incorporate a feature that allows readers to easily tweet or share quotes from your blog on Facebook.

Wi-Fi Accessibility

Many of today's customers expect Wi-Fi access during their travel experience so they can stay connected and share what they are experiencing in real time. The use of smartphones is replacing postcards as a way to brag back home. A recent study found that the number of people using smartphones has tripled, and that wireless use was higher on vacation (40%) than at home (25%) (Cameron 2012). While providing Wi-Fi access is not a problem in urban environments, many sustainable tourism businesses operate in rural or wilderness environments where it is costly and difficult to provide. There is also a moral dilemma. Some people feel that travelers need to be unplugged for hours, if not days, to get the most of their time in nature. Others may disagree or have practical reasons for needing to stay connected. Some people believe they need to stay in touch with the office or risk losing business or their jobs. As described in the sidebar Canadian Mountain Holidays, finding a balance between these needs can be tricky. You will need to find a way to meet the needs of your customers while maintaining the experience they are seeking.

Customer Service

As described earlier, social media helps travelers share their complaints with many people quickly. To minimize the damage this could do to your business, monitor social media networks and participate in the discussions. If someone is singing your praises, a simple thank you can suffice. If someone is unhappy with an aspect of your tourism product or his or her experience, respond positively and quickly. You can mention how the problem has been solved or if not solved, taken into consideration for future changes. By replying you let your customers know that you heard their concerns and are interested in maintaining a rela-

---

Canadian Mountain Holidays

Heli-skiing and hiking are the mainstays of Canadian Mountain Holidays (CMH). Lodges are located in remote locations in the Rocky Mountains and the ability to reach pristine wilderness areas is a cornerstone of the visitor experience. When CMH visitors first requested Internet access, there was some resistance within CMH and fears that connectivity would diminish the experience of being away from it all.

Many CMH customers work in managerial or professional jobs and believed they should not be out of touch with their work, so a compromise was made and Internet was offered in only a few lodge areas. Today, Wi-Fi is available throughout the facilities and each lodge's connectivity is described in detail on the company's website. This is proof that even adventure lovers want to be connected!

---

tionship with them. If the complaint is particularly egregious, you might want to offer a discount or a complimentary product.

Staffing

Social media provides opportunities and challenges with respect to staffing. You may find your cost of recruiting will decrease because you can advertise for staff on social media cheaper than by placing advertisements in the local paper. Conversely, you may find there are additional staff costs because your employees spend time on personal social media while on the job. Younger workers are more likely to be distracted by social media at work because it is an important part of their life. Some companies respond by banning the use of social media while on the job, but this strategy may not work. Research suggests younger employees would rather have access to social media at work than a larger salary, and 56 percent will not accept a job without access to social media (Conner 2012). Take the Ecochallenge "How Much Social Media?" with your friends to see whether this reflects your values.

Many tourism businesses are not able to offer high salaries, so perhaps they can attract better job candidates by allowing social media access during work hours. These companies could also use those social media skills in managing their company's social media activities.

MAXIMIZE YOUR WEB PRESENCE

Being visible on social media is an important part of marketing. If necessary, hire people who understand it and can help with the technology requirements. At times, social media can seem like a beast with an insatiable appetite. The need for constant content places a huge time demand on a tourism business. The rapid change makes it difficult to stay on top of trends and expensive to incorporate these technologies into your business.

Many books and websites are devoted to the issues of managing the daily demands of social media. This section outlines critical strategies for using Web 2.0 to build your business.

Ecochallenge
How Much Social Media?

Chances are you use social media and use your smartphone, tablet, or computer to stay in touch with friends and family several times a day. How much of your workday do you think can be spent on personal social media without affecting your work performance? You may find it difficult to estimate how much time you spend on social media, so for one day track the number of times you receive or send a text or post to a social media website. How important is it for you to be connected while at work? Would you have difficulty accepting a job in a remote location if it meant difficulty accessing the Internet? How do you think a tourism company could attract skilled staff if their location makes it difficult to offer reliable Internet connections? Does your current employer have a policy on social media use at work? If it does, consider whether you think the policy is fair or whether the company misses opportunities because of it. Identify ways you might change the policy or rules if you were allowed.

Focus on Your Own Content

Many social media websites are free for users and relatively easy to start operating. It takes minutes to set up a Twitter or Facebook account. In an hour, you can set up a free blog and start sharing your thoughts. But social media websites are run by businesses; to offer free services to participants, they must make money some other way. These websites can change their conditions and terms of service at any time. What is free when you sign up may no longer be free after you have invested hours in building your profile and following. Or you might find that information on your activity is being sold by the website owner to other businesses. A saying about the Internet states that if you are not paying for the product, you are the product. The loss of privacy may not be a concern if you are using social media for business, but you might be concerned with changes to the terms of service. Instagram caused turmoil among users in December 2012 when it announced it had the right to sell users' photos without payment or notification. This decision was quickly reversed but it highlights the problem you might face if the website you have used for your social media suddenly changes its contract with users.

You could also spend time developing a social media presence on a website that becomes irrelevant. When Myspace lost the popularity race with Facebook, anyone who had built a following on the former had to reestablish himself or herself on Facebook. A better strategy is to invest most of your time in content that you control, for example, a blog on your website (not a blog hosted by someone else's website). You can still use other social media venues, but develop different strategies for them. For example, it probably makes sense to use some social media to feed others. Twitter is a great place to connect with strangers, but once you have made initial contact you can direct them to your website. A trip-rating website may be where customers find your business, but if they enjoy your product, ask them to write a review that you can tweet, share on Facebook, or add to your website.

Manage Your Time

Although you have many options for engaging with social media, what counts is that you engage frequently and quickly. Managing your social media presence can take tremendous resources from your business, so it pays to be organized. You need to learn the ways of each new social media and, once established, invest time in maintaining your presence. If you have ever watched a Twitter feed for a few hours, you are aware of the huge amount of information being shared. If you are to be noticed, you need to be active daily, if not hourly. If you are starting to wonder where you will find time to keep up with social media, you are not alone.

A system that allows the same information to feed multiple social media platforms will help you manage your time. Programs like Hootsuite allow you to post to Twitter, Facebook, and LinkedIn from one place. If you will be in the backcountry leading a hike, you can schedule the release so people won't know you are away from your computer.

It may make sense for small companies to pick one or two social media websites and focus on those. It is difficult to manage all social media channels well, so pick those that meet your needs best and that you enjoy. Some people love the microblogging feel of Twitter, others complain it is an overwhelming and confusing mass of information. Find something that appeals to you and commit to spending time on it. What counts is that you build new relationships, not where you do it.

Technology Use Among Older Adults

Chances are the Internet has always been part of your life and you are comfortable with technology. However, senior citizens remember life before the World Wide Web and might take a different approach to technology. According to a recent U.S. survey, many have cell phones, but only 18 percent own smartphones, compared to the national average of 55 percent. Use of social networking sites, such as Facebook, for seniors is 46 percent, again below the national average of 73 percent, and just 6 percent use Twitter (Smith 2014). If active seniors are your target market, use the Internet in a way that matches their needs. You may need to offer options for payment besides online and use e-zines or print newsletters to share news instead of tweeting.

Consider Paid Placement

Even though one of the advantages of social media is its cost—free in many cases—you might want to pay for advertising to raise your profile. Many business owners are dismayed to find that even though they have a Facebook page and post frequently, many of the people who have liked their page never see their posts. One Facebook expert calculated that only 17 percent of Facebook fans see a post on a page they have liked (Carter 2012). Facebook has a sophisticated algorithm that includes factors such as which posts appeal to a user, their interests, and the number of comments on posts to determine whether a post shows up in the news feed. The result is that the posts you make to your Facebook page are seen by far fewer people than you expected. Facebook has a solution to this dilemma: pay for placement of your post so more people see it. You may decide this is a good use of your marketing funds, but try to measure the sales you are generating through social media so you can evaluate its effectiveness, just like any other marketing activity.

SUMMARY

Social media is a relatively new addition to the tourism world, but it is having large impacts. Travelers are turning away from traditional advertising in favor of recommendations from friends or trusted strangers and they want to interact with businesses on the Internet. You need to understand this societal change and evolving technology and allocate resources within your business to manage it. Measuring the effectiveness of social media can be difficult, but if you think of it as a way to build relationships with your customers, you will know you are succeeding when you can point to a loyal base of customers feeding your business more and more sales.

GLOSSARY

bulk purchasing power—Discounted prices negotiated with suppliers in exchange for large orders from big companies.

social media—Forms of electronic communication (such as websites for social networking and microblogging) through which users create online communities to share information, ideas, personal messages, and other content (such as videos).

Web 2.0—The second phase of development of the Internet, characterized by the change from static web pages to user-generated content and the growth of social media.

REVIEW QUESTIONS

1. How has the Internet changed since it was created? What are the implications for sustainable tourism organizations?

2. What is Web 2.0?

3. How can sustainable tourism organizations use social media to market their tourism experiences?

4. Many travelers expect to have Internet access when they travel. How might this affect the tourism experience in remote or natural environments? Do you think it enhances or detracts from the ability to get away from it all?

5. As social media and Internet use increases, describe the implications for sustainable tourism organizations in product development, marketing, and operations.

IIIIIIIIIIIIIIIIIIIIIIIIIIIII VIDEO CASE STUDY IIIIIIIIIIIIIIIIIIIII

Visit the web resource to watch the video "Social Media and Travel." After watching the video, answer the following questions:

1. How is social media changing how a tourism experience is marketed? What advantages does social media provide sustainable tourism organizations operating in remote locations?

2. Explain how your impressions of Antarctica changed after watching the video. What questions would you want answered before traveling to a new destination? List the social media applications you would use to gather information.

3. How important to tourists is the ability to update social media while traveling? Identify the positive and negative impacts travelers might experience if they update social media during the trip.

4. How can social media help tourists form friendships after a trip ends? How can a tourism organization use those friendships to increase sales?

5. Describe how people of different ages might use social media differently. How might a sustainable tourism organization align its marketing strategies to reflect generational differences?

IIIIIIIIIIIIIIIIIIIIIIIIIII YOUR BUSINESS PLAN IIIIIIIIIIIIIIIIIIIIIIIIII

Social media will be part of your marketing activities. Look at the work you have done on your business plan to date. If your marketing section does not already include social media, update it for the activities that match your business objectives and communication style.

Unless you have unlimited funds, be realistic about the social media activities that you will undertake. It is better to pick a few and build a presence than to set up accounts in a dozen and never use them. In your business plan workbook, estimate the costs of your social media activities. Although signing up is free in most cases, you will need time from your staff for social media. Make sure you include these labor costs in your budgets.

1. Provide website references or research studies that support your choice of social media channels. How can you convince a reader of your business plan that the methods you selected are those used by your customers and not chosen solely because you are familiar with them?

2. Document your assumptions regarding the time required for your business's social media activities. Talk to business owners about their social media programs to test your assumptions for validity.

3. Review the social media activity of a company similar to yours. Describe which posts generate the most likes, shares, and discussion. Give examples of similar posts you might create for your organization.

IIIIIIIIIIIIIIIIIIIIIIIIIIIIIIIII **REFERENCES** IIIIIIIIIIIIIIIIIIIIIIIIIIII

Cameron, L., and C. Vogt. 2012. More people staying connected on vacation. *MSU Today*, June 8. http://msutoday.msu.edu/news/2012/more-people-staying-connected-on-vacation.

Carter, B. 2012. Uh, oh! Facebook pages only reach 17% of fans. AllFacebook, January 18. http://allfacebook.com/facebook-page-17_b73948.

Conner, C. 2012. Employees really do waste time at work, part II. *Forbes*, Nov. 15. www.forbes.com/sites/cherylsnappconner/2012/11/15/employees-really-do-waste-time-at-work-part-ii.

Nielsen. 2012. Consumer trust in online, social and mobile advertising grows, April 10. www.nielsen.com/us/en/newswire/2012/consumer-trust-in-online-social-and-mobile-advertising-grows.html.

Voyager's World. 2012. U.S. travellers share trip experiences in real time, Dec. 21. www.voyagersworld.in/article/us-travellers-share-trip-experiences-real-time.

Smith, A. 2014. Older adults and technology use. PewResearch Internet Project, April 3. www.pewinternet.org/2014/04/03/usage-and-adoption.

Fleming, G. 2012. Global social technographic update 2011: US and EU mature, emerging markets show lots of activity. Forrester Research, Jan. 4. http://blogs.forrester.com/gina_sverdlov/12-01-04-global_social_technographics_update_2011_us_and_eu_mature_emerging_markets_show_lots_of_activity.

Wexler, E. 2009. Finalist – CTC's Greg Klassen: Canada's tourism superhero. *Strategy*, Dec. 1. http://strategyonline.ca/2009/12/01/moyklassen-20091201.

WORKING WITH THE TRAVEL TRADE

After reading this chapter, you will be able to do the following:

- Identify the components of the travel trade

- Understand how travel intermediaries sell tourism experiences

- Explain how a tourism business can help a travel agent sell sustainable tourism

As the manager of a tourism business, you will quickly become aware of the difficulties in selling your product. Marketing is time consuming and often requires considerable sums of money to execute. People who are interested in your tour or lodge may not book for several years, requiring you to cultivate a large pool of customers so you have sufficient bookings each year. The travel trade can be a valuable ally in your marketing efforts. They have access to large markets, understand what consumers seek, and can sell your product to many more people than you could reach individually. This service is not inexpensive; travel intermediaries want commissions of 10 to 30 percent of the package price, and great effort is required to access their services. However, because you only pay them if they bring you customers, allying yourself with the travel trade can be a good business strategy. This chapter explains how to decide whether the travel trade is a good fit for your business and how to develop your relationship with it.

UNDERSTANDING THE TRAVEL TRADE

The **travel trade** resells travel products that they have purchased or reserved in advance from tourism suppliers. It sometimes refers collectively to tour operators, wholesalers, and travel agents. To help you understand these players in the travel trade, each is described in the following sections.

Someone setting up a tourism business is called a tour operator. In the tourism industry, the vernacular is often shortened to operator. Tour operators are one of three types:

- **Ground operator** is the company that delivers the actual tourism product.

- **Inbound operator** is the company located at a destination that creates tour packages. **Tour packages** combine multiple elements of a vacation, for example, accommodation and activities, or multiple activities and meals. Inbound operators sometimes provide part of the trip as the ground operator, for example, uses their guides. But the delivery of some of the trip might be contracted through another supplier, for example, a lodge that supplies rooms and meals.

- **Outbound operator** is the company that packages trips and sells them to people leaving a destination. This category may include wholesalers, although some wholesalers do not deliver any part of a tour.

Wholesalers buy up large quantities of products, such as hotel rooms, airline seats, attraction admittance, and recreational activities. These components are packaged and sold either directly to the consumer or through another intermediary such as a travel agent or tour operator.

Travel agents work in businesses that provide trip-planning and booking services in exchange for a commission from the product provider. Prices for booking through a travel agent are in some cases lower for the consumer because a good travel agent is able to capitalize on special rates and various travel schedules.

Some convention and visitors bureaus function as booking agents for tourism businesses and can be considered a travel intermediary. A visitors bureau might be the first point of contact for people planning to visit your community. They may charge a commission to the tourism business for selling its product and sometimes they require businesses to become members of the bureau before promoting the product.

Travel associations such as motor clubs also function as travel intermediaries by selling tours, accommodations, and services. Thousands of people each year use the guides of the American or Canadian motor associations. A listing in such a guide can be helpful in selling your product.

You want to align your business with the travel intermediaries that are selling to the same people you identified when setting target market segments and that charge commissions commensurate with your ability to pay. To understand which organizations might be good marketing partners, you need to understand what the travel trade is looking for in a partner and how to establish a working relationship with the travel trade.

What the Travel Trade Wants

The travel trade looks for business partners that can provide tourism experiences and products consistently and at a quality that meets their customers' expectations. If you think a partnership with the travel trade would benefit your business, familiarize yourself with their requirements

Companies that deliver nature or cultural experiences are often called ground operators.

Travel trade members expect partners to meet industry standards for operations.

and take steps to remedy deficiencies before you approach the travel trade. Consider whether you are able to provide the following:

- Adherence to industry standards. This means that your business is fully licensed and insured and has all necessary permits to operate.

- Pricing for travel trade. You must be able to provide commissions and confidential pricing for your travel trade partners. Your partners will also expect you to guarantee your prices, perhaps one year in advance of your operating season.

- Quick booking. Travel trade partners will expect you to work with their booking and cancellation policies. You must also be prepared to respond within hours to booking inquiries. If you offer accommodation, travel trade partners may ask you to set aside blocks of rooms for them.

- Unique product. Established travel trade businesses will have partnership with many businesses. You need to convince them your product is sufficiently unique for them to add another business to their structure.

- Complete package. Your travel trade partner wants to sell a complete experience starting when the traveler reaches your destination. You need to have a multiday package of activities, accommodation, and

transportation ready to sell. More information is provided in the next chapter for building a complete package through marketing partnerships.

If you can meet the requirements of the travel trade, gather information showing how. Also be prepared to describe the following:

- The quality of the product you offer. Now is not the time to embellish. Be honest about whether you are ready for the market.

- What experience customers can expect. Describe whether customers will find physical activity, a contemplative journey through an ancient culture, or something else.

- Who might enjoy the product. Give your prospective travel trade partner descriptions of travelers who are well suited to your experience, for example, families or people who are physically fit.

- Sustainable tourism differences. Explain how your commitment to principles of sustainable tourism make your company a good travel choice and how your travel trade partners can highlight these with consumers who might have limited knowledge of sustainable tourism practices.

Be sure you are **market ready**, able to sell travel products that meet expectations of a national or international audience. Market readiness is subjective, but you can get an idea of the market readiness of your business by ensuring that your business does the following things:

- Maintain a good standing in all applicable licensing and insurance requirements
- Develop marketing materials such as a brochure, rack card, or website
- Provide a contact telephone number or e-mail contact year-round
- Publish a consumer billing, payment, and cancellation policy
- Publish a trade-orientated billing, payment, and cancellation policy for receptive, inbound tour operators and outbound, international tour operators

The travel trade looks for reliable suppliers because they stake their reputation on the trip they sell. If a tour wholesaler needs firm departure dates and prices two years in advance when preparing brochures for travel agents, a tourism business must be able to make this commitment. This is a challenge for some sustainable tourism businesses. If you operate in national parks or other protected areas where permits or fees are often not set until a few months before the season, it can be difficult to set departure dates or prices a year in advance. This is changing somewhat as park managers become more aware of their impact on tourism providers and try to provide more lead time on their decisions. A tourism business can also mitigate scheduling problems by developing contingency plans. Instead of promising a hike on a specific trail, it is better to develop a package around types of experiences. An alpine hike is easier to deliver than a walk along a specific ridge; if you encounter trail closures or restrictions on the trail you chose, you can switch to another trail without disappointing the consumer.

Meeting the Travel Trade

Once you have determined you are market ready and ready to work with the travel trade, you can begin to build your relationships. This process will take time and is best undertaken by meeting in person with representatives from the travel trade. Mass mailings are often ineffective because these companies receive huge quantities of mail. Some even use coded mailing labels to distinguish solicited from unsolicited mail. Direct selling by phone or in person is a better way to introduce your company.

You can easily set up meetings with your local convention and visitors bureau, but it will be more difficult to reach tour operators and wholesalers. Many of them are located in cities far from your business, so traveling to see each would be costly. Instead plan to attend trade shows for the travel trade, such as those organized by the National Tour Association or the American Bus Association. Most trade shows provide opportunities for brief meetings between wholesalers and suppliers. Schedule meetings with the wholesalers most likely to need packages in your region. Bring a short, organized presentation to the trade show, then send detailed material on trip itineraries and costs if asked, and finally, arrange familiarization tours for the people seriously interested in your product. To obtain information on trade show dates and locations, contact your local tourism offices or visitors bureau.

Tourism departments for many state and provinces also organize their own gatherings or marketplaces where travel suppliers can showcase their products to the travel trade and develop marketing partnerships. Attend these whenever possible and follow up with phone calls or e-mails and marketing materials if requested.

CONSUMERS' RELATIONSHIP WITH THE TRAVEL TRADE

The travel trade plays an important role in the tourism industry by making a large selection of products available to travelers around the world. It may seem that with so many people using the Internet to research travel, the role of travel agents or other travel intermediaries would be diminished. But as shown in table 7.1, travel trade players such as travel agents are important for overseas trips. It seems reasonable that people are more likely to use travel intermediaries as the itinerary becomes more complex or the distance between the visitor and the destination increases. According to Peter Yesawich, former president of Ypartnership and now vice chairman of MMGY Global, "three out of ten American travel agents use the services of a travel agent on a regular basis and this percentage is growing for two reasons: 1) many travelers now place a higher value on the time it would take to pick through multiple

Table 7.1 Information Sources for U.S. Travelers Visiting Overseas Destinations: 2011

Information sources	Percentage (%) of all U.S. travelers
Personal computer	42
Airline	28
Travel agency	28
Friends, relatives	16
Company travel department	6
Tour company	5
Travel guides and timetables	5
State and city travel offices	2
In-flight information systems	1
National government tourism office	1
Newspapers and magazines	1

Data from U.S. Department of Commerce 2012.

websites to find the best options/prices than the fee they have to pay the agent to do the work for them, and 2) consumers see agents as 'in the know' and a potential source of otherwise unadvertised deals" (Hotel News Now 2008). For an example of how the travel trade links consumers in the United States with tourism businesses in Central America, watch the video "The Travel Trade and You" in the web resource.

As shown in figure 7.1, consumers interact with the travel trade directly and indirectly. Although many consumers will book travel directly with tourism businesses or operators on the ground,

for distant destinations or more-complex itineraries with multiple destinations or activities, consumers use other travel trade players, sometimes without realizing it. A traveler who buys a hotel and airfare package on a website like Expedia is buying a simple package that has been created by a tour operator or wholesaler.

THE DIFFICULTY IN SELLING SUSTAINABLE TOURISM

Tourism businesses selling ecotourism or sustainable tourism experiences may find it difficult to work with the travel trade if they encounter companies unfamiliar with differences in the product or market expectations. Often people interested in sustainable tourism are looking for a variety of activities and may be fairly sophisticated in their requirements. An avid bird-watcher wants to visit a variety of sites and view as many species or rare species as possible. A travel agent unfamiliar with the requirements of avitourists—bird-watching tourists—might direct them to a tour that has great scenery but mediocre bird-watching. This mismatch can lead to dissatisfaction and a loss of future bookings.

To provide the type of experience a sustainable tourist seeks, a travel agent must be knowledgeable

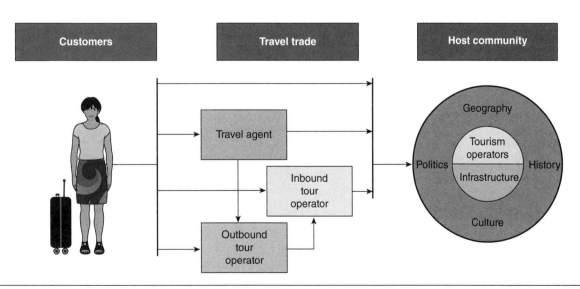

Figure 7.1 Travel booking channels.

about the attractions and services that appeal to nature, culture, and adventure seekers. Sustainable tourism clients are usually well educated and well read, delving into magazines on their favorite sport or interest. This makes for knowledgeable customers who expect the same or greater level of expertise from their travel agent. To sell sustainable tourism, a travel agent must determine which ground operators provide consistent high-quality service and adhere to sustainability principles.

A tourism business supplying these products can help its travel trade partners by providing detailed information on the unique features of its experiences and how they differ from conventional travel products. Explaining the care that has been taken to protect the environment or to deliver high-quality interpretation can be helpful shortcuts for the travel agent. Certification by a Global Sustainable Tourism Council accreditation organization can help.

Given the range of sustainable tourism activities and destinations available, and the pace at which companies enter and leave the business, it is difficult to stay on top of current developments. For this reason, some travel agents have specialized in ecotourism or adventure travel instead of trying to be all things to all people. You should target these agencies as marketing partners rather than trying to reach every travel agent, some of whom may never send you clients.

Imitation is the sincerest form of flattery. When a product sells, competitors try to mimic the success. The green sell, or the use of nature and the environment as a tour theme, is a way to attract customers to trips. Unfortunately, some tourism businesses use an ecolabel with little evidence they are embracing principles of sustainability. Worse, these products will disappoint discerning travelers. International standards may be one way to identify travel suppliers who deliver sustainable tourism.

The practice of describing a business or product as having environmentally friendly attributes when it does not is called **greenwashing**. To see how prevalent it is in the business world, take the Ecochallenge "Sustainable Tourism or Greenwash?"

HELPING THE TRAVEL TRADE SELL SUSTAINABLE TOURISM

Selling sustainable tourism is different from selling other travel products in several ways. You still need to know your markets in terms of age, gender, origin, motivations, and interests. As with other types of travel, you need to match your client's interests, personality, and budget to the right

---

Ecochallenge
Sustainable Tourism or Greenwash?

To find out how often the sustainability label is misused, do an Internet search for tours or travel experiences with the word eco in the description. Pick several items and investigate further. Can you find evidence that the product's supplier is adhering to sustainability practices? Clues that they are might include the following:

- A code of ethics
- Description of their environment or sustainability practices in the About section
- Awards for sustainable tourism practices from recognized organizations
- Press releases on support of conservation or cultural projects

In the absence of these things, how can travelers be sure they are not victims of a green-

wash? The following are signs that a product has been greenwashed to make it more appealing to consumers:

- There is little consideration of group size, and when there are large groups, steps have not been taken to protect the environment.
- The product is built or created in the same manner as other tourism products that do not make sustainability claims.
- The product supplier or industry has received bad press about its environmental practices

Once you have completed your research, determine whether greenwashing is widespread.

product. What is different in selling sustainable tourism is the need for a travel agent or other travel trade player to do the following:

- Screen tour operators, accommodations, and transportation suppliers to assess how sustainable their product is.
- Possess knowledge of the destination's ecosystems and cultures, preferably firsthand.
- Be familiar with activities you recommend, for example, sea kayaking or wildlife viewing, and the quality of the experience offered.

Given the variety of destinations and activities possible, it is understandable that travel intermediaries selling sustainable tourism or ecotourism often specialize in a region or type of activity. They need to demonstrate their value to a tourist to get their business. Technology is making it easier for consumers to research destinations, obtain information on tourism providers, and book trips—services that travel agents provided in the past. Sustainable tourism suppliers can help travel agents and other travel trade players compete by increasing their knowledge of sustainable tourism practices and their product. Some ways to do this are to help them evaluate suppliers they are considering as partners and help them prepare their clients for a sustainable tourism experience.

Evaluating Travel Suppliers

Until international standards are in place to certify sustainable tourism providers, it behooves a travel agent or wholesaler to develop its own screening practices for evaluating travel suppliers. If travel trade players do not understand the sustainable tourism industry, you might suggest they ask the following questions when selecting partners.

- Can you provide written material on your environmental policies or procedures?
- How do you support conservation or environmental organizations in the area where you operate?
- Do you buy your food locally?
- What steps have you taken to minimize energy and water usage?
- Do your vehicles meet or exceed vehicle-emission guidelines?

- What type of interpretation do you provide customers on local nature and culture?
- Do you hire local people and guides? What are their qualifications?
- Does your business have a recycling program? What items are recycled?
- What is your disposal policy at sea (for water-based operations)?
- What is your group size for tours? How do you determine this number?
- What pretrip information do you provide to tour participants about the local habitat and culture and on ways to be a responsible traveler?
- How often do you visit a particular site in a week? In a season?
- How do you monitor your impact on the local environment?
- What information do you provide on opportunities for tourists to support the local community after the trip?

These questions do not necessarily have one right answer. Some companies might operate in a remote protected area where they are unable to set up a recycling program. Better evidence of their sustainable practices might be the purchasing of bulk items or packing out garbage for disposal. But asking these questions will reveal the business philosophy and operating practices.

In your responses to these questions, you can highlight your sustainable tourism practices. This will show how a partnership with your organization will help your travel trade partners meet their marketing and sustainability goals.

Preparing the Client

Selling a tourism experience takes work. If you do it well, you will find it easier to sell subsequent trips to the same traveler. Helping your partners sell sustainable tourism experiences will help them sell the right products to the right customers and assure customer satisfaction. For many years, tourism planners have made changes to the destinations to meet the needs, real or perceived, of tourists. Perhaps less change to the host environment would be required if tourists received more pretrip orientation and were willing to adapt to the conditions they find at their destination.

By helping your travel trade partners supply information on the unique features of your sustainable tourism experience and ways travelers can contribute to sustainability while traveling, customers can select the trips that best match their needs and think about how they would be willing to change their behavior. If they are not willing or able to change to meet the tour requirements, they can switch to something else. Mongolia is a romantic-sounding destination to some travelers, but seeing the countryside means camping in yurts (the tents used by nomadic Mongols). Travelers who do not tolerate rustic conditions should select another destination rather than pressuring nomads to modernize their yurts.

Most tourism businesses provide pretrip information on their website, but the travel agent can provide similar information and use it to sell more trips. By pointing out the advantages of smaller groups, the ratio of guides to trip participants, or the access to remote locations, they can explain the benefits of a sustainable tourism experience to the traveler and show them how they can help the planet while having a more enriching travel experience.

Other ways that preparing the client can pay dividends include the following:

- Spark interest. Information on the geography, flora and fauna, history, and culture can spark interest in attractions and activities. By coaching clients on the best activities, tours, and destinations for them, the agent can deliver more information and better service to the customer. After all, every travel website has great photos, but the reality will feel different based on your background and physical abilities. Both agent and travel provider will benefit from a better match and a happy customer.

- Facilitate learning. Pretrip information is an integral part of the travel learning experience. A reading list is often appreciated, as are pretrip gatherings where people can listen to trip leaders or past participants.

- Avoid illegal activities. Facts about trade in endangered species help people avoid purchasing products made with animal parts or rare wood. As shown in chapter 3, a code of ethics for travelers can help suggest good behaviors. People will see how they can take a green philosophy on the road and hopefully shop for more-sustainable tourism products in the future.

- Smooth cultural relations. Pretrip information can help travelers understand what behavior might inadvertently cause offense with other cultures. For example, women dressed immodestly might cause

Tourism suppliers can help travel partners sell their product by explaining what constitutes a sustainable tourism experience.

offense, or pointing with fingers can be seen as a rude gesture in some cultures. If you visit indigenous people in Canada and the United States you might encounter cultural differences in conversational style. Pretrip orientation can help visitors feel more connected with the host community and perhaps make new friends.

Consider what information you want to share with your customers. This can include some of the information already discussed as well as packing lists, suggested background reading, and website references. You can list frequently asked questions on your website as a way to share pretrip information on topics causing greatest interest or concern. Sharing the right information will make it easier to provide good customer service because people will show up with more realistic expectations and prepared to enjoy the products and experiences you are offering.

SUMMARY

The travel trade is a valuable ally to a sustainable tourism business. They have access to vast numbers of consumers and are experts in tourism promotion. Building partnerships with these organizations will allow you to reach customers you cannot on your own. They can help you understand the needs of global travelers and provide avenues for growth. In the next chapter, marketing partnerships will be examined further.

GLOSSARY

greenwashing—The practice of describing a business or product as having environmentally friendly attributes when it does not.

ground operator—The company that delivers the actual tourism product.

inbound operator—The company located in a destination that creates tour packages.

outbound operator—The company that packages trips and sells them to people leaving a destination. This category may include wholesalers, although some wholesalers do not deliver any part of a tour.

market ready—Ability of a tourism business to sell travel products that meet the expectations of a national or international audience.

tour packages—The multiple elements of a vacation, for example, accommodation and activities or multiple activities and meals.

travel agents—People who provide trip-planning and booking services in exchange for a commission from the product provider.

travel trade—Organizations that resell travel products that they have purchased or reserved in advance from tourism suppliers. It sometimes refers collectively to tour operators, travel agents, and wholesalers.

wholesalers—Businesses that buy large numbers of products, such as hotel rooms, airline seats, attraction admittance, or recreational activities. These components are packaged and sold either directly to the consumer or through another intermediary such as a travel agent or tour operator.

REVIEW QUESTIONS

1. What is the travel trade? What are the main components of the travel trade?
2. How can the travel trade sell sustainable tourism experiences located in remote locations?

3. Identify possible challenges a small-business owner might face in trying to meet the needs of the travel trade.

4. Describe ways sustainable tourism organizations can help travel agents sell their products or experiences.

5. Explain how tourism organizations and the travel trade can educate travelers about sustainability and help ensure a better holiday.

IIIIIIIIIIIIIIIIIIIIIIII VIDEO CASE STUDY IIIIIIIIIIIIIIIIIIIIII

Visit the web resource to see the video "The Travel Trade and You." After watching the video, answer the following questions.

1. Identify all the members of the travel trade that you see evidence of. Explain what each might contribute to the tour experience of Texans visiting Costa Rica.

2. Describe the advantages Texas A&M AgriLife Extension might find from using the travel trade versus organizing the trip on its own.

3. What benefits are Texas ranchers and farmers hoping to gain from an educational trip to Costa Rica? How valuable do you think travel can be to knowledge sharing? Explain how an organized tour might help or hinder learning.

4. How difficult do you think it would be for a small sustainable tourism business in Costa Rica to market its product to a large U.S. organization? Describe how the travel trade could help small businesses reach larger markets.

IIIIIIIIIIIIIIIIIIIIII YOUR BUSINESS PLAN IIIIIIIIIIIIIIIIII

Hopefully, you will see a role for the travel trade in your marketing plan. It takes time to develop these relationships, so you should spread your marketing activities over several years. Review your market research for information on how your target markets make their travel decisions. Allocate money in your marketing and operating budgets in your business plan to building partnerships with the travel trade players they use. If you have not already done so, complete a pricing worksheet and include commissions in your calculations.

1. Identify the benefits you would seek from working with the travel trade. Describe attributes of a potential partner. Search the Internet for two or three organizations that might meet your criteria.

2. List the information you would need before meeting with a member of the travel trade, for example, brochures, sample itineraries, and guide qualifications. Note the amount of time required to prepare each.

3. Develop a timeline for developing a relationship with someone in the travel trade to sell your company's product. Include steps for identifying partners, preparing the material described in the previous bullet, setting up preliminary meetings, and creating joint marketing materials, promotion, and bookings.

REFERENCES

Hotel News Now. 2008. Y Partnership predicts 2009 travel trends. Dec. 23. www.hotelnewsnow
.com/Articles.aspx/439/Ypartnership-predicts-2009-travel-trends.

U.S. Department of Commerce, ITA, OTTI. 2012. Profile of U.S. resident travelers visiting
overseas destinations: 2011 outbound. http://tinet.ita.doc.gov/outreachpages/download_
data_table/2011_Outbound_Profile.pdf.

8

MARKETING PARTNERSHIPS

Marketing is important to the success of a tourism business, but you may find you cannot afford to market as much as you would like. The most effective way to make your marketing dollars go further is to form partnerships. Working with other businesses that are interested in the same types of customers allows you to share the cost of marketing and promotion.

A marketing partnership can also create a larger presence in the marketplace than an individual operator can. Most partnerships are loosely defined groups of companies working together to sell their products. Although in some situations legal partnerships are created, more commonly, businesses combine their products, time, or money to achieve a more marketable or cost-effective venture. The following are common ways to build partnerships:

- **Tour packaging** combines several elements of a travel experience, such as accommodations, food, and recreational activities, into one product and sells it at a predetermined price. A tour package can be developed by one company or through the cooperation of several tourism organizations.

- **Cooperative marketing** allows two or more tourism organizations to pool their resources to market an event, product, or destination.

- **Festivals and special events** are public happenings that celebrate a cultural, natural, or historical aspect of a community.

Partnerships can also provide community support for your tourism product. By drawing in people from many business and community sectors, your partners can create their own opportunity to benefit from the sale of your product.

Marketing partnerships are powerful, so most operators find them a valuable addition to a marketing plan. Because partnerships take many months or years to develop, a business cannot rely strictly on marketing partnerships, especially in a start-up situation. But if you want your business to reach its full potential, you need to pursue marketing partnerships. Ways to build these relationships are discussed in the next section.

TOUR PACKAGING

In the last chapter, the benefits of working with the travel trade were explained. For many sustainable tourism businesses, the travel trade comprises their most important marketing partners. To attract these partners, you need a good tour package. A tour package can be as simple as a romance special that offers a night's hotel accommodation, dinner, and a box of chocolates. But to work with the travel trade, you need to offer longer and more diverse experiences. If you are offering adventure experiences, you might find that people want accommodations or cultural activities. If you cannot provide all aspects of the tour package, you need to build partnerships with other suppliers or ground operators.

Tour packaging offers the advantages of price and convenience to the customer. Your tour package should provide a less-expensive and more-convenient holiday than if travelers bought each element separately and it should provide more time for pursuing special interests. The combination of greater value and more time for fun will make it easier to sell your product.

The packages can also be developed around a theme, such as hiking in several protected areas or a bird-watching trip to several communities along a waterway. Package tours can bring travelers to a major center or hub and then provide activities and short trips that originate from the hub. This can be a great arrangement for tourism in remote areas where accommodations are lacking.

Another type of package appealing to sustainable tourism operators is a holiday that incorporates a learning component. Many universities offer learning packages on subjects from archaeology to zoology. Other organizations have recognized the appeal of these packages. The Churchill Northern Studies Centre in northern Manitoba added learning vacations to its operations to promote public education. Programs give participants a chance to learn from professional scientists and develop a greater understanding of the northern ecology and astronomy.

Tour Package Process

To develop a tour package you need to invest time and money in the process. Although it usually takes one to two years to bring a tour package to market, it can strengthen your business once in place. Developing a tour package requires the following steps:

Tour packages combine amenities such as accommodation, transportation, meals, and activities.

- Set package objectives
- Research market needs
- Use your knowledge of community activities and services
- Build your package itinerary
- Assess the willingness of tourism operators to partner
- Price the package competitively
- Plan for development time

Each step is explained in the following sections.

Set Package Objectives

Your objectives for creating a tour package should be defined early so you attract the right partners and can measure your success later. If your objective is to make your town the main wildlife-viewing center for the region, you need to partner with other businesses offering wildlife viewing. You may want to include state or provincial conservation agencies as potential partners. If you are focusing on a cultural objective such as aboriginal tourism, partners will likely come from organizations involved in cultural tourism.

Research Market Needs

As explained in earlier chapters, you need market research to understand what customers are looking for. Travelers interested in sustainability can be attracted to tour packages as long as they incorporate elements that are important to them. In many cases, this means scenery and nature, a multitude of activities occurring in nature, an opportunity to engage with the host community, and interpretation of the environment. Many travelers like flexibility, so the ability to customize itineraries is desirable.

You will also need information on how much your customers are likely to spend and how they discover your community. If the average tourist is spending $1,500 over a two-week period, you need to find new markets if your tour package is priced at $3,000 for a one-week tour.

Consumers are used to getting things the way they like them. Some may be reluctant to buy a tour package if they think they will need to do everything in a large group. Companies like Anderson Vacations, a Canadian tour packager, started as a tour bus company but expanded its product offering with packages for independent travelers. Groups as small as two can visit the website and build their own package. So consider the group size you are targeting as you develop your product.

Use Your Knowledge of Community Activities and Services

Refer back to your objectives and then consider the activities and services your community has to offer. Comparing these to your objectives will help you identify possible components of your package. Look for unique activities to make the package more marketable; if the tourist cannot participate in these activities without purchasing your package, you create an incentive to buy. An example might be access to a restricted area, such as a tour of a little-known cave, or a behind-the-scenes tour of an organic winery.

Your trip package should have a theme that can be described in a dozen words or fewer. This will give it focus and identity as you develop the package and again when you market it. You can also use it in your marketing materials when you start promotion.

Nature tourism businesses should avoid the pitfall of developing a tour package similar to traditional tourism products. Historically, many tour packages were developed for the motor-coach industry. However, many nature lovers like to travel in small groups, so it is unlikely that you would attract them to a conventional bus tour package.

If you are located in a coastal community and have cruise ships stopping nearby, you may want to create a package for cruise passengers so you can take advantage of the revenue opportunities, but you need to adapt your small-group packages for the large numbers you will receive from one cruise ship. One strategy is to split large groups into smaller groups and partner with similar businesses to deliver a consistent experience for each group.

Look also for hotels and transportation companies, such as airlines or railways, to join your partnership, especially if you operate in a remote location. Adding accommodation and transportation gives your customers greater convenience and price savings, and your bookings will grow.

As you add components to your package, keep your market research in mind. Will customers want each day to be full of activities or will they want a less-structured approach to their holiday time? Will your customers be seniors with mobility issues or families requiring services that are child friendly? Adjust your itinerary and services accordingly.

Cruise ships can serve as travel partners with companies offering adventure, historical, or cultural tours.

Build Your Package Itinerary

A **package itinerary** is a detailed plan describing the elements of a trip. It lists the transportation, accommodations, and meals provided as well as activities and stops at attractions.

Using the possible elements you identified in the previous step, brainstorm how you might add them to an itinerary. Let your imagination go and come up with as many creative ideas for activities or combinations of experiences as you can. One of these may be the key to developing a product so unique it will command a higher price from travelers. A company offering polar expedition cruises, Quark Expeditions, offers a trip to the North Pole once a year. Billed as the chance to be "one of only 250 people to stand at the top of the world in 2013," the company charged a premium price for the trip.

Once you have identified the services and attractions that you want to include, set up an itinerary for each day of the trip. By walking through the itinerary, you will get a feel for the experience you are developing and can tell how many components need to be included in your price. Each component will potentially increase the attractiveness to the tourist but will also increase the complexity and cost. An example of a two-day trip itinerary is shown in figure 8.1.

If your product relies on natural phenomena, think about how you can ensure consistency. If wolves are not sighted, can you still deliver a tour experience that lives up to your theme of northern lights and wildlife? Perhaps you could add a meeting with scientists tracking wolves to your itinerary. If people do not see a wolf, they may be satisfied with hearing a wolf through a tracking headset, and there is a greater likelihood you can find a wolf through telemetry than visual spotting. If you are promoting aboriginal tours, some rituals or dances may be limited to specific times of the year. Your challenge will be to consistently deliver tours that provide the same quality of experience even though specific components are different.

Assess the Willingness of Tourism Partners to Package

With your itinerary concept defined, you can identify the services that your business cannot provide and you can approach other tourism organizations to determine their interest in developing and marketing the tour package with you. You may have specific providers in mind because their product is unique or because their environmental philosophies are consistent with yours.

For some, approaching industry partners can be difficult because they perceive a David-and-Goliath scenario. A large hotel chain might appear unlikely to be interested; however, even the biggest industry player is looking for newer and better ways to market. If you have an idea for a tour that gives hotel guests more to do in an area, chances are they will stay longer and hotel management will be interested. When approaching possible partners, explain how a partnership can benefit them. While

Figure 8.1
Sample Tour Package Itinerary

Tour Package Theme: Weekend Bird-Watching

Target market: casual bird-watchers, independent travelers

Day One

- Orientation held at local eco-lodge
- Nature walk through lodge grounds and surrounding woods
- Lunch at lodge
- Afternoon birding hike through local sanctuary
- Shopping at local craft center that features wildlife art
- Dinner at local restaurant followed by interpretative talk by ornithologist

Day Two

- Early-morning bird-watching at lake and wetlands
- Breakfast at country inn
- Visit to state park and interpretative center
- Picnic lunch
- Afternoon spent in the field working with scientist banding birds
- Farewell dinner at lodge

you want to be clear about your expectations of a partnership, you also need to be clear that everyone will win. Aim for specific benefits in your presentations. An extra 2,000 visitor days a year is a more convincing lure than the chance to make people more environmentally aware, although both are worthwhile goals.

While your partners may make bookings for your package, you also need their active participation in marketing the package. If they are willing to mention the package in their online advertising or social media, you will have the benefit of a combined marketing effort.

Price the Package Competitively

Packaging is a successful marketing strategy because it gives travelers a better value for their money than independent travel. It is critical that the package price never exceed the retail price of the items purchased separately. This will require negotiations with your partners to determine an acceptable price for each component. In addition, determine the conditions for bookings and cancellations with each company. If they require a 50 percent deposit, you need to ask your customers for the same deposit or you could find yourself paying if a customer cancels.

Many accommodation rates or entrance fees vary with the season, with higher prices for peak times and discounts in shoulder seasons, the time between peak and off-peak seasons. Package prices need to reflect these variances. Also consider discounts for special groups, such as seniors or members of conservation groups. Some tourism market segments, such as bird-watchers, attract people in their 50s or older. Offering a senior discount in these cases may be expected; however, given that they may represent a significant number of tour participants, you will need to account for the discount in the price. If you will be making a donation to a conservation group for each booking, include that in your pricing calculation.

Instructions on pricing were found in chapter 5. Once you have established your package price, compare it to similar products. Look at other package brochures and talk to your partners. Is your package priced competitively? If not, add extra value through added convenience, guaranteed prices against foreign currency fluctuations, or access to unique experiences.

You will endeavor to deliver each package consistently. However, anticipate the need for refunds or credits when severe weather or other unfavorable conditions arise. An unhappy customer is the worst form of advertising.

Plan for Development Time

Underestimating the amount of time required to develop and market a package is common. Most packages take 18 months to two years to develop. As you increase the number of parties in the partnership, you increase the time required to move through the process. As well, you need to incorporate the business cycles of your selling agencies. If you decide to tackle the motor coach market, you need to present a package to bus tour companies two years in advance of the first visit. Likewise, wholesale travel agents need to incorporate the package into their advertising material, brochures, and catalogues and market these to consumers. One of the challenges of the small and medium-size tourism businesses is being able to commit to tour dates two years hence.

Some tour wholesalers have the perception that nature or cultural tourism businesses are not easily incorporated into their packages because these businesses cannot handle large groups or cannot guarantee dates far into the future. There is some merit to this. Ecotourism, by its underlying principles, is not mass tourism and may require partnerships among several operators to handle large groups, but it can still benefit from tour packaging.

Sustainable tourism organizations may have difficulty planning years ahead for a tour package if they need permits from national parks and managers of protected areas. Government agencies are usually concerned with the upcoming year, and detailed bookings for one or two years may not be possible. As an alternative, a tourism business can build a tour package that includes tours to areas that don't require the same level of permits or advertise tours without specific departure dates and add the dates as permits are received.

Marketing Your Tour Package

If you have created a multiday tour package, you will likely want to work with the travel trade to market it. Methods for approaching the travel trade were described in the last chapter.

For shorter packages, marketing is better done through a variety of promotional activities direct to the consumer. You might use direct sales and print brochures or fliers and distribute these to past customers or use qualified mailing lists to reach potential customers. You might use newspaper or magazine advertisements to target specific markets, perhaps running an advertisement for a romantic getaway two weeks before Valentine's Day.

Your website is probably the best place to advertise and you can use your social media activities to spread the word, especially if your package has a human interest angle. For example, tourism businesses in Alaska and northern Canada have packaged and marketed viewing of the northern lights to Japanese tourists as shown in the sidebar Tour Packaging Capitalizes on Japanese Love of Northern Lights.

You may also want to promote your package by displaying brochures at local hotels, stores, tourist information centers, and visitor bureaus. Other ways to work with partners to market are explored in the next section.

Tour Packaging Capitalizes on Japanese Love of Northern Lights

Businesses in Alaska and northern Canada have turned the winter display of northern lights into a successful tourism package for Japanese tourists. Marketing the opportunity to see aurora borealis while staying in comfortable accommodation, Chena Hot Springs Resort in Fairbanks, Alaska, was booked from the end of December until the end of March for 2013 and was fully booked for next winter.

In the Yukon, easy connections between Japan and Whitehorse and more marketing in Asia have increased the number of travelers coming to see the northern lights. Northern Tales Travel Services, a Whitehorse-based tourism business, saw its business grow 80 percent in 2012 and has hired six Japanese guides to provide interpretation (CBC News 2012). Northern Tales Travel has created a popular Facebook page, with more than 21,000 likes in January 2015, to share information on solar flare activity, forecasts, and package specials. The company has developed a successful tour package and is building a loyal customer base.

COOPERATIVE MARKETING

Cooperative marketing allows collaboration between two or more tourism organizations to promote a product, service, experience, or destination. The marketing partners share expertise and costs to create a synergy and a larger presence in the marketplace.

An example of a cooperative marketing partnership is an advertising campaign aimed at the visiting friends and relatives market. Partners might develop a newspaper advertisement for regional papers that promotes tourism activities in the areas that suit families. Coupons or special rates for popular attractions might be offered to encourage visits to each of the businesses partners.

Other cooperative marketing partnerships are nature- or culture-based tour companies working with hotels or resorts to promote a specific destination. Adding a nature or cultural experience to an accommodation answers the question "What do we do?" for people looking at vacation choices.

Travel Alberta has been effective in developing a cooperative marketing partnership with KLM Royal Dutch Airlines to promote their region. By highlighting winter sports in a marketing campaign, they used online, radio, print, and social media placements to sell winter products to travelers in the Netherlands. The partnership exceeded all targets, increased the load factor for KLM, and resulted in increased flight service to Alberta in winter and summer.

Cooperative marketing partnerships can be helpful for sustainable tourism businesses operating in rural communities. When businesses are spread out geographically, it can be difficult to find marketing partners, but one region showed it can be done with their campaign to market events. Central Alberta is a region with many small towns and long driving distances between attractions. In 2008, the Central Alberta Tourism Committee created a cooperative marketing partnership between these towns and communities to reach more visitors. Historically, these towns had regarded each other as competitors, but people agreed to pool their resources for this project.

The partnership focused on the events in the region. One event for each summer weekend was selected as part of the Sweet 16. Although no new events were created, the cooperative marketing meant the creation of new marketing efforts.

A website was created to promote the Sweet 16 concept and events. Advertisements were placed on other websites to attract attention. Postcards showcasing the 16 major events were created and distributed at each of the events along with special Sweet 16 candy, highlighting the sweet theme.

In only a few months, visitation to the Sweet 16 website exceeded the marketing goals and the communities realized the benefits of working together. Participants also felt the project could serve as a model for cooperative marketing for other rural areas (Central Alberta Tourism Committee 2008).

The members participating in the Sweet 16 cooperative marketing agreed that they were more successful collaborating instead of competing and identified that as one of the most important benefits of participating. Take the Ecochallenge "Is Cooperative Marketing Easy to Do?"

There are other ways your business might participate in cooperative marketing. Some trade associations allow members to access mailing lists at a reduced cost. A small to medium-size

Ecochallenge
Is Cooperative Marketing Easy to Do?

It appears there are many benefits to cooperative marketing partnerships, yet successful examples are not common. See whether you can find one in your community. You might start your search on the website of your state or provincial tourism department. Look for industry awards for cooperative marketing for hints on successful partnerships. If you have access to newspapers or magazines, look for special inserts with advertisements from different businesses in the same region. If time permits, go to a visitors bureau and scan the brochure racks or look at the upcoming events. You might find an event aimed at attracting tourists that is also a cooperative marketing partnership.

When you have finished your research, review your findings and reflect on how easy or difficult it was to find evidence of cooperative marketing partnerships. Try to explain the underlying reasons for your results.

businesses can take advantage of this form of cooperative marketing to undertake direct mail promotions.

Another simple version of marketing partnerships exists on the Internet when businesses exchange web links. People visiting one sustainable tourism website are likely to be interested in related sites, so linking sites can increase exposure with little extra cost. Some larger sites such as visitors bureaus might charge to post links; however, the cost is justified if it increases sales. Building a network of links will also give you a higher ranking on search engines such as Google.

FESTIVALS AND EVENTS

Festivals and special events are a unique type of tourism partnership in which community partners come together to highlight a unique feature of their area. Events can be a great way to create destination awareness or create critical mass for a region with many small tourism businesses. Sustainable tourism businesses can use festivals and special events effectively because natural phenomena or cultural experiences are cornerstones of their businesses. For an example of a festival boosting destination awareness, watch the video "Marketing Cooperatively With Festivals" in the web resource.

Events require the cooperation of many organizations to succeed and are often started by a few people with a great idea such as celebrating wildlife migrations. Large numbers of birds or animals congregating can create engaging visitor experiences and provide compelling media images. The migrations occur in shoulder seasons when hotel owners want more business and can invest in marketing.

An example of one such festival can be found in Qualicum Beach and Parksville, British Columbia, where the Brant Wildlife Festival is held each spring to celebrate the return of thousands of geese as they move from Mexico to Alaska to nest. The HummerBird Celebration of Rockport and Fulton, Texas, was started to celebrate the fall migration of the ruby-throated hummingbird and has grown rapidly as people come to observe these jewel-like creatures each year.

Cultural festivals also offer opportunities to promote a sustainable tourism venture. Each year the Banff Mountain Film and Book Festival presents films and books focusing on mountain activities and communities. Located in Banff National Park, in Alberta, Canada, the festival has developed a following among adventure lovers around the world. People come from great distances to participate, boosting tourism in the mountain community. The best of each

Festivals celebrating wildlife migrations can be good ways to increase tourism in shoulder season.

year's films are combined into a minifestival that travels North America sharing the movies with people who missed the festival. It is a clever way to promote the next year's festival while creating another revenue stream.

Festivals are usually multiday events and provide activities that appeal to a wide range of people. Even people without an interest in the wildlife or culture being featured will often enjoy the dining, shopping, or music offered. While each festival is different, successful events include many of the following:

- Wildlife-viewing opportunities
- Interpretative talks
- Culinary contests such as cook-offs or best meals using local ingredients
- Sporting events (for example, a 10K run at a salmon run festival)
- Displays and sales by local artisans
- Theater performances
- Historical presentations
- Dedication ceremonies
- Children's games
- Parades
- Celebrity appearances
- Film screenings

Planning and running a successful event requires lots of manpower. For wildlife-themed events, it is usually community and environmental groups that provide much of the manpower for the planning and execution of the event. Volunteers are critical, but some paid staff is needed to keep momentum going from year to year and to provide reservation and financial infrastructure. Sometimes the local chamber of commerce will support a festival; other times, volunteers apply for grants and donations to hire seasonal staff.

It can be easier to attract volunteers and sponsors if the economic benefits of these events are measured and highlighted. To the extent that the festival can attract tourists from some distance away, the community will be the recipient of additional tourism spending. Creating a successful festival through marketing partnerships will generate significant economic benefit to the host community. For example, the communities in central Nebraska celebrate the return of the sandhill cranes each spring. Since 1971, Kearny, Nebraska,

has hosted the Rivers and Wildlife Celebration, now known as Audubon's Nebraska Crane Festival. Thousands of visitors come to see hundreds of thousands of cranes gather along the Platte River. Researchers estimate the economic impact of the sandhill crane migration on the central Nebraska economy is U.S.$10.33 million per year (Edwards and Thompson 2009).

Tourism businesses participate in festivals by helping to advertise the event on their website or social media. They can also offer tours or experiences during the event, or partner with accommodation providers to offer a festival package of lodging and activities. Guiding companies may work for conference organizers to offer community tours. These tours may not be large revenue generators, but they can be a good way to get exposure. Another way to benefit is to advertise your business during the event. Coupons can be effective. Providing a small discount or offering a partial reduction on multiple-person bookings during a festival can give people the belief they are getting a special deal and encourage them to spend.

If a festival does not exist in your area and you want to create one, look for a community or conservation group that might take on its organization. A festival is a large undertaking for any one organization, especially a business that needs to spend most of its time making money. The best festivals have widespread community support with volunteers from chambers of commerce, conservation groups, youth clubs, and so on working together. Tourism businesses can participate by donating money, supplies, or services and work with other partners to harness the power of cooperative marketing.

SUMMARY

In this chapter you learned how to work with other organizations to share marketing costs. Many of these activities require a business commitment of many years. You should now realize that your marketing plans need diversity, much like when planting a garden. You want marketing activities that generate results quickly to pay your bills in the first season. You also require marketing activities that give your business strength over the long term. Cultivating marketing partnerships is an effective way to develop medium- to long-term marketing activities that will extend your reach and reduce costs.

GLOSSARY

cooperative marketing—When two or more tourism organizations pool their resources to market an event, product, or destination.

festivals and special events—Public happenings that celebrate a cultural, natural, or historical aspect of a community.

package itinerary—A detailed plan describing the elements of a trip. It lists the transportation, accommodations, and meals provided as well as activities and stops at attractions.

tour packaging—Combining several elements of a travel experience, such as accommodations, food, and recreational activities, into one product and sold at a predetermined price. A tour package can be developed by one company or through the cooperation of several tourism organizations.

REVIEW QUESTIONS

1. What are the benefits of forming a marketing partnership?
2. Identify three forms a marketing partnership might take.
3. List two benefits of creating a tour package. Describe the main steps in creating one.
4. What role can festivals or special events play in a tourism organization's marketing plan?
5. Who might be potential partners for sustainable tourism organizations wanting to undertake cooperative marketing?

VIDEO CASE STUDY

Visit the web resource to watch the video "Marketing Cooperatively With Festivals." After watching the video, answer the following questions:

1. What natural feature does Salt Lake City use as the basis for its festival? Are you aware of other communities offering similar events?
2. Identify three activities that are part of the festival. Which organizations are likely to provide these activities?
3. Describe the challenges that multiple events and tourism providers might cause.
4. List steps a sustainable tourism organization might take to develop a festival in its community.
5. How might a festival like the Great Salt Lake Bird Festival benefit a sustainable tourism organization? Evaluate these against benefits of other marketing partnerships.
6. Would you recommend a festival as a good use of marketing resources? Explain your reasons.

‖‖‖‖‖‖‖‖‖‖‖ YOUR BUSINESS PLAN ‖‖‖‖‖‖‖‖‖‖‖

As you complete your marketing plans, consider whether you will include marketing partnerships in your business plan. If you will, identify which type of marketing partnership will provide the greatest benefit to your organization. Make notes describing your partnership objectives, potential partners, activities needed to build the partnership, promotion activities, and costs of establishing your partnerships.

1. Review the staff levels of your organization. Identify the amount of time available to develop marketing partnerships. Determine whether student intern programs or government grants or subsidies are available and would allow you to add staff for a partnership.

2. Find examples of three tour packages offered by business similar to yours. Note the abundance—or scarcity—of packages and the frequency with which they change. Determine whether you would be able to offer a competitive package.

3. Assess your destination's image for recognition by and appeal to your target market. If you feel the image is out of date or does not match the attributes you are promoting, describe how an event could change this perception. Brainstorm potential themes, activities, and partners for such an event. If you feel a festival or event is needed for your success, include activities and costs in the marketing section and financial forecasts of your business plan.

‖‖‖‖‖‖‖‖‖‖‖‖‖‖‖‖ REFERENCES ‖‖‖‖‖‖‖‖‖‖‖‖‖‖‖‖

CBC News. 2012. Japanese head to Whitehorse for northern lights. Feb. 22. www.cbc.ca/news/canada/north/story/2012/02/22/north-whitehorse-japanese-tourism.html.

Central Alberta Tourism Committee. 2008. The Alberta Sweet 16 marketing partnership. www.centralalberta.ab.ca/imagesedit/CAAAWeb_Sweet16%20Nomination.pdf.

Edwards, R., and E. Thompson. 2009. The economic impact of the Rowe Sanctuary and sandhill crane migration on the central Nebraska region. Bureau of Business Research, University of Nebraska at Lincoln, Sept. 8. www.bbr.unl.edu/documents/52009-Rowe%20Report%2009.08.pdf.

MANAGING THE BOTTOM LINE

IIIIIIIIIIIII LEARNING OUTCOMES IIIIIIIIIIIIII

After reading this chapter, you will be able to do the following:

- Understand why financial management is important for sustainable tourism

- Appreciate the challenges of financing sustainable tourism ventures

- Identify financial forecasting schedules

- Analyze financial performance

- Manage accounting records needed to meet your fiduciary responsibilities

- Find ways to improve cash flow

You have used strategic planning to create a wonderful tourism product and have crafted an innovative marketing plan. Now you need to manage your finances to keep your business profitable and generate positive cash flow while you execute your plans.

Many tourism operators struggle with their financial management. They often depend on weather conditions or school schedules and their business may be seasonal. According to a study by Research Services of Tourism British Columbia (2005), characteristics of nature-based tourism businesses make it difficult to generate a year-round, stable income:

- Employ fewer than three full-time staff
- Employ more staff in the summer and fall (warmer months) than spring or winter

- Generate most revenues from guided activities
- Spend most of their money on labor, fuel, and transportation costs
- Provide a package of activities that includes accommodation
- Many tourism businesses generate a high percentage of their income during peak months while some expenses are incurred year round. Value-added products like guiding or tour packages increase profitability but can only be offered during operating season. A large percentage of revenues are spent on labor, fuel and transportation, leaving a small amount to cover other costs.

A study by the Canadian Tourism Commission found that while tourism businesses account for approximately 1.5 percent of the country's operating revenues and costs and 1.8 percent of profits, tourism accounted for 13 percent of bankruptcies (CTC 2011). Most tourism businesses are **small or medium-size enterprises** with fewer than 500 employees and less than C$50 million in annual revenue. On average, they generate lower revenue and less profit and have less retained earnings than nontourism enterprises (Pierce 2011). They will face difficulty in obtaining financing. Add to this the need to deal with government regulations, record keeping, and tax preparation, and you can see that the business side of your tourism company requires attention from skilled people or you will diminish the profits created by your hard work.

To that end, you will need to be familiar with basic financial procedures and see that they are completed. This does not mean every tour operator has to become an accountant, but every owner and manager should possess basic business literacy. Day-to-day functions can be delegated to staff or outside experts, but it is important to have the knowledge to prevent fraud, avoid cash flow problems, and maximize return on investment. This chapter will help you acquire the knowledge needed to manage your business finances. For an example of a sustainable tourism business successfully managing its finances by targeting bird lovers and adventure seekers, see the video "The Bottom Line" in the web resource.

OBTAINING FINANCING

Nature- or culture-based tourism can be attractive to many would-be business owners and community planners because of the relatively small amount of capital needed for start-up. It is helpful the start-up requirements are small because obtaining financing from conventional sources is not easy for tourism operators. The tourism and recreation industries are not familiar to banks, and in many cases are not regarded as good risks. Part of this is because of the instability inherent in the industry and the lack of assets for collateral, but some of the skepticism arises from lack of preparation by business owners when meeting with prospective **investors**, which are organizations or people who will contribute money in exchange for an ownership share in the business, or **creditors**, which are organizations or people who lend money with the expectation it will be repaid with interest.

As a tourism owner or manager you need to present a sound business plan, collateral if asking for a loan, and the ability to sell your ideas. Banks will look at your background and how debt will be repaid. You must demonstrate experience in the tourism industry and management skills. Banks will also need assurance that you are willing to invest some of your own money in the business. Take the Ecochallenge "Making a Case for Yourself" to see how well you might fare in a meeting with a prospective lender.

Once you have convinced a bank to lend you money, you should be concerned with the cost

Many tourism businesses are seasonal and must make money in only a few months.

Ecochallenge
Making a Case for Yourself

If you were to meet a banker to seek financing for a sustainable tourism business, what work or volunteer experience could you say you possess that would convince him or her that you were qualified to run a sustainable tourism business? The course you are taking in sustainable tourism is one part of your background. Do you have other skills, training, or experience that you could mention in a meeting? Be prepared to describe situations in which you solved a problem or took initiative for a new product or service.

If you feel you lack experience or skills, is there a way to add to your resume before you graduate? Perhaps you could apply for summer jobs at sustainable tourism businesses. Or maybe you could volunteer at a special event that celebrates the environment. Getting involved in organizing the event will teach you even more because often you will need to find sponsors, tackle marketing on social media, or handle bookkeeping. Supplementing your classroom experiences with related work or volunteer experience will make you more credible with future employers as well as bankers.

of the debt. You will need to generate enough cash to pay the interest on a bank loan. If you are hoping a bank will provide a large portion of your start-up needs, be aware that a bank may want you to contribute 50 percent or more of the funds needed before approving the loan.

For these reasons, you will likely need to find financing sources besides traditional banks. You might consider your personal assets as a source of financing. You will need money to support yourself until your business is established. You are also the person with the most to gain from the business. Any investor or creditor will expect to see a financial contribution from you as a measure of your commitment and to ensure that you are sharing the risk. Your personal savings have the advantage of being the most flexible of funds. They do not require a repayment schedule and do not dilute the control of your business.

Another source of financing is family and friends who will lend money because of their relationship with you. They may loan you money outright or take an ownership interest in exchange for their investment. Be sure to spell out what the expectations are on both sides. Agree on what level of control your investors will have and the terms under which money will be repaid. Again, a business plan can help in these matters.

Some regions make seed money available from government programs to start small businesses. These funds may be easier to access and have better repayment terms than funds found at banks. In Alaska, the Forest Service organized 30 job-creation initiatives to help communities shift their revenue sources from forestry to tourism and ocean products (Dobbyn 2012). As you can see in the sidebar From Forestry to Tourism, government support can help entrepreneurs re-create communities as tourism destinations. Contact your economic development authority or tourism agencies to see what programs may be available. These programs change frequently and may require a considerable amount of paperwork, so do your homework carefully. Some businesses find them more trouble than help, but you might find a program to help you launch your tourism dreams.

Remember that you will likely need more money than you anticipate. Preparing a business plan will help you to anticipate these contingencies. Financing is difficult, so focus initially on minimizing your operating costs and on obtaining funds from personal resources, family, and friends. Many businesses fail not because they are short on ideas but because they are short on cash. In the next section, you will learn to prepare the documents that lenders and investors will require.

FINANCIAL FORECASTING

Financial forecasting is predicting the financial results and requirements for the future, usually one to three years from the present. The following are common schedules used in financial forecasting:

- Budgets
- Cash flow forecasts
- Financial pro forma statements

From Forestry to Tourism

The 17-million-acre Tongass National Forest in Alaska was the base for many years for a robust timber industry, but in recent times, timber sales have sharply declined. Now people are focusing on a "forest of fish" and the salmon produced from the forest habitat. Ocean products, sport fishing, and nature-based tourism are growing.

Jim Leslie owned a logging company but saw the timber decline coming in the 1990s. He noticed that cruise ships were bringing thousands of tourists to southeast Alaska and decided to switch businesses. Jim closed his logging business, got involved with the Wrangell Chamber of Commerce, and opened Alaska Waters Inc., a tour company that offers tours to view bears, birds, and seals and also offers access to aboriginal cultural experiences.

Now Wrangell, Alaska, is a community with new opportunities. A marine services center has replaced the downtown sawmill, a tribal house is being restored, and more residents are turning to tourism to make a living (Dobbyn 2012).

Budgets

Goal setting is necessary for successful businesses and a budget is a critical part of this process. A **budget** is a financial forecast of your operating and capital activities. An operating budget includes estimates of **sales revenue**, the amount paid to you by customers, and expenses, usually for a year. A **capital budget** is an estimate of expenditures for equipment, land, and buildings.

Most of the time you spend budgeting should be spent on the operating budget. An example of an operating budget is shown in table 9.1. To complete the budget you will need to estimate your sales revenue and expenses for the upcoming year, or more if you are preparing a multiyear budget. The sales forecast you prepared in chapter 5 will be a good starting point for your revenue forecast. Supplement that with your historical sales records if you have been in business for a few years, or look for secondary research sources, such as tourism forecasts for the industry or your region, to derive revenue estimates. A blank operating budget spreadsheet is provided for your use in the web resource.

You will also include your estimates of all costs for your business. If you have an existing business or have been in a similar business, you can use historical records. If you do not have this information, try to obtain estimates from major suppliers.

Once you have estimated the sales and expenses, you will be able to calculate **net income**, the excess of revenue over expenses. This income will be the surplus you need to repay creditors or make capital expenditures for equipment, land, and buildings.

Small and medium-size tourism organizations usually do not create capital budgets because their capital requirements are small. Larger facilities such as lodges or attractions should prepare capital budgets and use a cost–benefit analysis to guide their investment decisions. Reference books on finance concepts can provide more direction if you require a detailed capital budget.

Operating budgets are usually prepared annually. A sample operating budget worksheet is included in the web resource. It is relatively easy to develop a budget spreadsheet that enables you to easily change to your projections.

When you have completed your budget, give it a reasonability test. Remember, your budget is the financial blueprint that will translate your goals into reality, so allocate adequate resources to key areas. If improved customer service is one of your goals, include corresponding budget items to accomplish this goal, for example, extra funds for customer service training or wage costs to develop a customer-tracking system to determine whether you have increased your number of repeat visitors. Or perhaps you might decrease marketing costs because you expect your customer service improvements to generate more word-of-mouth sales. An absence of these types of relationships between revenue, costs, and your business goals will decrease your chances of accomplishing your goals. This will also cause confusion among your staff as they detect the inconsistency between what you say you want to do and what you are actually doing.

Cash Flow Forecasts

Once the budgeting process is complete, it is a good idea to do a **cash flow forecast**, an estimate of the amount of money received and spent by a business and the timing of inflows and outflows. It alerts you to cash shortages and to investment opportunities when you have cash surpluses. A cash flow forecast is important because of the

Table 9.1 Operating Budget

	Jan.	Feb.	March	April	May	June	July	Aug.	Sept.	Oct.	Nov.	Dec.	Year 1	Year 2	Year 3
							AMOUNT ($)								
SALES															
Rental					2,800	14,950	36,750	36,200	4,080				94,780	108,997	125,347
Tours					900	2,400	3,600	3,600	600				11,100	13,320	15,984
Packages													0	16,000	40,000
Total sales	0	0	0	0	3,700	17,350	40,350	39,800	4,680	0	0	0	105,880	138,317	181,331
EXPENSES															
Cost of sales					2,220	10,410	24,210	23,880	2,808				63,528	85,057	127,816
Accounting	100	100	100	100	100	200	200	200	100	100	100	100	1,500	1,530	1,561
Advertising	300	300	300	300	300	300	300	300	400	400	400	400	4,000	3,672	3,745
Computer supplies	100	100	100	100	100	100	100	100	100	100	100	100	1,200	1,224	1,248
Loan interest	0	167	167	167	167	167	167	167	167	167	167	167	1,837	1,600	1,200
Legal		500											500	510	520
Memberships		300											300	306	312
Office supplies	30	30	30	30	30	30	30	30	30	30	30	30	360	367	375
Postage	50	50	50	50	50	50	50	50	50	50	50	50	600	612	624
Promotion			1,000										1,000	1,020	1,040
Rent	00	00	00	00	350	350	350	350	350	00	00	00	1,750	1,785	1,821
Salaries	2,000	2,000	2,000	2,000	2,000	2,000	2,000	2,000	2,000	2,000	2,000	2,000	24,000	24,480	24,970
Telephone	100	100	100	100	100	100	100	100	100	100	100	100	1,200	1,224	1,248
Travel													00	00	00
Total expenses	2,680	3,647	3,847	2,847	5,417	13,707	27,507	27,177	6,105	2,947	2,947	2,947	101,775	123,387	166,480
Budgeted income	−2,680				−1,717	3,643	12,843	12,623	−1,725	−2,947	−2,947	−2,947	3,805	14,930	14,851

seasonality experienced by most tourism operators. You need to identify cash shortages and plan accordingly. For example, if you are conducting whale-watching tours from February to August, you will incur most of your marketing costs before the season start-up. You will need financing to cover expenses until revenues come, perhaps by setting up an operating line of credit with the bank. A blank cash flow forecast spreadsheet is provided in the web resource.

A problem encountered by some managers of small tourism businesses is that they use their bank balance as their only cash flow forecasting tool. With a large balance in the bank account at the end of their operating season, they might make a big expenditure during the winter months without taking into account the money needed for next season's start-up. By making expenditures without a cash flow forecast, at the very least, they have incurred additional interest expense, and at the worst, they could jeopardize the future of their business.

Preparing a cash flow forecast is similar to preparing an operating budget. The main difference is that it looks only at cash items and the timing of cash moving in and out of the business. For example, your operating budget would show trip revenues for the months when you expect sales to occur. On the cash flow forecast, you would show the sales when money is received. An example of a cash flow worksheet is shown in table 9.2. If you receive a deposit for a trip in June with the balance to be paid in July, you show the deposit as cash received in June (see cash receipts for March) and the remainder as cash received in July (see cash receipts for July).

Table 9.2   Cash Flow Forecast for Year One

	Jan.	Feb.	March	April	May	June	July	Aug.	Sept.	Oct.	Nov.	Dec.	Total
						AMOUNT ($)							
Cash on hand	8,500	33,500	30,420	26,373	22,126	22,579	34,112	60,355	72,248	49,051	42,546	39,199	8,500
Cash receipts:													
New investment	10,000												10,000
Cash sales					3,700	17,350	40,350	39,800	4,680	000	000	000	105,880
Bank loan	15,000												15,000
Total cash receipts	25,000	000	000	000	3,700	17,350	40,350	39,800	4,680	000	000	000	130,580
Total cash	33,500	33,500	30,420	26,373	25,826	39,929	74,462	100,155	76,628	49,051	42,546	39,199	139,380
Cash disbursements:													
Operating expenses	0	2,680	3,647	3,847	2,847	5,417	13,707	27,507	27,177	6,105	2,947	2,947	98,828
Bank loan repayment		400	400	400	400	400	400	400	400	400	400	400	4,400
Withdrawals													000
Capital expenditures													000
Total cash disbursements	0	3,080	4,047	4,247	3,247	5,817	14,107	27,907	27,577	6,505	3,347	3,347	103,228
Net cash flow	33,500	30,420	26,373	22,126	22,579	34,112	60,355	72,248	49,051	42,546	39,199	35,852	35,852

The same technique is used with expenditures. If you have credit with your suppliers, it is likely that you incur expenses a month before you actually pay for them. If you order brochures in December and pay a deposit in December with the balance due in January, you show cash spent on the deposit in December (see cash disbursements in December) and the balance in January (see cash disbursements in January).

Some businesses update their cash flow forecasts daily, others weekly or monthly. Frequency depends on the activity level of your business, the season, and your access to financing. If you are in the midst of your busy season and incurring large expenditures, you might do a forecast weekly or even daily. Having a line of credit allows breathing room in the event of cash shortages. If you are relying on cash inflows to cover your cash outflows, you may have to perform a delicate balancing act between paying suppliers and receiving payments from customers. Remember to save some of your cash surplus from one year to cover the start-up expenses or capital purchases for the next operating season.

Cash Flow Management

As you prepare your cash flow forecast you might be dismayed to find you have cash shortages or are not generating the surpluses you had hoped for. You can manage these cash flow problems by taking steps to minimize cash outflows.

Some of the most important cash management strategies for sustainable tourism organizations involve the following:

- Equipment acquisitions
- Contracting out services
- Cost minimization
- Deposits and cancellation fees

Ways to meet customer needs while managing cash are discussed in the following sections.

Equipment Acquisitions

Ensuring your customers' safety will require reliable equipment and trained personnel. This does not mean you have to buy all the required equipment or hire the employees needed. Equipment can often be rented or leased, although in a remote location, the range of rental options might be smaller. Many universities and colleges rent recreation equipment at reasonable costs and retailers may also rent outdoor equipment.

Vehicles and airplanes can be rented or leased, this is preferable if use is intermittent. If you need an office or storefront from which to start your tours or make bookings, you can link up with another business so that you are not paying the full cost of an office. You have probably been in a hotel that has an activity desk where you can book adventure tours. This is a good marketing practice not only because it makes it easier for tourists to plan their days, but also because it is an effective cash management strategy because the hotel and tour operator share building costs.

Contracting Out Services

Because labor costs are significant in most tourism businesses, it may be wise to contract out services instead of hiring employees. A contract situation enables you to bring in skilled guides for a short time without incurring the administrative costs associated with maintaining employees. It is important, however, to ensure that you are not violating labor or tax laws by classifying someone as a contractor when he or she should be considered an employee. This will be discussed in more detail in chapter 11.

Cost Minimization

Minimizing operating costs wherever possible is important to your survival and reduces cash outflows. Look at all areas of your business to find ways to trim costs and your cash flow will improve. For example, examine the way you market. Perhaps you can use an e-mail list to advertise your tours instead of mailing brochures. Or maybe you can advertise with a website banner ad rather than attend a trade show. Using voice over Internet Protocol telephone services can reduce telephone charges. Technology allows even the smallest companies to expand their reach while lowering costs. When searching for cost savings, talk to other business owners; they might share information on ways they have saved money or perhaps you can find ways you can work together to share costs.

Deposits and Cancellation Fees

An important part of your cash management is ensuring money received from customers is greater than money paid to suppliers. One way to accomplish this is asking customers for deposits at the time of booking and final payment before the tour date. This will provide money for expenses incurred before the tour and protect you if someone cancels after you have spent money. The amount of deposit you ask for will vary depending on the length and cost of the tour; shorter tours may require a 50 percent deposit, while longer, more-expensive trips may ask for a deposit of several hundred dollars when booking and additional payments at subsequent dates. Talk to your suppliers to determine what your financial obligations will be and establish a deposit policy that matches these outlays.

You also need protection from people who sign up for a trip and then withdraw shortly before the tour date. In many cases, you will have spent money that cannot be recovered. A cancellation policy will help transfer those costs from your business to the customer. Usually a cancellation policy requires a customer to give a certain amount of notice to receive a full refund. Again, depending on the length and nature of a trip, this can vary from a week to several months. Often the cancellation policy refunds less of the trip fee as the cancellation date gets closer to the departure date and more has been spent on trip preparation. Even in cases of full refunds, a handling fee to cover administration costs is often charged.

Travelers are able to buy cancellation insurance that protects them from losing money because of illness or accident and should be encouraged to do so. Although you want to protect your cash flow, you do not want to ruin a relationship with a customer who must cancel for unexpected health reasons. If the customer has cancellation insurance, the customer can recover his or her deposit, you will still be paid for your outlays, and you keep a good relationship that will hopefully translate into future bookings.

Financial Pro Forma Statements

If you are in a start-up situation or applying for financing, you need **pro forma financial statements**, usually a balance sheet and a statement of income, created with forecasted transactions. You may also prepare pro forma statements as part of your annual planning process.

A **statement of income** includes the revenue and expenses for a business for a defined period, usually a year. It is sometimes called an income statement, a profit and loss statement, or simply

Table 9.3 Pro Forma Statement of Income

	Jan.	Feb.	March	April	May	June	July	Aug.	Sept.	Oct.	Nov.	Dec.	Year 1	Year 2	Year 3
							AMOUNT ($)								
SALES															
Rental					2,800	14,950	36,750	36,200	4,080				94,780	108,997	125,347
Tours					900	2,400	3,600	3,600	300				10,800	13,320	15,984
Packages													0	20,000	50,000
Commissions													0	−4,000	−10,000
Total sales	0	0	0	900	5,200	18,550	40,350	36,800	4,080	0	0	0	105,880	138,317	181,331
EXPENSES															
Cost of sales					2,220	10,410	24,210	23,880	2,808				63,528	85,057	127,816
Gross margin	0	0	0	0	1,480	6,940	16,140	15,920	1,572	0	0	0	42,052	53,260	53,515
Accounting	100	100	100	100	100	200	200	200	100	100	100	100	1,500	1,530	1,561
Advertising	300	300	300	300	300	300	300	300	400	400	400	400	4,000	3,672	3,745
Computer supplies	100	100	100	100	100	100	100	100	100	100	100	100	1,200	1,224	1,248
Loan interest	0	167	167	167	167	167	167	167	167	167	167	167	1,837	1,600	1,200
Legal		500											500	510	520
Memberships		300											300	306	312
Office supplies	30	30	30	30	30	30	30	30	30	30	30	30	360	367	375
Postage	50	50	50	50	50	50	50	50	50	50	50	50	600	612	624
Promotion			1,000										1,000	1,020	1,040
Rent	00	00	00	00	350	350	350	350	350	00	00	00	1,750	1,785	1,821
Salaries	2,000	2,000	2,000	2,000	2,000	2,000	2,000	2,000	2,000	2,000	2,000	2,000	24,000	24,480	24,970
Telephone	100	100	100	100	100	100	100	100	100	100	100	100	1,200	1,224	1,248
Travel													00	00	00
Total expenses	2,680	3,647	3,847	2,847	3,197	3,297	3,297	3,297	3,297	2,947	2,947	2,947	38,247	38,330	38,664
Net income	−2,680				−1,717	3,643	12,843	12,623	−1,725	−2,947	−2,947	−2,947	3,805	14,930	14,851
Net profits to sales													4%	11%	8%
Return on equity													43%		

the P&L. An example of a pro forma statement of income is shown in table 9.3. It is similar to the operating budget and may include information from the same sources.

The revenue and expense categories shown in the example in table 9.3 can be modified to suit your business type, but use enough detail for an accurate forecast. Use the same estimating techniques you used for operating budgets.

A **balance sheet** is a schedule that shows your business **assets**, debt, and **equity** in the business. It summarizes the net worth of your business. A pro forma balance sheet is a forecast of your business'

net worth at a particular point in time. An example is shown in table 9.4.

Balance sheets for sustainable tourism businesses differ from those of non-tourism businesses. Many tour companies do not maintain large inventories, perhaps only food or promotional items such as T-shirts. An ecotourism lodge conversely could maintain larger inventories of food and beverages plus housekeeping and maintenance items. Many tourism operators will receive payment for services by cash, check, or credit card. They would not extend long-term credit to their customers, so they would not have

Table 9.4   Pro Forma Balance Sheet for Year One

Assets	Amount ($)
Cash	22,460
Inventory	100
Total current assets	22,560
Equipment	20,000
Incorporation costs	500
Total assets	**43,060**
Liabilities	
Accounts payable	4,700
Bank loan: current portion	3,900
Total current liabilities	8,600
Bank loans	14,000
Other loans	10,000
Total liabilities	32,600
Shareholder's equity	
Share capital	100
Retained earnings	10,360
Total shareholder's equity	10,460
Total liabilities and shareholder's equity	**43,060**

accounts receivable. Compiling pro forma statements can be difficult, so you may want to engage professional help.

Sensitivity Analysis

Guesswork is involved in completing any type of financial forecast. You use your experience to shape your predictions of sales volumes and revenues. You project capital and operating expenditures based on suppliers' estimates. Often though, the best-laid plans go awry. A spell of bad weather can decrease sales during your peak season. A key guide might leave suddenly, requiring skilled contract help at a premium. One of your trips might receive favorable mention in a national publication and bookings increase by 200 percent.

To be sure you are prepared for these events, perform a sensitivity analysis on your forecast of key variables. A **sensitivity analysis** is a "what if" examination of the assumptions underlying your financial pro formas and operating budgets. Some questions you might face as a sustainable tourism manager or owner could be What if your sales volume is 10 percent greater than forecast? What if it is 10 percent less? Will you still generate a profit? Will you still be able to pay the bills? What if you have to decrease prices by 5 percent to sell the number of trips targeted in the marketing plan?

You need to be able to answer questions like these. If you are taking your financial forecasts to bankers for financing, they will often want to see evidence of sensitivity analysis. Some businesses make the mistake of assuming that a 10 percent increase in sales volume will translate into a 10 percent increase in profits and, therefore, a sensitivity analysis is not needed. This is not the case because all costs may not vary directly with sales volume. Profits may not increase by 10 percent because the additional volume may require additional staff or acquisition of new equipment to handle the demand. This can be demonstrated in the following sensitivity analysis.

Assume you forecast the sale of 10,000 admissions to your natural history museum at $10 each. You have an operating cost of $6 per customer and annual administration cost of $25,000. Your net income is forecast as $15,000.

Base Case *(the amount included in your budget and pro forma income statement)*

Total revenue	10,000 × $10	= $100,000
Operating costs (10,000 customers × $6)		– $60,000
Subtotal		$40,000
Administration		– $25,000
Net income		$15,000

A sensitivity analysis determines what happens if you are incorrect in your sales forecast. If the number of visitors is 9,000 instead of 10,000, your net income is calculated as follows:

Total revenue	9,000 × $10	= $90,000
Operating costs (9,000 customers × $6)		– $54,000
Subtotal		$36,000
Administration		– $25,000
Net income		$11,000

You see a 27 percent decrease [($11,000 – $15,000) ÷ $15,000] in net income arising from a 10 percent decrease in volume.

You can conduct a sensitivity analysis on price forecasts. A price that is 10 percent greater than your initial forecast means admission should be $11 instead of $10. The sensitivity analysis is as follows:

Total revenue	10,000 × $11	= $110,000
Operating costs (10,000 customers × $6)		– $60,000
Subtotal		$ 50,000
Administration		– $25,000
Net income		$25,000

This 10 percent price increase resulted in a 66 percent net income increase [($25,000 – $15,000) ÷ $15,000]. These examples tell tourism business operators that both price and volume are sensitive to change.

As a manager, you should look for ways to maintain or increase prices, perhaps through extra services such as pretrip briefings, because any price increase will have a favorable impact on the bottom line. Conversely, in a competitive market, a small decrease in price could have a disproportionate impact on profit.

An area where tourism businesses often perform sensitivity analyses is foreign exchange. If

If you are conducting business in other countries or buying products overseas, your business will be affected by fluctuations in foreign currency.

foreign exchange rates increase dramatically and your trip becomes very expensive for a key geographic market segment, you may see significant decreases in net income. You can prepare by setting up a bank account in foreign currencies that are more stable and protect funds from foreign currency fluctuations, or you might decide to switch your marketing efforts to domestic markets. Undertaking a sensitivity analysis will help you anticipate these challenges and make plans for mitigating negative impacts.

FINANCIAL ANALYSIS

In addition to forecasting your business sales and expenses, you need to read your financial statements so you can make informed decisions about future events. This will also give you a better idea of whether a banker will lend you money or not. You will know whether you have sufficient cash to expand and offer tours next year to Annapurna, or perhaps your sales were not what you expected and you might consider offering a larger commission to travel agents to increase sales.

As explained in earlier sections, the balance sheet summarizes the assets, liabilities, and equity of your business. A statement of income summarizes revenue and expenses. To build your business literacy, review these two statements. You can analyze the data presented in several ways to learn more about your business. In this book we focus on the following methods:

- Comparative analysis
- Common-size analysis
- Ratio analysis
- Break-even analysis

Knowing how to perform these analyses will help you assess the health of your tourism business. It will also allow you to speak the same language as your banker.

Comparative Analysis

A **comparative analysis** simply compares this year's (or month's) financial statement to last year's (or month's). Not all accounting software provides comparative information, but financial statements prepared by a professional accountant will show the current and previous years' financial results. Compare sales from this year to last year's or look at the cost of wages this year versus last year. By looking at changes from one year to another, you can spot trends and see whether your business is moving in the direction you want.

Common-Size Analysis

This is a fancy name for a common-sense review. A **common-size** (or vertical) analysis looks at your revenue and expense items as a percentage of sales. Table 9.5 shows an example of common-size analysis. Common-size analysis is used routinely in the hospitality industry where operating margins are very small. Rather than focusing on absolute dollars, each item is viewed as a percentage of sales. These percentages can then be compared to previous periods to determine whether the business is becoming more or less efficient.

Salaries and wages are a large part of a tourism business' expenditures, so monitoring labor costs can be helpful. Tracking the percentage of wages against sales will tell owners whether they are using their guides and other staff members effectively. Food can be easily wasted or stolen. Monitoring food cost percentages will let you know whether there is excessive waste. Sales depend on money being spent on marketing programs. Keeping your marketing expenditures at the same percent of sales each year will ensure you maintain a presence in the marketplace without going overboard.

Table 9.5 Common-Size Analysis of an Adventure Travel Operator

Expense category	Percentage (%) of sales
Labor	$24,000 ÷ $105,880 × 100 = 23
Marketing	$(3,600 + 1,000) ÷ $105,880 × 100 = 4
Other	$(63,528 + 37,547 − 24,000 - 3,600 − 1,000) ÷ $105,880 × 100 = 68
Gross profit	$4,509 ÷ $105,880 × 100 = 4
Total sales	$105,880 ÷ $105,880 × 100 = 100

Ratio Analysis

Investors and bankers will use **ratio analysis**, the relationship between one number and another, to review the performance of your business. By looking at key ratios, investors and bankers are able to determine whether you have enough money to meet your debt obligations or whether your profitability is as good as other businesses in the industry. Owners can also use financial ratios to spot potential problems in time to take corrective action. The following areas of your financial health should be evaluated with ratios annually:

- Liquidity
- Profitability
- Growth

Liquidity

Liquidity refers to the ability of a business to pay its bills. Assessing liquidity focuses on the current assets and liabilities on the balance sheet. A **current asset** is an asset that is cash or that which can easily be turned into cash, such as inventory or accounts receivable. A **current liability** is a debt that must be paid within the next year.

A banker considering a short-term loan to your business or a trade creditor investigating your credit position will look at your **working capital**, the current assets minus current liabilities. Working capital represents the surplus you have to reinvest in your business, undertake expansion, or repay investors.

A ratio often used to assess liquidity is the **current ratio**, expressed as current assets to current liabilities. If you have $40,000 in cash, short-term investments, and inventories (your current assets) and $20,000 in accounts payable (your current liabilities), your current ratio is $40,000 to $20,000, or 2:1. Ideally, a banker would like to see a 2:1 current ratio to ensure you have the resources to meet debts as they come due. A ratio less than 1:1 means you cannot meet your short-term debts. A ratio significantly greater than 2:1 could mean that you are missing opportunities to invest in your business.

The debt-to-equity ratio is used if you are applying for financing to determine how much additional debt your company can sustain. The **debt-to-equity ratio** is calculated as **debt** (the total money owed to creditors) divided by **equity** (the difference between the value of assets and liability of a business).

If you have debts of $100,000 and equity of $20,000, the debt-to-equity ratio would be ($100,000 ÷ $20,000) or 5:1. This would be a high debt-to-equity ratio. A lender will want assurances that you are sharing the risk. If your company has a high debt-to-equity ratio, it means that you are risking more of your creditors' money than your own. This is acceptable if you can make your loan payments. However, in an uncertain business environment you could lose control of your business if payments cannot be made.

Profitability

Performing ratio analysis on profitability helps you determine whether you are making sufficient surplus on your core business activities. The first ratio you need to calculate is **gross profit** to sales (It is usually expressed as a percentage).

$$\text{Gross profit (sales less cost of goods sold)} \div \text{sales} \times 100$$

Cost of goods sold are expenses that vary directly with sales activity. For example, in a hotel, each additional guest requires more housekeeping staff time, electricity to light the room, and coffee in the morning. These costs are considered cost of goods sold.

Gross profit is also called gross margin. It is an indicator of how efficiently you run the business. If, like in the sensitivity analysis described earlier, sales were $100,000 and operating costs were $60,000, gross profit ($100,000 – $60,000) is $40,000. Gross profit to sales ($40,000 ÷ $100,000 × 100) is 40 percent. This means you have 40 percent left over from each dollar in sales to cover administration costs such as marketing, insurance, management salaries, and taxes. If you have a large gross profit, you have more money to expand or pay back debt. If you have a small gross profit, you must control costs carefully as you walk a fine line between making and losing money.

The next ratio calculation you should look at is net profit to sales (shown as a percentage). Net profit is the same as net income; on a financial statement net income is the preferred term, in financial analysis, net profit is the term commonly used. It is calculated as follows:

$$\text{Net profit} \div \text{sales} \times 100$$

Net profit is the money left after all expenses have been subtracted. If your net profit (or net income) is $15,000 and sales are $100,000, net profit to sales ($15,000 ÷ $100,000 × 100) is 15 percent. As with the ratio of gross profit to sales, a larger number provides more flexibility and financial security. However, many businesses compensate for a low ratio of net profit to sales by selling high volumes. You may also want to compare your net profit to sales against other businesses in the industry to assess your performance.

If you hope to attract investors to your business, you will need to be familiar with the concept of **return on investment (ROI),** the profit made from an investment. It is usually expressed as a percentage of the amount of the investment. A common way of calculating ROI is as follows:

$$ROI = Net\ profit \div equity \times 100$$

For example, if a company has $75,000 in equity and net profit of $15,000, return on investment is 20 percent ([$15,000 ÷ $75,000] × 100). There is no right return on investment, but an investor would expect to receive a return greater than that from a risk-free investment such as a term deposit with a bank. In the example, the business generates a 20 percent return on equity, which is a good rate of return and considerably higher than that earned by risk-fee investments. While this does not mean that an investor will receive a payment equal to the ROI each year, it does indicate that the company is creating wealth from the investment and over time should be capable of repaying the investment.

Growth

With proper planning, your business will grow. One of the fastest ways to determine how well your business is growing is to calculate growth ratios for sales, profits, assets, and debts. In each category, calculate the difference between this year and last year and then determine the percentage change from the starting point, last year's results. For example, to calculate growth in sales, use the following formula:

$$Sales\ growth =$$
$$(sales\ this\ year - sales\ last\ year)$$
$$\div sales\ last\ year$$

If sales were $95,000 last year and $100,000 this year, sales growth [($100,000 – $95,000) ÷ $95,000] × 100 is 5 percent.

The same formula can be modified to examine performance in profits:

$$Profit\ growth =$$
$$(net\ profit\ this\ year - net\ profit\ last\ year)$$
$$\div net\ profit\ last\ year$$

If net profits were $14,000 last year and $15,000 this year, profit growth {[($15,000 – $14,000) ÷ $14,000] × 100} is 7 percent.

With proper planning, your business is more likely to grow.

The formula should be adapted to identify the growth in **assets**, things your business owns that have significant value, and debts as follows:

$$\text{Asset growth} = \frac{(\text{assets this year} - \text{assets last year})}{\text{assets last year}}$$

If assets are $100,000 this year and $97,000 last year, asset growth {[($100,000 – $97,000) ÷ $97,000] × 100} is 3 percent.

$$\text{Debt growth} = \frac{(\text{total debt this year} - \text{total debt last year})}{\text{total debt last year}}$$

If debt is $25,000 this year and $30,000 last year, debt growth {[($25,000 – $30,000) ÷ $30,000] × 100} is negative 17 percent, indicating a decrease of 17 percent in money owed to creditors.

In general, a business would like to see similar growth in all four areas. A 5 percent increase in sales and a 1 percent increase in profits indicates a positive trend in sales, but could mean that you have become less efficient because you are keeping less of your sales. Unless start-up, marketing, or operating expenditures are required to generate additional sales, you want sales and profits to grow equally.

Debt may grow as fast as assets or sales, but you do not want to see debt growing more than assets. This could indicate that you are using debt to finance operating expenses.

In the example shown earlier, growth appears to be well managed because sales have increased by 5 percent, but profits are growing faster at 7 percent. The business was able to grow 5 percent in sales with only a 3 percent increase in assets and debt has decreased, evidence that cash is being well managed.

Break-Even Analysis

If you are seeking financing, you may be asked to perform a **break-even analysis**, a calculation to determine at what point your business makes money. Start-up or small businesses often assume that money in the bank means they are making money; if there is no money in the bank, they assume they are losing money. As a rough guide, these observations can be valid, but there is a difference between cash flow (money in the bank) and profitability (the excess of revenues over expenses). If your business is growing rapidly or if you have used funds to finance capital expendi-

tures, you might experience a cash shortage but still be profitable.

A break-even analysis will tell you at what point you will start to make a profit and how much incremental profit you will make with each sales dollar once you break even. This understanding of your cost structure will help you make better decisions. The analysis requires you to determine your forecasted sales, variable costs, and fixed costs.

- Forecasted sales (your prediction of your sales income).

- **Variable costs** are expenditures that fluctuate directly with the activity level of your business. If you provide overnight hiking trips, costs that vary with the number of participants are food, park fees, guide or camp staff wages, equipment rental, and printing costs of pretrip orientation packages. In each of these cases, the costs vary directly according to the number of trips sold. On your financial statements these might be called cost of goods sold.

- **Fixed costs** are expenditures that do not vary directly with the activity level of your business, such as marketing costs, management salaries, and building rent. These types of costs are tied to increases or decreases in overall business activity, but they do not vary directly with the number of people on a trip, visiting an attraction, or staying at a hotel. While you may need to spend more on marketing if your business is to double in size, a direct relationship between marketing costs and individual trips does not exist. For example, your listing in a tourism directory will cost the same whether you offer 10 trips a year or 12. Brochures are printed for an entire season's trips and cannot be tied directly to one trip, so they are considered a fixed cost. Some individual costs, such as newspaper advertisements or special promotions, may be directly related to a particular trip, but for the most part, these are treated as fixed for a break-even analysis.

Two methods can be used for calculating a break-even point. If you have information on a per unit basis, you can calculate a break-even point for each product or tour. More often however, tourism businesses aggregate sales for many tours and products, so break even must be calculated using overall sales dollars. Either method generates the same answer, so select the method that works best for you.

To calculate the break-even point in units sold, use the following method if you have collected cost information by trip. If not, skip to the second method. The first method is as follows:

1. Contribution per unit = selling price – variable cost per unit

2. Break-even point in units = fixed costs ÷ contribution per unit

If you operate a natural history tour company and charge customers $99 for a one-day geological tour, you could calculate your break-even point using the previous formula. You may estimate the variable costs for the lunch, van rental, and guide services as $45 per person and your fixed costs for marketing, rent, telephone, insurance, and salaries as $40,000 per year.

Your break-even point is as follows:

1. Contribution per unit [selling price ($99) – variable cost per unit ($45)] = $54

2. Break-even point in units [fixed costs ($40,000) ÷ contribution per unit ($54)] = 740.74 trips

The break-even point would be rounded up to 741 trips because you cannot sell part of a trip. Now you know you need to sell 741 trips to break even. When you sell the 742nd trip, you will have covered your fixed costs and start earning your first profits. Note that each unit sold after the break-even point does not generate $99 in profit, but $54 because each sale has a variable cost of $45, a point often overlooked by business owners.

If you do not know your costs by trip participant, you can use the following formula to calculate a break-even point in dollars:

1. Variable cost per sales dollar = variable costs ÷ sales

2. Contribution per sales dollar = $1.00 – variable cost per sales dollar

3. Break-even point = fixed costs ÷ contribution per sales dollar

If you estimate sales for the year are $98,000; variable costs for van rentals, food, and contract guide services are $45,000; and fixed costs are $40,000, the break-even point would be calculated as follows:

1. Variable cost per sales dollar [variable costs ($45,000) ÷ sales ($98,000)] = $0.46

2. Contribution per sales dollar [$1.00 – variable cost per sales dollar ($0.46)] = $0.54

3. Break-even point [fixed costs ($40,000) ÷ contribution per sales dollar ($0.54)] = $74,074

In this example, 46 cents of each sales dollar would be needed to cover variable costs, and 54 cents would be available from each sales dollar to cover fixed costs. The business would break even when the contribution from each sales dollar has covered the fixed costs of $40,000. This occurs when sales reach $74,074. From this point on, each sales dollar will generate 54 cents in profit. Because you are forecasting sales of $98,000, your business will reach its break-even point of $74,074 and generate a profit when it exceeds this amount.

This is a simple example of a break-even analysis. When completing such an analysis for your business, you may encounter problems classifying costs as fixed or variable. When it is difficult to decide whether something is variable or fixed, err on the side of caution and classify it as a fixed cost. This will give you a higher break-even point, but planning for a higher break-even point will motivate you to make more sales.

ACCOUNTING

By now you have realized you need complete and accurate financial records for financial analysis and to satisfy information requests from investors or creditors. To create reliable records you need to monitor the following:

- Bookkeeping
- Payroll
- Taxes
- Internal controls

Each of these is discussed in the following sections.

Bookkeeping

Most entrepreneurs have great ideas and a desire to make things happen. The need to track expenditures and revenues in detail is usually not seen as an enjoyable part of the business.

Well-maintained finances will free you to spend more time working with your customers.

However, to make your business successful and to stay out of trouble with the government, it is critical to have a well-functioning accounting system.

Your accounting system does not have to be expensive or elaborate, but it is imperative that all items are recorded and charged to the correct account. There are many accounting software packages on the market, from simple to elaborate. Choose one that fits your needs and find someone to update it.

You may hire a friend or relative who has bookkeeping experience to do the daily or weekly record keeping, but hire a professional accountant to help you get started and to review your records annually, more often if your volume is high. Not hiring an accountant can be one of the most expensive decisions you make. You might overlook deductions or take them incorrectly because you are not familiar with tax laws. If you have family members involved in the business, there may be opportunities to take advantage of income splitting. Given that many tourism operators are small to medium-sized businesses, they can benefit from sheltering as much income as possible.

Another reason for getting professional assistance is to ensure that your records are accurate. By analyzing your financial records as discussed earlier, you can determine the most profitable tours or products. To do this, you need accurate financial information. If you record the new van as a trip expense instead of a capital equipment purchase, you will find your net income unusually low and may overprice products based on this erroneous accounting. Make sure to separate personal expenditures and income from the company's records.

Payroll

As your business grows, the number of people working for you will increase. Many tourism entrepreneurs start out doing many business functions themselves and quickly realize they need additional guides, camp staff, or sales people. Preparing payroll accounting for hourly workers is time consuming and comes with numerous regulations surrounding deductions, taxes, and wages.

A cost-effective way to maximize your time is to contract out payroll accounting as early as possible. Contact firms that specialize in payroll services. Usually they charge a small fee to set up each employee's account and then a modest fee for each pay period. Even large companies will contract out payroll because the task is time consuming and it is expensive to maintain in-house expertise. Use the time saved on marketing your newest bear-viewing trip. You will be more successful in the long run.

Taxes

No one likes to pay taxes; however, collecting, recording, and remitting taxes are part of being a business owner. As mentioned earlier, keeping good records and conducting tax planning can minimize the amount of income tax you pay. It is also important to set up procedures to collect and remit sales tax, if required. Tax rates vary between and within countries and states or provinces. Your accountant can provide information on tax rates and a list of items that are taxable. If you are doing business in other countries, you also need to become familiar with those tax rates and collection requirements. Make sure all required tax payments to the government are made on time. Assessed penalties are an unnecessary expense.

Internal Controls

As a tourism business owner or manager, one of your obligations is to protect the company from waste, fraud, and inefficiency. Internal controls are the safeguards needed to meet that obligation. Smaller operators may not have an elaborate system of internal controls, but basic controls can be implemented.

If you are the only person working in the business, most of your controls will be aimed at ensuring the accuracy of the financial records. Providing a receipt for each sale and keeping invoices for cash expenditures are examples of internal controls you should adopt.

When you grow to the point that you hire staff, you will need to add more controls. No one wants to think their employees may be dishonest; however, when cash or assets are easily consumed, theft and fraud increase. Businesses that accept cash payments or have food service operations are at a greater risk of theft or fraud. Simple internal controls start with hiring the right people and checking references during the hiring process. Make sure no one employee handles a transaction from beginning to end. If one of your guides is also marketing tours and receiving the mail, have another employee make bank deposits and record revenues. By comparing the sales ledger against the tour roster, you can make sure all payments have been deposited.

Set policies on who can order materials and who can select stops for tours. Use specific suppliers to maximize discounts and to prevent problems of employee collusion. Other companies might offer rewards, in either cash or in-kind merchandise, for bringing customers to their business. Guides might be promised free meals for bringing a group to their restaurant. Car rental agencies may tip lodge staff that recommend them. While you might not discourage these practices, you should be aware of them. You do not want your tour groups diverted to restaurants or shops solely because of deals offered to your staff. Your customers are savvy travelers and will detect a compromise in quality or a feeling of being funneled into a business for someone else's benefit.

As well, prepare a budget and review your monthly or financial statements against it. This simple step can be one of the best internal controls you can implement. Even a rudimentary budget will give you some idea of what to expect for the coming year.

SUMMARY

Learning to manage financial affairs is necessary for all businesses. It is more difficult for managers of sustainable tourism businesses because they must juggle environmental and social benchmarks in addition to financial goals, but breaking even and generating surpluses are critical for success. To achieve the strategic goals set out for your business means translating vision, goals, and strategy into dollars. You must balance the desire for the best facilities and unlimited marketing with the reality of your sales inflow. Although you may hire trained accountants to handle financial tasks, ensure you understand where your costs originate, how you make money, and what your financing needs are. Participate in your financial planning process and your staff will have better information for making decisions and you will create an entity with lasting financial strength.

|||||||||||||||||||||||||||| GLOSSARY |||||||||||||||||||||||||||||

assets—Things a business owns that have significant value. Examples are cash or investments. **Capital assets** are assets that last longer than a year and form the infrastructure of your business. Examples include land, buildings, computers, and furniture.

balance sheet—A schedule that shows the business assets, liabilities incurred, and equity in the business. It summarizes the net worth of a business.

break-even analysis—A calculation to determine at what point a business makes money.

budget—A financial forecast of operating and capital activities. An operating budget includes estimates of sales revenue, the amount paid to the business by customers, and expenses, usually for a year.

capital budget—is an estimate of expenditures for equipment, land and buildings.

cash flow forecast—An estimate of the amount of money received and spent by a business and the timing of inflows and outflows.

common-size analysis—An analysis that looks at revenue and expense items as a percentage of sales. Sometimes called a vertical analysis.

comparative analysis—An analysis that compares this year's (or month's) financial statement to last year's (or month's) financial statement.

cost of goods sold—Expenses that vary directly with sales activity. For example, in a hotel, each additional guest requires more housekeeping staff time, electricity to light the room, or coffee for the morning drink. These costs would be considered cost of goods sold.

creditors—Organizations or people who lend money with the expectation it will be repaid with interest.

current asset—An asset that is cash or that which can easily be turned into cash, such as inventory or accounts receivable.

current liability—A debt that must be paid within the next year. Examples are accounts payable or taxes payable.

current ratio—The ratio of current assets to current liabilities.

debt-to-equity ratio—The ratio of liabilities to equity in a business.

debt—The total money owed to creditors.

equity—The difference between the value of assets and the value of liabilities of a business.

financial forecasting—Predicting the financial results and requirements for the future, usually one to three years from the present. Common schedules used in financial forecasting include budgets, cash flow forecasts, and financial pro forma statements.

fixed costs—Expenditures that do not vary directly with the activity level of a business, such as marketing costs, management salaries, and building rent. These types of costs are tied to increases or decreases in overall business activity, but they do not vary directly with number of people on a trip, visiting an attraction, or staying at a hotel.

gross profit—Sales minus the cost of goods sold. Sometimes called gross margin.

investors—Organizations or people who will contribute money in exchange for an ownership share in the business.

liquidity—The ability of a business to pay its bills.

net income—The excess of revenue over expenses. Sometimes called profit or net profit.

pro forma financial statements—Usually a balance sheet and a statement of income, created with forecasted transactions.

ratio analysis—An analysis that looks at the relationship between one number and another. Often used by bankers and investors to evaluate a business.

return on investment (ROI)—The profit made from an investment. It is usually expressed as a percentage of the amount of the investment.

sales revenue—The amount paid to a business by customers. Sometimes referred to as revenue or sales.

sensitivity analysis—An analysis that includes a "what if" examination of the assumptions underlying financial pro formas and operating budgets.

small and medium-size enterprises—Businesses with fewer than 500 employees and less than C$50 million in annual revenue.

statement of income—A financial statement that includes the revenue and expenses for a business for a defined period, usually a year. It is sometimes called an income statement or a profit and loss statement or simply the P&L.

variable costs—Expenditures that fluctuate directly with the activity level of a business.

working capital—The current assets minus current liabilities. It is the amount of surplus available to invest in new marketing activities, buy new capital equipment, and so on.

||||||||||||||||||||| REVIEW QUESTIONS |||||||||||||||||||

1. Why is financial management important to sustainable tourism organizations?

2. Identify possible financing sources for sustainable tourism ventures. Do you think it might be more difficult for sustainable tourism organizations to find financing than for other industries? Explain your reasoning.

3. Describe the main forecasting schedules tourism organizations use.

4. What are three methods for analyzing the financial performance of sustainable tourism organizations?

5. How can a business benefit if financial records are well maintained?

6. Define cash flow. What are three steps a sustainable tourism organization can take to improve cash flow?

|||||||||||||||| VIDEO CASE STUDY ||||||||||||||||

Visit the web resource to view the video "The Bottom Line." After watching the video, answer the following questions:

1. What unique activity does the Casa de San Pedro Bed and Breakfast offer its customers?

2. Activities such as the ones shown in the video could be included in the room rate, perhaps with a higher rate, or sold as a separate activity. List the advantages and disadvantages of these two approaches. Which would you recommend from a financial perspective?

3. Describe the type of travelers who would be interested in this experience. Explain what role the product–market match has played in Casa de San Pedro Bed and Breakfast's success.

4. Identify the tourism partnerships in the video. What costs might a business owner incur in developing and maintaining these partnerships?

5. The bed and breakfast charges different rates for each room, depending on its location and decor. Discuss how this pricing strategy can add to profits and the potential problems you foresee.

6. How do you think this bed and breakfast could have benefitted from a strategic plan? Give examples of market or economic trends mentioned in the video that may have led business owners to pursue bird-watchers as a profitable market segment.

7. Provide evidence of competitive barriers you observed that would prevent a competing bed and breakfast from establishing its own activities for bird-watchers. How might the Casa de San Pedro Bed and Breakfast establish a competitive advantage in that situation?

|||||||||||||||| YOUR BUSINESS PLAN ||||||||||||||||

It is time to tackle the financial forecasts in your business plan. With the techniques you have learned in this chapter, gather the information you will need and prepare an operating budget and cash flow forecast. You will also need to complete a pro forma balance sheet and statement of income. In your preliminary schedules, look carefully for months where your net income is negative or where the cash outflows are greater than cash inflows. You may need to find additional revenue sources or trim costs or both. Now is the time to decide whether your marketing plan is generating the revenue needed to cover costs and grow your business as envisioned in the business plan.

Think about how you will attract investors and ways you can make your business appear attractive to them; a good return on investment and sufficient cash flow to repay loans will help. Calculate some of the financial ratios described in this chapter to provide evidence your business is a good investment choice.

1. List the cost categories you require for the operating budget and cash flow forecast. Identify the information (e.g., number of employees, minimum wage, or rental rates) you will require and possible sources.

2. Prioritize the decisions you will need to make as you prepare your financial forecasts. If you are uncertain of which products you will offer, perhaps start with a break-even analysis to determine which tours offer the greatest profits. If you want to know whether you have sufficient financing, a cash flow forecast will highlight periods with cash shortages or periods of surpluses for debt repayment.

3. Determine how you can build flexibility into your financial forecasts. Perhaps you will want to prepare different forecasts for different levels of sales or for different combinations of products. This can be helpful in answering "what if" questions when potential investors review your business plan.

IIIIIIIIIIIIIIIIIIIIIIIIII REFERENCES IIIIIIIIIIIIIIIIIIIIIIII

Dobbyn, P. 2012. Transition for Tongass. *American Forests*, summer. www.americanforests. org/magazine/article/transition-for-tongass.

Canadian Tourism Commission. 2011. Tourism competitive benchmarking study: Where does tourism rank in the context of the Canadian economy? Nov. 30. http://en-corporate. canada.travel/sites/default/files/pdf/Research/Industry-research/Economic-political-impacts/tourism_competitive_benchmarking_study_en_2011.pdf.

Pierce, A. 2011. Financing profile: Small and medium-sized enterprises in tourism industries. Industry Canada, December. http://www.ic.gc.ca/eic/site/061.nsf/vwapj/SBFProfile-ProfilFPE_Dec2011_eng.pdf/$file/SBFProfile-ProfilFPE_Dec2011_eng.pdf.

Tourism British Columbia. 2005. Characteristics of the commercial nature-based tourism industry in British Columbia. January. www.wilderness-tourism.bc.ca/docs/Commercial_ Nature-Based%20Tourism.pdf.

10

CUSTOMER SERVICE

LEARNING OUTCOMES

After reading this chapter, you will be able to do the following:

- Understand why customer service is important
- Describe the process needed to deliver consistent customer service
- Understand how interpretation enhances customer service
- Resolve common problems in customer service
- Qualify customers for the best match between products and their abilities

ustomer service is the ability to meet your customer's real and perceived needs through the actions of your staff and suppliers. Customer service occurs every time tourists come into contact with your business. It is the way they are treated whether they are calling for trip information or to make a booking. It is the impression they receive when they drive into your parking lot. It is the experience they have when they take one of your guided nature walks.

Unless your business is small enough that you can personally take care of every tour detail, you have to develop a customer service process that delivers a consistent level of customer service to each visitor. As all aspects of your operation affect customer service, managing it is one of the biggest challenges for an owner or manager.

As mentioned in earlier chapters, a business has a difficult time competing on price alone and, if operating under rustic conditions, a somewhat difficult time competing on quality. Where a sus-

tainable tourism business can distinguish itself is on its ability to deliver *great* customer service. For an example of a sustainable tourism business using great customer service and interpretation as a competitive advantage, watch the video "Elkhorn Slough: Enhancing Experiences With Customer Service" in the web resource.

CUSTOMER SERVICE PROCESS

Tourism organizations that successfully provide exceptional customer service understand that means meeting or exceeding customer expectations. Customers expect basic customer service, such as taking reservations quickly, preparing tasty food, and leading safe outdoor activities. Fail to meet their expectations and they will tell all their friends how poorly your business did. If you meet their expectations, you will have satisfied customers. If you exceed their expectations, you will create fans that will sing your praises on their social media channels and do some of your marketing for you.

Unless your business is so small that you are the only employee, you will need to create a **customer service process**, a series of actions leading to an expected outcome, in which you document your policies and procedures, train employees to deliver customer service, follow up to ensure the process works, and recognize performance.

In addition to basic customer service, such as taking reservations or preparing and delivering food, a sustainable tourism business often needs to provide interpretation, evidence of environmental and cultural sensitivity, and a high level of safety management. This complexity means a customer service process is even more important to ensure your messages and procedures are consistent and that you have a strategy to manage expectations. If your lodging is rustic but it is the best place to watch a caribou migration, be honest about the amenities—it is not a four-star hotel—and focus on the wildlife experience in your marketing materials. You may want to plan pleasant surprises or extras for your guests. If you tell your visitors everything that you provide, you cannot exceed their expectations because they will have expected everything you delivered.

When you develop your customer service process, refer to your market research to determine what your customers expect. Consider as well where you have positioned your product. If you are offering a premium product and a higher price, your customers will likely anticipate a higher level of service and your process must ensure you meet expectations.

Keep in mind that your customers' perceptions are everything. You might feel you provide great customer service, but if your customer feels you are lacking in some area, you will lose business to others who meet that need. As Sam Walton, Walmart founder, said, "There is only one boss. The customer. And he can fire everybody in the company from the chairman on down, simply by spending his money somewhere else" (Entrepreneur 2008). So do not expect to issue an edict saying that you have great customer service and then expect it to come true. You must plan for it and your success in delivering great customer service will depend to a great extent on your ability to manage the following elements:

- Policies
- Procedures

- Standards
- Recruiting
- Training
- Controls
- Recognition

The role of each of these in customer service will be examined in the following sections.

Policies

Customer service **policies** are broad, guiding principles describing your approach to customer service. Examples of areas in which you might create customer service policies might be hiring standards, dispute resolution, and dress code.

Policies give staff an idea of what is expected of them. A policy that empowers a guide to adapt spontaneously to changes in weather, road conditions, or business closures has a better chance of making sure customers have a fun and safe trip. A guide caught in unusually bad weather can decide to substitute a restaurant meal for a picnic lunch, knowing that he has the authority to do so.

A policy that says you provide guides with the highest level of skill or knowledge may result in a different level of service than a policy that says you will employ people with a specific license or diploma. For example, if your nature-based tour company employs only graduates from forestry technology programs, your policy may result in tours with a strong focus on forest ecology. Conversely, if many of your customers are families, you might set a policy of hiring staff with drama or theater backgrounds, knowing they will be entertaining presenters. You can train them in guiding skills and natural history. Some companies have a policy of hiring people with little training so they can teach them their methods and avoid "untraining" the habits and techniques an experienced person might bring.

Procedures

No one likes procedures, and often they are loosely defined for small businesses, but they are important to ensure consistency in customer service. A **procedure** describes in detail how something is to be done. Often your customer service process will consist of many procedures, which will help standardize behavior. As a sustainable tourism business manager, your big challenge is not in delivering a great tour the first time, it is in delivering that great tour the 100th time with the same enthusiasm.

You should take the time to describe what good customer service looks like for your business and document it so everyone knows what is expected. For example, do not take a haphazard approach to your initial communication with customers. Decide how promptly the phone should be answered or how quickly e-mail will be replied to. The number of times your phone rings before it is answered and the greeting used may determine whether you get the booking in the first place. Make sure you convey the impression you intended.

A simple procedure list can go a long way toward describing good service and it is invaluable in training new staff. An example of a procedure list is shown in the sidebar Tour Guide Greeting Procedure. The list is used when a tour guide first meets a group for a tour.

Identify all the processes that will affect your delivery of customer service, determine what actions will result in the desired customer experience, and develop the procedures that ensure staff can consistently deliver it.

Standards

Customer service **standards** define the goal or result expected from the customer service procedure, for example, the number of rooms cleaned by one housekeeper. Standards can also measure the effectiveness of customer service processes, for example, what percentage of reservations come from repeat customers. For traditional tourism products, standards might include the number of meals served by a food and beverage server in one shift. For a sustainable tourism business, other standards often apply. Examples include the following:

- Length of time to reply to trip information requests
- Percentage of time people spend engaged in core activity (e.g., trekking) versus noncore activities (e.g., travel days or orientation)
- Number of contacts before and after a trip to properly brief the client
- Number of partnerships with community organizations and opportunities for guests to become engaged
- Quantity of waste material diverted from landfills
- Energy savings from energy-efficient appliances and lighting

One standard often used for sustainable tourism businesses delivering tours is the guide-to-client ratio. This is important in determining the quality of customer service and the visitor experience. For a low-risk activity, tourism businesses may have one guide for 12 people or more. High-quality tours or activities in a higher-risk environment might schedule one guide for every three or four people. This standard will significantly affect your service delivery. A low guide-to-client ratio offers more flexibility in tour activities. People will have more opportunity to ask questions and learn about the environment and may create a stronger bond with your guide and your company. This level of customer service will cost you more, so make sure you set your prices high enough to cover extra wages.

It may be difficult to set standards for all areas of your business when you are starting or if you have a small business, but identify the areas where customer service is most important and develop standards. For example, if you are offering guided one-day tours, you might start with simple standards for delivering high-quality customer service:

- All customers will be asked about their special dietary requirements when booking, and trip cooks will provide meals for special dietary requirements on all trips.

Tour Guide Greeting Procedure

Your customer service procedure for a guide might include the following steps:

- Welcome the people to the tour.
- Have the guide introduce himself.
- Have tour members introduce themselves.
- Describe the trip, when and where there will be breaks, and when the group will return from the trip.
- Make sure everyone has proper equipment.
- Brief everyone on correct behavior for viewing wildlife, interacting with locals, and moving through sensitive environments.

Guide-to-client ratio can be an important customer service standard.

- All tour participants will be greeted within five minutes of arrival.
- Operation of trip equipment will be explained and demonstrated to all group members before the trip starts.
- No trip members will be left behind. A guide will stay with slower participants, or the group will slow its progress so the slowest members can keep up.
- Each customer will be thanked for choosing the tour company and provided information on the frequent booking program.

Recruiting

Policies, procedures, and standards will only be effective if the people you hire to work at your business are capable of delivering good customer service. As mentioned earlier, you may need to hire people with specific skills, or not, or you might need specific personality or leadership traits. For some sustainable tourism businesses, guides will be the company representatives with whom customers spend the most time. Stories of the guide will be retold back home and may serve as the most vivid memories of a tourism product. Selecting the right person to be the guide is critical. While it is easy to hire on the basis of formal qualifications, you must also take into account less-tangible attributes, like leadership ability and communication skills. You can train people to per-

form a technical skill, such as kayaking or historic interpretation, but you cannot teach someone how to smile. Identifying and hiring the right staff is discussed in more detail in the next chapter.

Training

By hiring qualified people, you can minimize training requirements, but you will still want to provide customer service training. Staff need to be familiar with your way of doing things; this includes your policies, procedures, and standards. If your employees' skills are deficient, you need to provide training to develop their skills. You also want to keep your staff up to date in their areas of expertise and make sure people are informed about the latest developments in the areas you operate. Ensuring consistency of procedures through ongoing training and reinforcement also provides protection against lawsuits if a tour goes wrong. Training will be discussed in more detail in the next chapter.

Controls

No one wants to be the watchdog for customer service, but someone must ensure that quality service is delivered. Controls give you assurance that a desired level of customer service is being delivered. Preparing job descriptions or completing background checks for new staff are two simple, but effective, controls. Ensuring everyone receives basic training is another. A further control may have you, or a senior member of the team, participating in trips from time to time to see that guides follow procedures and are interacting with a group in a professional and competent manner. Some companies use people unknown to the guides to take tours and assess the level of customer service. The key here is to ensure timely feedback to staff on their performance, both good and bad.

Recognition

To keep your customer service system working well, make sure to recognize your staff when exceptional customer service happens. You can explain what levels of customer service are expected through policies and procedures and put controls in place to ensure compliance, but recognition of people who make extra effort with your customers will boost morale and help empower employees. You cannot anticipate every situation your staff and customers will encounter, so there will be times when staff must make their own decisions on how to handle a problem. Reward them if they show creativity and empathy in keeping everyone happy. You do not need a large budget; you can use intangible or low-cost rewards such as a verbal thank you in front of their peers or a humorous certificate. The chance to borrow equipment in off-hours or the opportunity to lead choice tours can show staff that you appreciate their efforts to make your business more successful and keep your customer service system running smoothly.

Take the Ecochallenge "Finding a Good Reward" to see how easy it is to motivate employees with the right choices. Because many tourism businesses cannot offer large salaries, intangible recognition is necessary to attract and retain good employees.

CUSTOMER SERVICE AND INTERPRETATION

A visitor traveling through a natural area without interpretation is having an experience similar to watching television without the sound. Everything looks pretty, but it is difficult to tell what you are seeing and you miss much of the detail. **Interpretation** is communication that makes connections between the audience's interest and the meanings inherent in the resource. For

Ecochallenge
Finding a Good Reward

Think about what you would consider an appropriate reward if you had delivered great customer service. Limit your choices to nonsalary items. Perhaps you would appreciate time off to pursue leisure activities. Maybe you would like the chance to bring your family to your place of work for a free tour or visit. Some people find it satisfying when other people are made aware of their contribution through a mention in a company newsletter or an employee-of-the-month program. Or you might like the chance to direct donations from the company to a conservation or community group. List three or four rewards you think would be an incentive to deliver great customer service. Show your list to other people to see whether they agree. You may discover that employers need to adjust recognition to reflect employee age, family situation, and personal interests.

a sustainable tourism business operating in natural areas or featuring cultural experiences, offering interpretation as part of customer service is critical. Even accommodation providers who do not offer tours may want to include interpretative elements to explain their sustainability practices.

Interpretation serves two primary roles: one, it encourages interaction between trip participants and between participants and their environment and, two, it can supplement physical activities undertaken as part of the trip. Often tourism professionals think they do better at interpretation than they actually do. A guide will often memorize the names of common plants and animals but not be prepared to discuss the land use issues in the region visited. Give interpretation extra attention and you will have a customer service advantage as you exceed visitor expectations. If interpretation is new to you, contact someone at your university or college to coach you through the process or contact the National Association for Interpretation for training or publications.

To optimize your interpretation and customer service, develop an interpretative plan. This plan will identify the following:

- Information to convey
- Themes and subthemes

- Audience characteristics, such as age, culture, attitudes, interests, special needs, and expectations
- Methods of interpretation, such as demonstrations, living interpretations, signs, lectures, storytelling, and videos
- Evaluation methods

Each of these is discussed briefly in the following sections. For more detail, consult books and websites devoted to interpretation.

Information to Convey

Develop a list of topics you think your customers would find interesting or that make your product or destination unique. While most interpretation includes information on the natural setting, culture, and history, you should also consider land use and political issues. A principle of sustainable tourism is to provide opportunities to involve people in local communities. By fully informing your guests about the challenges an environment is facing, tourists can make informed choices about their actions. They may alter their buying habits after learning about the business practices of certain companies or they might make donations to nonprofit groups providing school programs on environmental education.

Themes and Subthemes

An **interpretative theme** is a key point or message about a topic that an interpreter wishes to convey to the audience. Themes will help you group information so that visitors can make connections between dissimilar information. As you develop your interpretation script, ask "Why does a visitor care about this information?" If you can answer, the "so what?" question, you will develop interpretation that engages your visitors. An example of an interpretative theme might be "local plants were used by aboriginal people for healing before modern medicine was available."

Audience Characteristics

The characteristics of your trip participants are important to your interpretative planning. You need to know how much they know about the topic and perceptions or misconceptions they bring. If your trip participants have master's degrees (many ecotourists are highly educated), do not focus on simple, identification interpretation. Incorporate discussions of more complex issues and local nuances. If you will have young children in your audience, the amount of content may be reduced as you spend more time introducing concepts.

Identifying your interpretative theme will help you decide what information to share with visitors.

Interpretative Methods

You can use many interpretative methods to convey your message. If you are offering tours, you will likely have your guides deliver interpretative talks, but other methods exist, some of which do not require staff. Some destinations, like the Boomtown Trail in central Alberta, are developing smartphone applications that provide interpretative information as travelers drive by on the highway. Small bed and breakfasts can provide interpretation through a brochure that outlines best places to see local wildlife or a walking tour of downtown historical sites. Hotels may choose to develop an interpretative card left in each room that explains its green practices and how guests can participate further.

If you decide to deliver interpretation through formal or informal oral presentations, consider developing an interpretative script your guides can follow. Business owners unfamiliar with interpretative scripts may find colleges or universities a source of help. Professors can sometimes develop class projects to build student skills and develop interpretative resources for a business in the process. In the sidebar Interpretation and Standards for a Continent, the International Association of Antarctica Tour Operators shows how consistent interpretation standards ensure greater awareness and better behavior by visitors in sensitive environments.

Evaluation Methods

Once you have developed your interpretative methods, create opportunities to evaluate them. Ask customers whether they took advantage of your interpretative opportunities. Add questions to your customer service surveys or ask visitors at the end of a tour whether there were topics they would have liked more information on. Use this information to keep your interpretation fresh.

As conditions change or new opportunities arise, plan to bring these elements into your interpretation. If a group spots a rare bird or sees a comet, the guide should be able to work these events into the trip experience. Customer preferences should also guide changes to your interpretative plan. If people enjoy your discussions on specific plant species but would like more information on environmental or social issues in your area, add these topics to future trips.

PROBLEMS IN CUSTOMER SERVICE

If you follow the steps in the previous sections, you will be well on the way to providing good customer service. However, if you have implemented a customer service system and are still receiving a

---

Interpretation and Standards for a Continent

Antarctica is a continent owned by no country. The Antarctic Treaty, an agreement signed by 50 countries, provides for cooperative governance among nations for peaceful purposes and scientific investigation.

More than 100 tourism operators are voluntary members of the International Association of Antarctica Tour Operators (IAATO), an industry group that, according to its website, has resolved to set the highest possible tourism operating standards in its effort to protect Antarctica.

An important part of the group's activities is the interpretation it supports among members. Visitors can find guidelines on the website for wildlife watching. Tour operators can access various interpretative materials to convey key messages. For example, preventing the introduction of invasive or nonnative species is a high priority for responsible tourism operators. IAATO has developed posters outlining guidelines for decontaminating boots, clothing, and equipment. Tour operators can use IAATO PowerPoint slides to explain decontamination protocol and environmental issues. After cleaning their gear and attending an interpretative session, visitors are asked to sign a biosecurity declaration, saying they have attended the interpretative sessions and have taken the necessary steps to comply with IAATO guidelines.

These measures may seem extreme to tour operators in other environments, but the consistency in the interpretative message to over 30,000 visitors a year, is a best practice that tour operators in other destinations could adapt for their sustainability objectives.

lot of complaints, the problem can often be traced to one of the following:

- Owner or managers did not start with a clear vision of customer service.
- Owner or managers started with a clear customer service vision but did not turn that into easy-to-understand and measurable performance standards.
- Owner or managers have rewarded employees for doing something that does not result in good customer service.

If you do not have a clear vision of good customer service, you will not be able to develop effective policies, procedures, and standards. It will be difficult to decide what training is required and what performance to reward when it occurs. If your customer service is not meeting your expectations, look at the business practices of tourism companies you admire. Think about what makes them attractive and how their customer service is different from your own. Perhaps they include a video in their pretrip information or they use more guides than you do. Seeing specific evidence of good service will help you clarify your own vision, identify your shortcomings, and make corrections.

If you have a clear vision of customer service but are having problems delivering it, make sure you have clear performance standards. To be effective, you need standards that state specifically what good customer service means. Some things may seem obvious, but if you are dealing with other employees, you need them to understand what is expected of them. Having a guide arrive before tour participants at the staging point may seem to be an obvious standard of customer service behavior, but other people's perception of time or organizational skills may result in guides arriving late. Some organizations specify that a guide will arrive 15 minutes before the trip start time to finalize arrangements and welcome early arrivals. Reviewing your processes for weak points and setting standards or procedure lists will often resolve problems.

Sometimes customer service slips because managers inadvertently reward the wrong performance. If an employee takes extra time to talk to an unhappy customer, but you reprimand him or her for being slow in getting to other tasks, your actions tell the employee that productivity is more important than customer service. In the final weeks of your season, after many guests have asked the same simple question (for example, why

can't I feed the wildlife?) and guides have given the same interpretative talk many, many times, it is easy for customer service to slide. Your guides may be tired and their sense of humor stretched thin and, if they think no one notices, they may be tempted to cut corners. If you do not comment or correct the situation, staff may think it is okay to lower the level of customer service. Do not let this happen. Let employees know you expect the standards to be met for the full season but that you understand the demands of the job and appreciate the effort they put in. To maintain the desired customer service levels, perhaps you can plan a special end-of-the-season party to recognize their hard work during the season.

In situations where your customer service system has failed, customers will be unhappy. If you are lucky they will take the time to complain. Many will simply take their business to your competition. Although no one wants to talk to angry or unhappy customers, it can be an opportunity to improve your tourism experience and strengthen your customer relationships.

Provide customer feedback forms to gather information. Read the comments on social media channels. Listen to complaints on the trip. Many customers get more upset when they feel their concerns are ignored. Listen intently and ask what would make the situation better. Often your customers will help you solve the situation by telling you what they need to feel satisfied. If it is within your power to grant, you may want to offer that compensation. If you cannot, at least let the customer know his or her complaint has been heard and steps will be taken to avoid future problems. Provide your staff training in dealing with problems in customer service.

QUALIFYING CUSTOMERS

Sustainable tourism businesses offering tours face a unique facet of customer service that is not found in other businesses. That is **qualifying customers**, ensuring your customers have the proper training, physical condition, and mental attitude to complete a tourism experience safely and without undue stress. Qualifying is done for several reasons. One is safety. You want people to select trips that match their physical conditioning and comfort level. In this way they do not endanger themselves or the group and they enjoy the experience. Part of the qualifying procedure can also involve educating the client about the risks

Qualify your customers to ensure they can handle the physical and emotional demands of the tour.

inherent in the activity they are undertaking. This may absolve the company of liability should an accident occur. An equally important reason for qualifying clients is to make sure people select a trip that matches their interests. This will enhance group dynamics and give you a better chance of meeting customer expectations and delivering great customer service.

It can be difficult to qualify customers correctly. People can either overestimate or underestimate their physical condition. Their idea of a nature experience may not be yours. To prevent negative feelings, spend time learning about your prospective customers. In the competitive world of tourism marketing, the temptation is to book every person who calls. By understanding a little about the customer's interests and lifestyle, you can help him or her choose the best trip. In some cases, that may be with your competitor!

It is also important to assess a person's physical ability to participate on a tour. Focus on identifying health conditions that may cause problems on the trip. Specific questions about physical conditioning, preexisting medical conditions, special medications, and severe allergies will help match people to a particular tour or activity level. Questions should be standardized and asked of all prospective clients. While someone might look healthy, a bad back or a severe allergy to bee stings will require special preparation by your company

to meet his or her needs. The following are questions you may want to ask:

- Do you understand the risk associated with (*activity*)?
- Is there a reason you may not be able to complete the tour?
- You understand that if you were unable to keep pace with the group, we would need to (*return to starting destination, radio for an airlift out of the backcountry, and so on*)?

Standardized questionnaires help avoid violating legislation that prohibits discrimination against the elderly or people with disabilities. On a more opportunistic note, if you find several prospective clients you are unable to accommodate for health reasons, you may be missing a marketing opportunity to provide an alternative experience.

A quick way to gather the information to assess the interest level of prospective clients is to ask questions about their previous vacations or recreational activities. Someone who is active in outdoor sports or who has previously taken camping or adventure trips is likely to be a good fit for an ecotourism or nature-based experience. People who have never been active in outdoor recreation or who have traveled very little should not be ruled out; however, you have an obligation to spend more time explaining the tour components and the activity levels.

SUMMARY

Customer service is a critical component of every sustainable tourism experience. As a manager you will spend much of your time training staff and monitoring customer service delivery and dealing with customer service complaints. Life will be easier if you approach customer service with a system of policies, standards, and procedures that can be made part of each employee's daily routine. Hiring the right staff will be an important part of your customer service success. In the next chapter you will learn more about recruiting the employees you need.

|||||||||||||||||||||||||| GLOSSARY ||||||||||||||||||||||||||||||||

customer service—The ability to meet customers' real and perceived needs through the actions of staff and suppliers.

customer service process—A series of actions leading to an expected outcome, in which you document your policies and procedures, train employees to deliver customer service, follow up to ensure the process works, and recognize performance.

interpretation—Communication that makes connections between the audience's interest and the meanings inherent in the resource.

interpretative theme—A key point or message about a topic that an interpreter wishes to convey to the audience.

policies—Broad, guiding principles for a business function.

procedure—A detailed description of how something is to be done.

qualifying customers—Ensuring customers have the proper training, physical condition, and mental attitude to complete a tourism experience safely and without undue stress.

standards—the goal or result expected from the procedure.

||||||||||||||||||||| REVIEW QUESTIONS |||||||||||||||||

1. What is customer service? Why is good customer service important for the success of a sustainable tourism organization?

2. List seven elements of a customer service process and briefly describe each.

3. How can interpretation enhance customer service for a sustainable tourism organization that offers natural or cultural attractions?

4. Identify three possible causes for problems in customer service. How might these be avoided?

5. Explain how qualifying customers can prevent problems in customer service.

|||||||||||||||||||||| VIDEO CASE STUDY ||||||||||||||||||

Visit the web resource to watch the video "Elkhorn Slough: Enhancing Experiences With Customer Service." After watching the video, answer the following questions:

1. First impressions are important to good customer service. What steps does Whisper Charters take to make a good first impression?

2. Many people visiting Elkhorn Slough choose to forgo guides and tour by themselves. How is Whisper Charters using customer service to create a competitive advantage and encourage people to take a guided tour?

3. What evidence did you see that the owner of Whisper Charters understands his customers' needs? How do you think he gathered this information?

4. List the steps you think Whisper Charters must take to maintain great customer service as it expands to more boats or more captains. What are problems small-business owners might face as they try to convey their approach to new staff?

5. Interpretation is an important part of customer service at Whisper Charters. How difficult do you think it would be to find more people qualified to captain a boat and deliver great interpretation? Describe other situations in which sustainable tourism organizations might need staff with an unusual combination of skills.

|||||||||||||||| YOUR BUSINESS PLAN |||||||||||||||||

At this point you can fill in more details on the operations section of your business plan. Start to consider the number of staff you will need and the skills they must have to deliver the desired level of customer service. The next chapter will discuss staffing in more detail, but for now, make notes on the staff and training you will need to meet your customer service goals. It is unlikely you will have large financial incentives to ensure customer service standards are met, so think of other ways you can deliver results. Perhaps you can provide intangible recognition for good service, such as publicly acknowledging good behavior, or maybe you will formalize many of your procedures to ensure consistency.

1. Describe the personal characteristics you will seek in staff to deliver customer service at your desired level. Distinguish between elements you must hire, such as a winning smile, versus elements you can train, such as the best way to answer the phone.

2. List areas where you expect your customer service to be above average. List areas where you may experience weakness. Identify strategies for turning your best customer service into a competitive advantage and minimizing your limitations.

3. Brainstorm five ways you can reward your staff that incur little financial cost and situations where you might use each.

|||||||||||||||||||||||| REFERENCE |||||||||||||||||||||||

Entrepreneur. 2008. Sam Walton: Bargain basement billionaire. Oct. 8. www.entrepreneur.com/article/197560.

11

HIRING AND RETAINING STAFF

LEARNING OUTCOMES

After reading this chapter, you will be able to do the following:

- Hire the right person for the job

- Identify the training required to overcome skill gaps or ensure service consistency

- Understand why policies in human resources are important

- Develop techniques to reduce employee turnover

Many sustainable tourism businesses are very small and have just one employee: the owner, who also serves as manager. Other businesses employ a handful of people, while a few companies may have several hundred employees during peak seasons. If you have employees, you will often find hiring staff a challenge. The process can be uncomfortable, and if the wrong person is hired, it is expensive to replace the employee and restore goodwill if it was lost as a result of the employee's behavior. As an employer, you are responsible for employees' actions unless you can show otherwise. Given that many nature tourism employees lead groups into wilderness settings, the potential exists for physical harm and associated lawsuits if guides are not good at their job; therefore, hiring the right person is critical.

HIRING

Hiring new staff should follow a logical order. The first task is identifying what work the new employee will perform. Many owners of sustainable tourism businesses have deep knowledge of natural history or culture, or are skilled at outdoor activities. These skills are important, but many others are needed for success. Perhaps you need help with sales or bookkeeping or social media and marketing. Group similar tasks and estimate the amount of time required to perform each. This will help you decide whether your new hire should be full time or part time, permanent or seasonal.

Next write a job description similar to the example in figure 11.1, outlining work to be done, performance standards, and level of supervision expected. Many small companies do not develop job descriptions, but a list of duties can clarify qualities and experience required of employees. This makes it easier to recruit and interview. It also helps ensure employers do not discriminate against applicants because job duties and skill requirements are clearly described.

Job descriptions can also point out holes in your organization, those tasks no one gets around

Figure 11.1
Sample Job Description

Job title: River guide
Job description: To lead one-day and overnight rafting trips

Job Duties

- Provide input into trip planning and packaging
- Assess river conditions before trip launch and alter routes or launch points accordingly
- Ensure proper equipment is available and in good repair
- Provide safety briefing to all trip participants
- Guide rafting trips incorporating historical and natural interpretation as conditions permit
- Coordinate meal times and camp setup
- Educate trip participants on low-impact travel techniques
- Monitor group dynamics and provide leadership, as required, to ensure the safety and enjoyment of all guests
- Provide social media updates before and after the trip

Requirements

- Three years of rafting experience
- Wilderness first aid certification
- Wilderness survival training
- Natural history knowledge
- Familiarity with social media platforms

Attributes

- Strong interpersonal and leadership skills
- Ability to remain calm in times of crisis
- Responsible

to, such as prospecting corporate customers for incentive tours. These gaps may represent missed revenue opportunities. Identifying tasks that are not being completed allows you to assess the value of adding a new employee.

Once you have developed your job description, you can start advertising the position. You may place ads in newspapers or on your website. Social media can also be a great place to find job applicants. If you are located close to a large urban center or popular recreation area, chances are there will be candidates who will meet your requirements. In other situations, you will find a limited pool of qualified employees, especially guides, in the local population. If your sustainable tourism business operates in

remote areas or in developing countries, finding qualified employees can be especially difficult. One of the global sustainable tourism criteria is to hire local people whenever possible to benefit the community. This poses a dilemma: do you bring in experienced people to get your product to market quickly, or do you develop guides and other personnel locally?

Each situation requires its own solution. Some organizations hire experienced outside guides and hire local people for entry-level positions, training them over time to take senior jobs. An alternative is to establish an intensive training program and train local people to be guides from the beginning. This takes more money and effort to set up but has the advantage of providing more economic and social benefits to the community.

You might reorganize job tasks to attract non-traditional labor sources by offering flexible hours. Seniors might enjoy working at your business if they still have lots of leisure time for their other interests. You can also structure your business so less labor is required. For example, if you are planning a food service establishment as part of your business, it could be a cafeteria instead of a full-service restaurant. Or perhaps, you will make food preparation one of the guest activities. Diamond Willow Artisan Retreat, in the foothills of the Rocky Mountains, offers pizza-making parties as evening entertainment. It is a great team builder and reduces staffing needs.

Another special challenge for sustainable tourism businesses is finding people with both interpretation and customer service skills for guide positions. You may find someone with a biology degree or certification in paddling, but he or she is not trained in interpretation or familiar with customer service. To provide a high-quality tour, your staff needs training in guiding, interpretation, and customer service. If your guides are taking casual bird-watchers on a tour, you want to ensure they provide interpretation on the habitat and behaviors of birds and have stories planned for times when a species is not visible. Or you want guides who know when not to talk as Melanie Elliott describes in the sidebar The Role of a Good Guide.

Interviewing Techniques

Conducting a fair interview is important for making sure you hire the right person and avoid legal problems. You do not want to engage in discriminatory behavior—intentional or not—and if a customer were injured in an accident, you want to prove that you hired the right person for the job. You may want to supplement your knowledge of hiring techniques with additional reading; however, the steps that merit special attention for sustainable tourism businesses are as follows:

- Use standard interview questions
- Include behavioral interview questions to assess personal attributes
- Perform a skills test
- Conduct a peer interview
- Avoid interview errors
- Make reference checks
- Verify qualifications

Use Standard Interview Questions

Standard interview questions are questions used in every interview and asked of each applicant in the same order. They establish a basis on which to compare candidates' education, experience, skills, and training. It can be helpful to develop a range of acceptable answers in advance and give

The Role of a Good Guide

As program manager for the University of Saskatchewan's Ecological and Travel program, Melanie Elliott has been leading trips for years. She understands that good guides sometimes have to follow their hunches and depart from conventional guiding techniques. In her own words, Melanie describes what happened when she challenged a group to focus on being instead of doing:

"A few years ago I led a group on an eastern, Red Centre tour of Australia. And yes I'm the yoga/meditation type but never broached it or forced it on clients. We were at a sacred water hole in the Red Centre, a springs, and it just seemed too neat to hike in, then out. So I suggested we find a spot away from each other and just sit for 15-20 minutes. One of the men said

"this isn't some new age stuff is it?" and though I'd hoped to have time to meditate, I just wanted them to sit and be quiet, stop the friendly banter. Quickly thought of Ernest Thompson Seton and explained that a nonactive way to watch wildlife was just to sit. He seemed to accept this. It was lovely. You could hear the birds, wind in leaves, so peaceful and got some sense of why the Aborigines viewed it as a sacred water hole. At the end of 15 minutes Rock Wallabies came out of some crevices in the rocks and moved around, grooming and looking for food. Because everyone was still and quiet we had a marvelous wildlife encounter that we surely would have missed if we were just walking and talking."

Courtesy of Melanie Elliott.

each a numerical rating. By developing questions and answers in advance, subjectivity can be reduced considerably. Candidates are asked the same questions and their answers are numerically scored. This prevents the common error of jumping to conclusions or hiring people because they are similar to the interviewer. It protects business owners legally as well, because the interviewing process can be demonstrated to be fair.

When developing your list of questions, be sure to probe for specific experience in previous jobs. Just because someone has been associated with a project or a special activity, do not assume the interviewee played a major role or has a particular skill.

Keep in mind employment and disabilities legislation precludes you from asking personal information that could be interpreted as discriminatory. The items that are often off limits include age, marital status, ethnic background, religion, family, disabilities, sexual orientation, and criminal record. Instead of asking interviewees whether they have a physical disability, ask whether they can perform the requirements of the job. If you explain that the job requires them to hike three hours a day and they state that there is no reason why they cannot meet this requirement, you have some legal protection. If later they are unable to perform this task, you have grounds for dismissal because they gave you assurance they were able to perform the job duties.

Include Behavior Interview Questions

Behavior interviews are based on the premise that the best predictor of future behavior is past behavior and use questions based on past behavior to assess work experience and personal attributes, including initiative and leadership. If you want evidence that someone will deal well with customers, look for situations where they have demonstrated that skill in the past. This does not mean that someone has to have experience in exactly the same job; what you are looking for is an indication that in a similar situation, whether it is volunteer work, other jobs, or school activities, the candidate has worked well with customers.

An example of a behavior interview question might be "Working as a hiking guide in remote situations can require you to resolve group conflicts without assistance from other people. Can you describe a situation where you resolved a conflict between customers in an isolated situation and what actions you took?" By asking for specific examples from the past, you have an idea of how

that person will react in a specific situation. This is different from interviews where you ask a theoretical question such as "Can you describe what actions you *would* take if you *were* faced with a conflict between customers in an isolated situation?" The answer may not reflect how someone has actually behaved. In addition, you can also standardize behavior interview questions by anticipating a range of acceptable answers and assigning corresponding numerical scores.

Perform a Skills Test

A **skills test** is asking a job applicant to demonstrate a skill required on the job as part of the interview process. If you are hiring a river guide, you might ask a potential candidate to demonstrate paddle skills or perform public speaking. If you are trying to assess applicants' communication skills, you might give them an unusual object from nature and ask them to give a short, impromptu interpretative presentation. You will get a quick idea of their speaking skills and their ability to think on their feet.

You will also want to verify licenses and educational qualifications by contacting the issuing agency. But your best assessment of personal attributes, such as interpersonal or communication competencies or ability to perform job-specific skills, comes from a skills test.

Conduct Peer Interviews

If you have a small, closely knit team, it is important for new staff members to be accepted by everyone. Including key staff members on the interview panel helps select candidates that fit the organization's culture. People who score well on the initial interview could then be invited to an interview conducted by staff members. This interview can provide additional information on the candidates and ease their acceptance into the group. Peer interviews need to follow the same standards of interviewing mentioned earlier. To find out how you would fare if you were asked to do a peer interview, take the Ecochallenge "What Would You Ask?"

Avoid Interview Errors

If you have a small pool of job candidates, you may be tempted to select one who does not meet your basic requirements rather than pursue additional candidates. You may also make a snap judgment about a candidate without going through a complete interview. You may place too much emphasis on nonverbal behavior; this can be especially problematic when hiring from cultures other than your own. For example, western culture values eye contact; other cultures may consider this disrespectful.

Most people will find they are more comfortable with people they perceive as similar to themselves. This preference can translate into hiring someone who has your skills and personality traits. If you are a capable fishing guide, what you require may not be a person knowledgeable about fish, but someone who knows how to sell your catch-and-release fishing trips. Think of your weaknesses and hire people who can compensate for them.

Check References

Take time to check the candidates' references. A few phone calls can confirm your impressions or smash them to bits. Ask questions that give you the information you want but do not violate employment and disability laws. Assess the person providing the reference. If his or her comments sound reserved or cautious, ask more questions to find out whether there are behavior limitations you need to consider.

You may find that some companies will not provide references over the telephone. Legal action by employees who received bad references without proper documentation has led companies to limit references to confirmation of employee position and dates of employment. In these cases, you will

have to rely on information from the interview process or consider social media. Before you use social media to do background checks, make sure you are aware of the legal implications.

Employers may turn to social media for background information on potential new employees, but be sure to stay within legal hiring guidelines. The safest way to get information from social media is to look at a candidate's public postings; however, the timing can be important. You may discover a candidate's age or family situation by looking at their social media profile, but you cannot let this information affect the questions you ask. According to the recruiting and hiring website Monster.com, "once you review a candidate's online profile, a court will assume you are aware of that person's protected characteristics." The site suggests that if you are going to use social media in your hiring process, wait until after you have met the candidate to view their social media postings. David Baffa, a labor and employment lawyer, suggests that you conduct the same searches on each candidate and at the same time in the selection process, and if you see something that concerns you, take screen shots for your records (Berkowitz 2014).

Verify Qualifications

When specific qualifications are a prerequisite for good job performance, verify that applicants hold the qualifications they claim. Transcripts will confirm degrees or diplomas. Licenses or special training can be verified by contacting the licensing or delivery agency. Protecting your tourism business from legal risk requires you to hire people who are properly qualified. If an accident were to occur, you would not want to be found negligent because you had not taken reasonable steps to ensure your employees were licensed and trained for the job.

Using Contract Help

Higher payroll taxes and associated costs have made hiring employees an expensive process. Small and medium-size tourism businesses are often seasonal or operating below capacity. If hiring full-time staff is a financial commitment you cannot afford, you might consider engaging a contractor to deliver a service such as interpretation, sales, or catering, rather than hiring an employee.

Contracting services can remove some administrative burden and costs such as payroll taxes. However, caution is required. With the boom in self-employment, there are more and more people working in businesses who may not be actual employees. The contractor must be a valid business and not an employee presenting himself as a business. A problem arises when there is an employer–employee relationship but the employee is invoicing the company as a separate entity. While people may prefer to be treated as a contractor for tax reasons, the onus is on the employer to ensure that an employer–employee relationship does not exist.

In the United States, the Internal Revenue Service says someone is an independent contractor if the payer controls or directs the result of the work, not what will be done and how it will be done (IRS 2014). Revenue Canada has similar rules and will look for evidence of an employer–employee relationship. This includes the ability to direct to a large extent the activities of the person doing the work. Employers need to determine whether they are hiring a contractor rather than an employee. The following are characteristics of contractors:

- Has no fixed hours or work
- Is free to work for other companies while performing work for your company
- Hires their own assistants if required
- Controls their day-to-day activities (i.e., how the work will be done and timing of activities)
- Is employed for a specified time to complete a specified task
- Does not use company equipment or a company office

If an employer is found to have treated an employee as a contractor, the employer may be liable to pay all employee withholdings and the associated employer portions, including various penalties and interest payments. Because fines can run in the thousands of dollars, it pays to review the employer–worker relationship carefully. Check employment and income tax legislation where you will be operating. And you must ensure that contractors acting on your behalf meet your standards for customer service and safety management because you could be liable for their actions.

TRAINING

If you are unable to hire people with all the skills you require, you may need to provide **training**, a transfer of specific skills and behaviors to build proficiencies. There are other reasons you will want to make training part of your human resource activities. You may need regular training to keep your staff up to date on research, local events, or skills. Adequate training can also be a safeguard to prevent accidents and minimize liability. For an example of an organization using training to ensure they have the right person for the job, watch the video "Staffing for Success" in the web resource.

Areas where a sustainable tourism business might need training for its staff include the following:

- Equipment operation (e.g., boats, vehicles, radios)

Training remedies skill deficiencies and imparts knowledge on new trends and research.

- Safety
- First aid
- Natural history and conservation research
- Local culture and history
- Code of ethics and sustainable travel behaviors for guides and travelers
- Customer service
- Leadership and conflict-resolution skills

Training is not the solution for all performance deficiencies, however. Before you put time and money into training, ask yourself whether the employee cannot do the task or does not want to do the task. A deficiency in ability requires training; a lack of motivation requires goal setting, feedback, and recognition. To establish regular training in your sustainable tourism business, you will want to follow the process outlined in the following sections.

Establish Objectives

Determine what you want employees to be able to do when training is complete. Be specific. Do not say you want to develop great customer service. You need a measurable, observable activity. A training objective for the staff at an eco-lodge might be "To learn to clean a room within one hour while adhering to sustainable tourism practices as set out in the company's environmental policy."

Complete a Needs Assessment

Once you know what you want staff to do, complete a needs assessment to identify the training **baseline**, the starting point used as a basis for comparison. In a training needs assessment, this will be the skill level of your current employees and skill gaps you want to remedy through training. You should also identify barriers to training, such as distance to training facilities, so you can compensate and make your training more effective. For example, if some staff are working in a language that is not their native tongue, you may need to allow more time for training or include language interpreters in your training courses.

In a larger organization, a needs assessment may require the use of a standardized survey tool. In a smaller company, the owner or manager can probably gather this information through informal meetings. Your needs assessment might reveal that not all employees need immediate training; some may have the skills they currently need and

will require only a refresher course every other year. Once you have the results of your needs assessment, you can select the best delivery methods for your training.

Select Methods for Training Delivery

Training can be delivered in many ways. It may be on the job with an experienced person training a less-experienced person, or it can be in the form of seminars or courses held in house or off-site. Some institutions offer courses online, and many sustainable tourism organizations offer webinars that provide inexpensive training regardless of your location. Colleges and technical schools often offer continuing education courses that are relevant for tourism professionals, such as guiding, first aid, customer service, and marketing. Asking experienced staff or outside experts to speak at staff meetings can provide training in your ongoing operations at a very low cost.

The following are methods that you are most likely to use as a sustainable tourism business owner or manager:

- On-the-job training
- Job-instruction training
- Seminars
- Online courses
- Informal presentations
- Training videos

Each of these is described in the following sections.

On-the-Job Training

On-the-job training is the most common technique and involves a knowledgeable employee teaching a new or inexperienced employee skills or behaviors. It is usually informal and costs are limited to the time required by both parties. Select people who have good training skills, not necessarily the most experienced. If you are training a new guide, assign training to a guide who provides interesting, enjoyable tours and can articulate how a successful trip is conducted. Because people will also be transferring values and ethics, select employees who present your company in the best possible light. You do not want someone who circumvents your policies or procedures to train your new staff, or you will end up with a team of people delivering your customer service in a manner you had not intended. Where commitment to environmental sensitivity is a business foundation, the transfer of values through policies and procedures is important.

Job-Instruction Training

Job-instruction training uses a list of written sequential task descriptions. A well-known example of job-instruction training is the checklist that pilots use before each flight to ensure the plane is ready to fly. Job-instruction training works well for jobs that are task orientated because it breaks the job into functions and describes what is to be done for each step. This type of training can be helpful for people familiar with technical skills, but not familiar with operating in an environmentally sensitive location, for example, a camp cook. Job checklists are relatively easy to prepare, provide consistent instruction, and do not require as much time from other employees to deliver training. The disadvantages are that you cannot ensure people use them, and in some cases, they may not understand the instructions.

Seminars

Training seminars and workshops gather employees in a structured setting where an expert provides concise, organized information on specific skills or behaviors. Training seminars usually include a variety of techniques, such as role playing, lectures, discussion, and case studies.

If your organization has only a few employees, it can be cost effective to use external resources for training seminars. Tourism industry associations, chambers of commerce, and universities may offer training appropriate for sustainable tourism businesses. Larger organizations may develop their own training or use a combination of in-house and external training (see the sidebar Training for Interpretation and Research). Select training techniques for their suitability in transferring skills. For example, role playing is helpful in training people in customer service skills such as dealing with dissatisfied customers.

Online Courses and Webinars

Online courses and webinars can be attractive to businesses that operate in remote areas or have little money available for travel. Check with tourism industry associations and regional colleges and universities for upcoming offerings. You might also be able to find older presentations online or as podcasts that you can use for training.

Informal Presentations

Ongoing training can be accomplished through informal but regular presentations at staff meetings. Asking staff who have special skills or guest experts to speak are great supplements to formal training. A local park ranger or historian can provide interesting insights on natural or historic points of interest. A staff member with a knack for photography can help guides understand how to situate guests so they can take photographs under the best lighting conditions.

Training Videos

Many training videos are now available online, some at no cost on websites like YouTube. Training videos are helpful in explaining routine tasks or

Training for Interpretation and Research

Pacific Whale Foundation (PWF) is a nonprofit organization located on the Hawaiian island of Maui; its mandate is to protect the oceans through science and advocacy. Established in 1980 by researcher Greg Kaufman, the organization has grown into one of Maui's largest whale-watching organizations with over 3.5 million people taking its eco-adventure tours since its inception.

The guides on these trips are highly trained naturalists. All are graduates of marine biology, environmental education, or related science majors. They undergo more than 100 hours of PWF training in lifeguard skills and first aid, seamanship, Hawaiian culture and history, and marine mammal research. In addition, several employees have participated in the National Association for Interpretation (NAI) program to achieve recognition as certified interpretative guides (Pacific Whale Foundation 2012).

The combination of in-house training and certification by an industry association means visitors have access to expert knowledge on trips. And staff are able to participate in ongoing professional development.

illustrating concepts such as the need for sustainable business practices. Check with training companies, tourism associations, educational institutions, and special tourism education councils for videos on topics relevant to your employees.

Deliver the Training

The actual delivery of your training should be scheduled as close as possible to the employee's need for it. Shortly before the season starts would be a good time to provide customer service training or train staff in low-impact camping techniques. The effectiveness of training is diminished when the skill is not used. Critical skills that are seldom used, such as first aid or search and rescue, need to be kept current through regular practice sessions or drills each season.

Evaluate Training

At the simplest level, evaluation consists of asking people for their reactions to a training program. This will usually tell you whether they enjoyed the experience. However, that provides no indication of whether they actually learned from the program. You may want to include a test at the conclusion of training to see whether participants learned the desired skills or behaviors. If they have learned the skill during training, track how effectively the person transferred these skills to the job. Finally, ask yourself whether the training brought the result you were seeking. After customer service training, you might see whether feedback from customers is more positive or whether the number of repeat customers increased. If you are evaluating safety training, look at whether the number or severity of accidents has decreased.

POLICIES IN HUMAN RESOURCES

In addition to hiring the right employees and training them on core skills, you need to ensure you have policies in human resources that make your business a good place to work, present your business professionally to customers, and protect your company against lawsuits in employment disputes or accidents. As explained in the previous chapter, a policy is a broad, guiding principle for a business function. The following are areas you might want to address through policies:

- Sick leave
- Rates of pay
- Uniforms and dress codes
- Education, reimbursement, and payment
- Hiring practices
- Termination procedures
- Benefits
- Work hours
- Safety

This is a basic list; there are many other areas where you could develop policies. Policies do not have to be documented in great detail, but as your business grows, so will your need to develop and document your methods and principles. If you only have one employee, you may not need a policy on dress code, but as you add employees you may start to outline a policy that says employees will wear clothing with the company logo when dealing with customers. Guidelines on hairstyles and body markings can be difficult to develop, so you may want to get input from employees or consult with other business owners. For more samples of policies in human resources, search the Internet for policies you can adapt for your business.

MANAGING TURNOVER

Tourism in North America is an industry characterized by high turnover. A 2005 study by Statistics Canada found that turnover for all Canadian industries was 19.9 percent, but within tourism it was much higher at 37.7 percent (CTHRC 2011). Low wages and unusual work hours cause many to leave. Others enter the industry to gain experience or earn income to pursue other goals. Staff turnover is a cost that most businesses do not like to absorb. Losing employees is disruptive to business operations and adds to recruiting and training expenses. Ensure your policies help you retain as many trained staff as possible.

Many people may want to work for your company because they like the lifestyle that often accompanies tourism careers. The reality is they must still make enough money to support a base standard of living, and small tourism businesses are often not able to provide full-time or year-round work. This can mean staff will work part time at other businesses, which may reduce your scheduling flexibility, or it could mean that staff will be hired away. To avoid losing your staff, you might look at policies that accomplish the following:

- Provide more earning opportunities—If you have a policy of pursuing extra business opportunities in shoulder seasons, you can provide staff with longer employment and retain your best staff. You might consider tours that focus on the fall foliage, visit cranberry festivals, or observe fall or spring migrations.

- Provide experience in a wider range of business activities—Many people realize that a long-term career in the ecotourism or adventure travel industry often leads to self-employment. You can keep employees longer if your policies promote training for senior staff in a wide range of business skills such as marketing, trip planning, and training.

- Recognize employee efforts—Many people leave a company because of a lack of recognition from their employer. You may not be able to pay staff an exceptional wage; however, you can "pay" them with a large amount of recognition. Create a policy to deliver regular nonfinancial performance recognition. Catching people doing something right and showing your appreciation can go a long way toward motivating people to go the extra mile and maintaining a stable work force. Tourism businesses are also blessed with the opportunity to offer in-kind products or services as a staff reward. Allowing employees to bring family or friends on a tour may not add much to your costs but can be a powerful reward. Some tourism companies swap products among themselves to reward employees for great customer service.

These policies can help you reduce turnover. You may also find it helpful to stress the sustainability initiatives you are undertaking. People who enter the field of sustainable tourism often believe a career in this field can make a difference. The emotional appeal of a sustainable tourism business and the chance to combine conservation and business principles for the benefit of employees and environments can garner employee loyalty that may not exist in other tourism organizations.

SUMMARY

Although they do not appear on your company's balance sheet, trained and talented staff are your biggest asset. To build the workforce your sustainable tourism business needs, identify your requirements with detailed job descriptions and hire the people with the necessary characteristics, experience, and skill. Often further training is required to ensure staff can do the job in the way you want. Training is a large investment for your organization, so take time to identify your needs and gather baseline information. Take advantage of new technology that allows you to deliver training frequently and cost effectively. And once you have created a good workforce, protect your investment by developing policies in human resources that will make your company a great place to work and keep employees from leaving.

|||||||||||||||||||||||||||| GLOSSARY ||||||||||||||||||||||||||||

behavior interviews—Interviews based on the premise that the best predictor of future behavior is past behavior. They use questions based on past behavior to assess work experience and personal attributes including initiative and leadership.

baseline—The starting point used as a basis for comparison.

job-instruction training—Training that breaks the job into functions and describes what is to be done for each step.

skills test—Asking a job applicant to demonstrate a skill required on the job as part of the interview process.

standard interview questions—Questions used in every interview and asked of each applicant in the same order. They establish a basis on which to compare candidates' education, experience, skills, and training.

training—A process of transferring specific skills and behaviors to employees.

|||||||||||||||| REVIEW QUESTIONS ||||||||||||||||

1. Explain how writing a job description helps a sustainable tourism organization hire the right people.

2. Identify seven steps in the interview process.

3. Describe two reasons a business might undertake staff training.

4. Identify three methods of delivering training and the advantages and disadvantages of each.

5. What is a policy in human resources? Why are policies important to tourism businesses?

6. Do you believe staff turnover is a problem for sustainable tourism organizations? What steps can an organization take to reduce turnover?

|||||||||||||||| VIDEO CASE STUDY ||||||||||||||||

Visit the web resource to watch the video "Staffing for Success." After watching the video, answer the following questions.

1. What roles do paid and volunteer staff undertake at the Rowe Sanctuary in Nebraska?

2. Explain the steps Rowe Sanctuary takes to hire the right people for the job. Describe differences you think there might be between the processes for finding people applying for paid work versus volunteer jobs.

3. Identify the ways the Rowe Sanctuary uses training to build skills in its volunteer staff. Comment on whether you think these techniques could be used by other sustainable tourism organizations.

4. How might volunteer workers help a sustainable tourism organization achieve its goals? What is Rowe Sanctuary able to accomplish with volunteers that it might not be able to if it relied only on paid staff?

5. Describe the incentives that would be important to you if you were to volunteer at a sustainable tourism organization. Do you see evidence of these rewards at Rowe Sanctuary?

|||||||||||||||| YOUR BUSINESS PLAN ||||||||||||||||

Continue completing the sections of the workbook that pertain to staffing. Based on what you learned in this chapter, identify the workforce you need and the training, policies, and compensation you want. Ensure your financial forecasts have sufficient funds to hire the number of staff needed to meet your marketing and customer service objectives and that you have allocated enough money for training and hiring functions.

1. Develop a list of interview questions you will use for key positions. Explain how they will help select the right person for the job.

2. Delineate work to be done by employees and by contractors. Describe the reasons for contracting out functions. Consider including this information in the financial section of your business plan.

3. List the training methods your organization will use and the estimated annual cost. Include these figures in your operating budget.

|||||||||||||||||||||||||||| REFERENCES |||||||||||||||||||||||||||||

Berkowitz, M. 2014. Social media recruiting: Understand the legal guidelines. http://hiring. monster.com/hr/hr-best-practices/recruiting-hiring-advice/acquiring-job-candidates/so-cial-media-recruiting-guidelines.aspx.

Canadian Tourism Human Resource Council. 2011. Workplace matters panel report: Turn-over in the tourism sector. http://cthrc.ca/en/research_publications/~/media/Files/ CTHRC/Home/research_publications/workplace_matters/PanelReport_Turnover_ CurrentEN.ashx.

Internal Revenue Service. 2014. Independent contractor defined. www.irs.gov/Businesses/ Small-Businesses-&-Self-Employed/Independent-Contractor-Defined.

Pacific Whale Foundation. 2012. PWF naturalists complete NAI training. March 6. www.pacificwhale.org/content/pwf-naturalists-complete-nai-training.

MANAGING BUSINESS RISK

After reading this chapter, you will be able to do the following:

- Identify where risk originates

- Understand why legal liability should be limited for business success

- Examine areas that may require insurance

- Explain how safety management can reduce accident risk

- Describe how risk management can help protect assets

ustainable tourism can take travelers to foreign lands and out-of-the way places closer to home. Many activities occur outdoors where nature is at her best, but severe weather conditions, unexpected route changes, and encounters with wild animals can also be part of the experience. This does not mean that sustainable tourism is dangerous; however, there is an element of **risk**, a likelihood of loss or damage to a business, its employees, or its customers. In fact, there is some degree of risk in all travel and in most daily activities, including the drive to the airport to start an adventure. Problems arise when insurance companies perceive the industry as being riskier than it actually is or when tourism organizations do not undertake sufficient risk management.

Identifying your risk and managing it will be one of the most important things you do to ensure a long and prosperous future for your business. This chapter discusses some of the areas where your organization may face risk and steps you can take to minimize it.

LOSS CATEGORIES

Risk is the likelihood of loss for your business or your customers or employees. Some losses will involve damage to property, others interruption to income, and, unfortunately, some losses can involve injury or death to people. The most common areas where your business faces risk and the possibility of loss are as follows:

- *Property damage*—This includes damage or loss to the physical assets of your business, such as a boat, building, or vehicle from theft, fire, vandalism, weather, and so on.

- *Business interruption*—This is the loss of earnings arising from a temporary stop to your business activity. If your company was put out of business temporarily, for example, if your eco-lodge was destroyed by fire, the earnings from your business would be interrupted and you might not be able to meet your financial obligations while you rebuild your business.

- *Disability*—Although many people can claim good health today, it is highly possible that they will be disabled at some point in their working lives. Most often the disability will be short term, like when one is recovering from surgery or a car accident, but in other cases the disability will be long term or permanent. In both cases, employment income and sometimes, business income, is interrupted.

- *Loss of key individuals*—Many companies rely on one or two talented people in critical positions. In an ecotourism business, it may be the owner of the company who started as a guide and who is still the most popular guide for your upper-end clientele. The loss of these key people could jeopardize the operation of the business until a replacement can be found.

- *Medical*—If an employee were to become injured or ill in a remote location, the evacuation of that person and his or her ongoing medical treatment could become your responsibility.

- *Public liability*—If, for example, someone is injured during a rafting trip or comes down with food poisoning on a day hike, you could be held responsible for the losses and stress suffered by that person or in worst case scenarios by that person's surviving family.

Losses in many of these areas could severely affect your ability to continue the business. To prevent this, you can take action in two ways. First, you can assess the areas where you have the greatest risk and obtain insurance to absorb the financial cost of an illness, accident, or property loss. Equally as important, you can undertake a program of safety management to minimize the potential for accidents occurring in the first place. These are discussed in more detail in the following sections.

Damage to physical assets can present a large risk to your business.

INSURING AGAINST THE ODDS

Insurance is a contract in which the insurer agrees to compensate the insured for specific losses and specific risks. Insurance can be a voluntary expenditure, for example, disability insurance in case you are unable to generate income, or it may be mandatory, for example, you often need proof of public liability insurance before you are granted permits and licenses for outdoor activities in national parks or other protected areas.

Insurance for sustainable tourism operators offering adventure activities can be expensive and difficult to obtain. Many people in the insurance industry do not understand ecotourism, nature tourism, and its close relative, adventure travel, so finding a company that will insure your organization can be difficult and the rates may shock you. Obtaining insurance for a start-up business may be one of the biggest challenges you face.

To find a company to insure your business, ask other tourism businesses in your area what insurance companies they use and inquire with them. Or contact the association for your activity, for example, the America Outdoors Association website provides a list of insurance providers that work with recreation businesses (AOA 2014). If your insurance agent is willing to walk through your business operations with you, he or she might be able to identify ways you can minimize your risk and save money on premiums. If possible, compare rates among different carriers to ensure you receive the best rate. Be prepared to spend several hundred dollars annually on public liability insurance for low-risk activities such as guided nature hikes. Riskier activities, such as white-water

kayaking or roped climbing, will move premiums into the thousands of dollars. Be sure to include these costs when you calculate your prices.

Unfortunately, some operators are unable to obtain insurance for an activity or cannot afford the premiums. They might elect to operate in areas where insurance is not required to obtain a license or permit and hope that no accidents occur. Often they have few assets or have structured their company so that their personal liability is minimized. This practice only harms the industry as a whole because consumers are not properly protected and the reputation of all adventure businesses suffer if an accident occurs.

Categories of insurance you might want to purchase correspond to the types of loss discussed earlier and include the following:

- Property damage
- Public liability
- Business interruption
- Disability
- Loss of key individuals
- Medical

In each situation, evaluate what the likelihood of loss is, the impact of such a loss on your business, and whether you are legally required to carry this type of insurance. You may be required to carry public liability insurance but decide that property damage is something you will not insure. If your assets are small and you could replace the equipment and carry on in the unlikely event of fire or vandalism, you might decide to use savings to self-insure against possible losses. Table 12.1 can be used to plan your insurance requirements. The figures shown are for illustrative purposes only. You

Table 12.1   Examples of Insurance Requirements for a Tourism Business

Category	Insurance coverage required ($)	Estimated annual cost ($)
Property damage	50,000	350
Public liability	2,000,000	2,200
Business interruption	200,000	200
Disability	50,000	1,000
Loss of key individuals	Not required	
Medical	Not required	
Total cost		3,750

should meet with an insurance agent to explain the nature of your business and determine what type of coverage you require and the estimated annual cost. Ask tourism businesses in your area for the name of their insurance agent. Someone familiar with the tourism industry and its risk can help you find insurance coverage at the best cost.

RISK MANAGEMENT STRATEGIES

Ensuring the safety of your customers is one of the most important functions you will undertake as a sustainable tourism operator. In fact, in its guidelines for hotels and tour operators, the Global Sustainable Tourism Council suggests as part of demonstrating effective sustainable management that "all personnel receive periodic guidance and training regarding their roles and responsibilities with respect to environmental, social, cultural, economic, quality, health and safety issues" (GSTC 2013, p. 3). Most business owners also recognize that while they can insure for lawsuits arising from accidents, there is no insurance in the world that covers the financial cost from lost customer goodwill.

Some tourists look for an element of adventure in their trips. However, with the exception of some hard adventure activities, most people expect to enjoy mild excitement on their outdoor experiences without facing serious peril. If you place your customers in unexpectedly dangerous situations, accidents or death could occur. Even if you avoid physical harm, the damage to your reputation may take considerable time to overcome because a guest can complain on social media within minutes of reaching safety and a Wi-Fi connection.

The secret to successful risk management is to provide the desired experience to the tourist, sometimes including perceived risk, while minimizing real risk to the customer. Climbing schools have balanced these risks successfully for years. They know that by top-roping clients, they can provide people with the thrill of scaling rock faces or walls without any real danger of the climber falling. The customers might perceive that they are overcoming the risk of falling while the reality is that they will only fall a few inches if they were to lose their grip.

Your business needs a **safety management system**, a business program to manage potential risk, health, and safety concerns and the associ-

ated losses. A detailed program for health and safety management is outside the scope of this book, but it will be helpful for you to understand how accidents arise and some of the steps you can take to reduce your risk.

How Do Accidents Arise?

Contrary to what you may have told your parents when you broke something at home, accidents do not just happen. Accidents usually occur when poor planning meets opportunity in the form of bad weather, equipment failure, or human activity. Some of the risk factors that sustainable tourism operators face are shown in table 12.2.

Where a greater number of hazards are present, the probability of an accident occurring is greater. Because most sustainable tourism businesses will find themselves facing multiple hazards, it makes sense to minimize the risks through sound planning and ongoing review and training.

Steps for a Safer Trip

When you break down accident potential into human, equipment, and environmental factors, you realize that tourism operators can take many actions to make their trips as safe as possible. For example, everyone knows the weather cannot be controlled, but you can control your business' reaction to it. Establish procedures that require guides to obtain a weather forecast before setting out, or insist that guides and participants carry clothing that is waterproof or insulated for snow. Set a policy that stipulates that no trips will be undertaken if temperatures drop below a certain level. In the event that rain, mud, or snow makes a route impassable, develop alternative routes. Conduct practice events, announced and unannounced, to test your contingency plans in the event a tour group is overdue from a trip.

The following are basic steps you can take to make your activities safer:

- Planning—Select alternate trip routes and activities that can be used in inclement weather or if the energy level of the group is waning.
- Setting policies—Set policies on how many guides will accompany a trip (in some sports and states, minimum guide numbers are set out by governing agencies). Develop safety policies that provide direction for bad weather, approaching

Table 12.2 Sustainable Tourism Risk Factors

Human	Equipment	Environment
Skills and experience: Lake of training and previous encounters with similar situations can lead to poor decisions	Clothing: The wrong clothing can lead to problems, such as exposure.	Terrain: Natural environments pose many hazards, (e.g., falling rocks, riptides, avalanches).
Age: Younger participants may not have the same judgment skills as older adults.	Gear: Equipment that is poorly maintained or fails under stress will hinder safety.	Weather: Unexpected storms can quickly turn routine activities into hazardous outings.
Fitness level and health: Inability to perform necessary activities can jeopardize safety.	Safety equipment: Operating without safety equipment, such as personal flotation devices or avalanche transceivers, can increase risk of injury or death.	Flora and fauna: Encounters with animals can cause bites or mauling; getting too close to poisonous plants can cause illness or death.
Group size: Larger groups make it difficult for guides to monitor everybody.	Communication: Guides without communication technology appropriate for remote locations may not be able to access backup quickly.	Built infrastructure: Structures built by humans can create environmental hazards, (e.g., road conditions can lead to car accidents or bridge decks may be slippery to walk on).
Attitudes: Customers unwilling to listen to guides cause problems.		Climate change: Unexpected seasonal weather events, such as snow in summer, can create dangerous situations for people outdoors or cause property damage from large storms or floods.

Based on Province of British Columbia. 2003.

wildlife, communicating with the base location, and other practices that are relevant to your operation.

- Hiring—Look for personal attributes such as judgment, leadership, and communication skills, as well as appropriate certification, when hiring guides. Check references from previous employers to assess the guide's performance under difficult conditions.
- Training—Provide training in leadership skills so that guides can maintain control over a group under stress. If inclement weather is encountered and disagreements arise over the best way to continue the trip, your guide must be able to prevent part of a group from trying to find its own way home. Ensure staff are trained in wilderness first aid and survival as well as map reading and radio communication.
- Qualifying clients—Ensure that all clients have completed a questionnaire and, in cases where physical condition is critical or a person has had medical problems, insist on a doctor's examination before the trip departs. Match the customer's abilities and interests to activities and

tour itineraries. Help customers select the tour that is the best choice for them. Resist the temptation to add them to a trip that is beyond their capabilities because you need the extra people in order to run the trip.

- Maintaining equipment—Mechanical failure of equipment can significantly increase the potential for accidents. Make it a priority to examine all equipment and restore it to good working order. When equipment is nearing the end of its life, budget funds to replace it.
- Practicing—Give your staff the chance to practice their safety skills, especially procedures that are used only in times of crisis, such as first aid or rescue drills.
- Preparing legal releases or waivers—Require customers to sign legal releases or waivers advising them of the risks of the activity they are about to undertake and absolving you of responsibility in the event of an accident, injury, or illness. While waivers and legal releases may not prevent lawsuits, they can reduce the likelihood that someone will win a claim because you have made them aware of the potential risks and dangers.

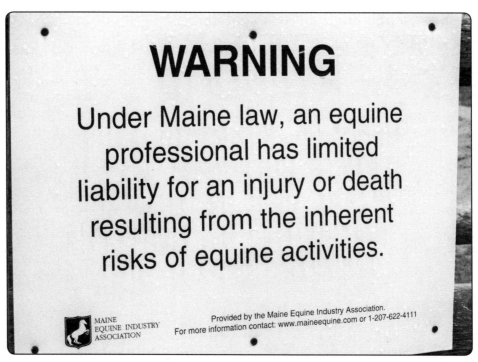

WARNING

Under Maine law, an equine professional has limited liability for an injury or death resulting from the inherent risks of equine activities.

MAINE EQUINE INDUSTRY ASSOCIATION

Provided by the Maine Equine Industry Association. For more information contact: www.maineequine.com or 1-207-622-4111

Warnings and waivers can make travelers aware of risks.

For an example of a sustainable tourism organization managing its risk through safety management watch the video "Managing the Risk" in the web resource.

This chapter serves as an introduction to safety management. You might want to explore each area in more detail in your business once you have talked to your insurance company or lawyer. Start by identifying the hazards for your business and the training and processes you can use to mitigate risk. Be sure to take into account industry best practices as well as all legal requirements to keep your employees and customers safe. This includes occupational health and safety guidelines.

IF THE WORST HAPPENS

Even with proper planning, policies, and training, accidents happen. When they do, it is important to react appropriately. Document events and existing conditions, use a standardized form to gather pertinent accident information, and take pictures. It is easy to forget important details. Contact your insurance company and the proper authorities in a timely manner. A contact person for media inquiries should be determined in advance so your business presents a consistent message. Concern for the person who is injured or suffered a loss is a priority. While you do not want to admit liability or assign blame, companies often exacerbate the situation by giving the impression they do not care what has befallen their client.

In addition to securing insurance and continually improving your safety management program, you can also protect your company's assets through its legal structure. A **sole proprietorship**—a structure that does not distinguish between the individual and the business —exposes both the owner and the business to legal action. Personal assets could be lost in a successful lawsuit. **Incorporation**—forming your business into a corporation—can remove some of this risk by limiting liability, in most cases, to the assets of the company. Some entrepreneurs take this step further and create several companies, holding their major assets in the company with least risk. A company that offers tourism activities would hold few assets because it is the company that is most likely to be sued if an accident or loss occurred. Another company, often the parent or holding company of the first, would hold the majority of the assets. While this may not offer complete protection in a legal action, it can provide added safety for a business owner.

Although corporate structure can protect business assets if an accident or lawsuit arises, it raises ethical concerns. Take the Ecochallenge "What's Fair?" and examine the moral concerns business owners face when they try to manage risk.

Ecochallenge
What's Fair?

Some corporations move their assets to holding companies to prevent losing them in legal action. Some people feel that having significant wealth in a company can encourage people to take legal action. After all, if a company has no assets to settle a legal claim, most people will not spend money on a lawyer to take legal action. Other people believe that companies that shelter assets, especially if they are held in offshore locations, are not good corporate citizens. The reduced tax base can affect the community's ability to offer educational or social programs. Also, if an environmental problem is caused by a tourism company that has few assets, the community cannot use legal action to gain financial reimbursement for cleanup costs or social assistance for people losing jobs.

Do you think it is ethical for a company to hold its assets in a separate company? Consider how you would feel if you were a customer who had suffered an accident while on a trip. Or if you were a fisherman living downstream of a hotel incorrectly disposing of sewage. Conversely, put yourself in the place of the business owner who has invested many years in building his or her company. Do you think travelers have a realistic understanding of the risk they face when undertaking adventure activities? Do you think they should share in the risk and not be able to take legal action after an accident? Do you think sustainable tourism companies have an ethical obligation to maintain sufficient assets to pay damages for accidents or environmental problems?

There are no right and wrong answers to these questions, but pondering them will illustrate the dilemma many business owners face.

SUMMARY

Managing risk to avoid loss to your business or customers is an important responsibility of managers and owners of sustainable tourism businesses. People's lives can be at stake, so put senior people in charge of assessing your risks and developing a safety management program. It is a complex field facing many legal implications, so talk to insurance and legal experts to ensure you understand your obligations. Insurance premiums can be a significant expenditure, so ask other business owners for tips on reducing risk and premiums or finding insurance at a lower cost. Managing business risk will safeguard the hard work you put into developing your business.

GLOSSARY

incorporation—Forming a business into a corporation. Setting up a separate legal entity limits the liability for shareholders of the corporation.

insurance—A contract in which the insurer agrees to compensate the insured for specific losses and specific risks.

risk—A likelihood of loss or damage to a business, its employees, or its customers.

safety management system—A business program to manage potential risk, health and safety concerns, and associated losses.

sole proprietorship—A structure that does not distinguish between the individual and the business.

|||||||||||||||||| REVIEW QUESTIONS ||||||||||||||||

1. List six categories in which a sustainable tourism organization might experience loss. How can insurance help mitigate loss? What types of insurance might a tourism business obtain?

2. Identify the main areas where risk originates. Give three examples of a potential risk and steps a tourism organization could take to reduce the chance of an accident.

3. What is a safety management plan? How can it be used to reduce risk?

4. How can a company protect its assets through risk management?

|||||||||||||||||| VIDEO CASE STUDY |||||||||||||||

Visit the web resource to see the video "Managing the Risk." After watching the video, answer the following questions.

1. List several risks you think a dogsledding company like Sundogs Excursions faces. Identify the source of each risk as human, equipment, or environmental.

2. What steps does Sundogs Excursions take to prevent accidents? Identify processes you observed that would ensure consistency in risk management from trip to trip.

3. How might the presence of animals make it more difficult to prevent accidents?

4. Describe the responsibility customers should take for their own safety when participating in a dogsledding trip. Give examples of background research a customer might undertake before signing up for a trip.

5. Sustainable tourism organizations often operate in the wilderness. Explain how operations in these environments might require different safety management plans than those of a businesses located closer to urban environments.

|||||||||||||||||| YOUR BUSINESS PLAN |||||||||||||||

Continue completing the business plan workbook, focusing on the sections dealing with insurance and organizational structure. Test the hiring and training assumptions you used earlier to make sure you will have sufficient staff and people with the right qualifications to develop and implement a risk management program. Where necessary, budget for additional resources and be ready to describe unique features of your risk and safety programs in your business plan.

1. Describe the risks your business may face and the safety management steps you will take to mitigate them. Identify how many staff days are required to implement your plan or undertake safety training.

2. List the losses your business could face and distinguish between those that you could self-insure (i.e., cover losses through savings) and those that would require you to purchase insurance.

3. Explain how your organization would react if an accident occurred. Include your plans to protect your organization's image and goodwill with the customer. Include these costs in your business plan's financial forecasts.

|||||||||||||||||||||||||||| **REFERENCES** ||||||||||||||||||||||||

America Outdoors Association. 2014. America Outdoors Association service and supplier. https://www.americaoutdoors.org/america_outdoors/vacation/commercial_members.php.

Global Sustainable Tourism Council. 2014. http://www.gstcouncil.org/images/pdf/HTO-CRITERIA_and_INDICATORS_6-9-14.pdf.

Province of British Columbia. 2003. Risk management for outdoor programs: A handbook for administrators and instructors. Ministry of Advanced Education. http://embc.gov.bc.ca/em/hazard_preparedness/Handbook_for_Administrators_and_Instructors_PDF_Nov_04_with_cover.pdf.

13

BUSINESS PLANS

After reading this chapter, you will be able to do the following:

- Identify why a business plan is important

- Describe the main sections of a business plan

- Understand how to write a business plan

Many small and medium-size tourism businesses operate with small margins and must make enough money in the peak season, often only a few months long, to maintain the business from year to year. Competition for the consumer's disposable income and free time is fierce. Add to this the government legislation you must understand and comply with, and you have a business that requires detailed planning and careful management to succeed. One of the most important planning tools for achieving success is a business plan. It is a written blueprint outlining the product development, marketing, and financing you will undertake for the next few years to achieve your goals.

NEED FOR A BUSINESS PLAN

Failing to create a business plan can keep your business from thriving as it should. In fact, Australia's Sustainable Tourism Cooperative Research Centre has identified the lack of effective business planning as one of the most pressing needs of small to medium-size tourism businesses (Sustainable

Tourism Online 2014). Business plans are prepared for a variety of reasons:

- To document business concepts, marketing strategies, operating activities, and financial forecasts

- To obtain external financing

- To communicate goals and strategies within the organization

Writing a business plan forces you to look at possible problems and prepare for the unexpected. It will not prevent all problems but can head off many by making you aware of areas where you are vulnerable. For example, if your business plan identifies a cash flow problem at the start of your operating season, you can plan ahead and obtain a line of credit instead of dealing with angry creditors or harming your credit rating when you should be focused on leading tours. For more reasons to prepare a business plan, watch the video "Why Learn Business Planning?" in the web resource.

Your Audience

When writing your business plan, keep in mind your reasons for preparing it and the people who will read the document. If you are hoping to attract investors, the plan has to function as a marketing tool. You must excite the reader about your business while demonstrating that you have done your research. You do not want to stretch the truth, but you should use a colorful style of writing that conveys the specialness of your product. In tourism, you are often selling the experience. Describing the intangibles by which people will remember your trip requires a bit of effort, but it is necessary to communicate the attributes that make your business special. Take the Ecochallenge "Writing for Different Audiences" to see why different writing styles are needed.

If you want your business plan to guide your staff's daily activities, it must be detailed enough that your staff understands your goals and business strategies. This information will provide the context they need to make smaller decisions and represent your company properly.

Sustainable Tourism Difference

Your business plan will differ from other business plans because of your commitment to the environment and responsible operating practices. The mission statement and your description of your products and services should reflect this commitment. For example, are you selling kayaking tours or are you selling lifetime memories of a natural history experience? The subtle ways in which you look at your product can make a big difference in how you promote your product and how you distinguish your tour or service in your business plan.

Discuss alliances with nonprofit organizations or community groups you are creating to help you develop authentic experiences or undertake conservation or community outreach activities. Your environmental commitment might require extra description in a business plan. Permits or special equipment might be required for sensitive areas; you need to identify them and the steps you will take to secure them. You may also discuss your policies and controls that ensure staff operates in an environmentally responsible manner.

Document the unique features, problems, and opportunities and your strategies for managing them. Your business plan will inform the people reading it about sustainable tourism and make them more confident in your abilities to run your business.

PREPARING A BUSINESS PLAN

When writing your business plan, include information on each major business function as well as an overall summary of your business. This will require the following sections:

Ecochallenge
Writing for Different Audiences

Different writing styles are required for different audiences. For university or college courses, you have probably become skilled in writing in a passive voice and referencing your sources. If you look at tourism brochures or websites, you will see a different writing style. It is more active and conveys a sense of engagement or excitement. When writing a business plan, you will need elements of both. You have to convey lots of information, but it must be done in an engaging way. You may also have to overcome skepticism about sustainable or green tourism concepts. Take a paragraph that you have written recently and rewrite it to be more exciting and evoke enthusiasm in your audience. Notice how difficult or easy it is for you to switch between writing styles.

Be creative in conveying the selling points of the sustainability features you are most proud of. If there are cost savings because of your waste management program or lower marketing expenses because you can join a sustainable tourism marketing partnership, highlight them. A banker will be impressed by your frugality. Add references or statistics to give your business case more impetus. Saying that the local chamber of commerce gets three inquiries a week about local birding guides is more convincing than saying potential customers are seeking greener tourism. Ask someone else to read your copy and comment on his or her impressions. Are his or her reactions what you expected?

Sustainable tourism businesses need to convey their environmental commitment in their business plan.

- Executive summary
- Description of products or services
- Marketing plans, including the sustainable tourism market and your targeted customers, an analysis of your competitors, marketing strategies, and sales forecasts
- Management and legal structure of company
- Operations comprising location, equipment, human resource management, and environmental best practices
- Financial forecasts including a projected income statement, projected balance sheet, projected start-up costs, and financing requirements
- Appendixes

Each aspect is described briefly in the following sections. Detailed information on marketing, financing, human resources, and operations is found throughout this book and can be referred to as you develop your plan. If you have been working with the business plan workbook as you read each chapter, you will have much of the information you need to start writing.

Executive Summary

This section is a short synopsis (one to two pages) of your business, highlighting your business con-cept, marketing plans, forecasted financial requirements and results, and operations. By condensing the key elements of your business plan into a few pages, the executive summary gives readers a powerful introduction to your business and the unique features that distinguish it.

For companies using the business plan to secure outside financing or investment, it is critical that the executive summary be well written. It should be a concise, thoughtful outline, written in a manner to catch the reader's attention. Investors are often faced with scores of business plans; yours must capture their interest quickly.

Description of Products or Services

This section describes the products or services you will provide. This may sound so obvious that it does not bear mentioning; however, many people are unable to explain their business concept clearly and succinctly. You should be able to describe your business in a few sentences. If it takes you several pages to describe the concept, chances are the product will require lengthy explanation to sell it to customers, or it may not sell at all.

Remember that people reading your business plan may not be familiar with tourism or sustainable tourism practices. Explain how your products are different from the competition and how they are the same. Introduce underlying strategies that will help you address weaknesses and external threats.

Marketing

The marketing section includes the most important information from your marketing plan. Include your situation analysis, market analysis, and competitive analysis to explain why your product is marketable and to estimate market size. The marketing description will provide details on target market segments, product pricing, advertising strategies, potential market share or sales volumes, and information on competitors.

This section should describe the overall characteristics and size of the sustainable tourism industry, with a focus on the tourism market in your area or activity, and on the portion of the market you think you will capture. Include a brief description of other sustainable tourism operators in your area and their strengths and weaknesses. This competitive analysis will show how you plan to compete against other tourism or recreation organizations. Without that distinction and evidence that a market exists for that uniqueness, your tourism dreams may be over before you get started.

While the financial forecasts may be the first thing people read in your business plan, a savvy investor knows that the accuracy of those numbers depends on the marketing plan. The forecasted sales volumes come from the marketing plan and are the starting point for financial forecasts; therefore, sales forecasts are important when assessing the viability of your business. Make your forecasts credible through enough marketing research to support your conclusions.

Management

This section discusses the structure of your business and includes the background of key personnel. Having management personnel with industry or management experience is a critical predictor of success. Investors look carefully at key people for experience in related businesses, so if your background has gaps in knowledge or experience, compensate. If you are not good at marketing or do not know a debit from a credit, include other people in your management team who can add the depth you need.

This section also includes a description of your business' legal structure; possible options are sole proprietorship, partnership, or an incorporated entity. Each has its own advantages and disadvantages as described in table 13.1. A nonprofit organization may be created for a community-based venture. Consider which structure meets your needs. Many tourism ventures are small businesses that operate seasonally. A sole proprietorship offers ease of start-up and lower costs; however, an incorporated entity or limited company will provide more protection in the event of legal action. Discussing your situation with your accountant, lawyer, and insurance agent will help you decide.

Operations

This section describes the physical activities and location of your business and the people and processes needed to run it. For some sustainable tourism businesses, you may need to include an office or storefront and the protected area or public facility where the trips occur. Sustainable tourism's emphasis on the environment presents unique operational challenges as follows:

Table 13.1   Legal Structures

	Sole proprietorship	Partnership	Limited company
ADVANTAGES	Easy to start up Fewer costs associated with maintenance (e.g., annual returns)	More growth opportunities than a proprietorship Investment by two or more people	Liability limited for third parties Existence not limited to shareholders' lives Can have one or more owners
DISADVANTAGES	One owner Unlimited owner's liability Limited to owner's life Personal income tax rates apply to withdrawals of profits	Limited to partners' lives Liable for partners' actions Personal tax rates apply on withdrawal of profits	Company profits taxed at corporate rates Investment possible in several forms Incorporation costs incurred to establish; other costs required to maintain

- How will you operate your business using sustainable tourism business practices for equipment, human resources, and supplies? Refer to resources from tourism organizations such as the Global Sustainable Tourism Council or its members for direction on best practices.

- How will your business manage dissimilar activities or profit centers, such as gift shops and outdoor recreation, or catering and accommodation? Make sure you have included all costs in your business plan and that staff have the skills needed to manage disparate activities.

- How will you obtain required permits and licenses, and what will be the impact on your business if you cannot obtain them or if the cost is greater than expected? By identifying where you hold or can reasonably expect to obtain licenses, you provide support for sales forecasts.

- How will your business evaluate its environmental and social impact? If you are required to conduct an environmental impact assessment, you should include time and money for this process in your forecasts. If you are not required to conduct an environmental impact assessment, decide on indicators you will use to measure your impact. You might consider tracking number and type of wildlife sightings, or monitoring your energy consumption and waste output. Your contributions to community or social programs may be another way to monitor impacts.

- How will you handle transportation systems to move building or operating supplies to remote locations? You might consider using people with backpacks or wheelbarrows, pack animals, or helicopter drops. Be sure to include additional costs in the financial forecasts.

Financial Forecasts

Financial forecasting presents special challenges for many tourism businesses because of their seasonal nature and smaller group sizes when operating in sensitive areas. This can mean lower revenues and higher operating costs, which translate to reduced profits and slower paybacks for creditors and investors. This may require creativity in repaying investors. Perhaps you can offer trips at cost for the families of investors until you have the cash flow for dividends.

When preparing the financial section of your business plan, include the following schedules:

- Pro forma balance sheet
- Pro forma income statement
- Cash flow projections
- Break-even analysis
- Sensitivity analysis

Descriptions of these items are provided in chapter 9. You will find it helpful to review the chapter before starting your business plan. You should supplement these schedules with the following statements:

- Statement of net worth (a summary of the assets and liabilities of the owner)
- Summary of start-up costs and capital improvements and proposed financing sources

A worksheet for start-up costs is shown in the business plan workbook in section 6.3. Table 13.2 uses information from a fictitious company to show you how you might summarize financial requirements and possible funding sources.

When completing your start-up cost schedule, include all possible costs, including the following:

- Equipment
- Land or buildings

Table 13.2   Financial Requirements and Proposed Financing Sources

FINANCIAL REQUIREMENTS	
Costs	**Amount ($)**
Licenses and permits	5,000
Marketing campaign	10,000
Computer	5,000
Operating costs until break even	30,000
Total financial requirements	50,000
PROPOSED FINANCING	
Bank loan	5,000
Line of credit	10,000
Government subsidy	3,000
Trade credit	2,000
Owner investment	30,000
Total financing	50,000

- Vehicles
- Advertising campaigns
- Inventory (food, spare parts, clothing, promotional material, and so on)
- Licenses, permits
- Environmental impact assessment
- Operating costs until break even is reached (rent, electricity, payroll, insurance)
- Contingency amount
- Management draws and salaries

The summary of start-up costs and financing is an important part of your business plan because it communicates your financing requirements to lenders or investors. It also shows where you have invested capital and secured other investors.

The following are financing sources you might want to include in your planning:

- **Trade credit** is the amount of time vendors give to pay a bill, usually 30 days.
- **Mortgage loans** are long-term credit offered on real property, such as land or buildings.
- **Leasing** vehicles or office equipment instead of purchasing an asset is a way to preserve cash flow even though a business pays a financing cost. Businesses usually do not assume ownership of a leased asset but are responsible for operating costs and some maintenance.
- **Commercial loans** are the loan of money by a bank to a business. These loans may be secured (backed by collateral) or unsecured. Small or start-up sustainable tourism businesses may find it difficult to obtain a commercial loan.
- **Line of credit** is a more flexible form of bank credit. Businesses only borrow money against their line of credit as they need it. Interest is usually not charged on the unused portion.
- **Government subsidy** is usually a grant that does not require repayment, but businesses must meet qualifying requirements.
- **Owner's investment** (when owners put their own savings into their businesses) shows lenders and investors that owners have invested their own money before asking for other people's money.

- **Equity investment or loans by private investors** is the money that high-risk investors lend to or invest in start-up entities. They expect high returns and possibly equity or control of the business or both.

Once you have completed the financial forecasts for your business plan, you would be wise to conduct a break-even analysis or a sensitivity analysis to answer questions from potential investors about the outcomes if you miss your forecasted targets.

Appendixes

Some of the information for your business plan will be too long to include in the main document, but it is still relevant to investors or creditors. Include this information as an appendix. These materials might include the following:

- Permits
- Contracts
- Licenses
- Purchase contracts
- Marketing agreements
- Maps
- Brochures or website mock-ups
- Earlier financial statements
- Resumes of key personnel
- Letters of support from community organizations
- Environmental impact assessment studies
- Primary market research
- Surveyor certificates
- Proof of insurance coverage
- Background of community partners
- Details of your competitor analysis

BUSINESS PLAN WORKBOOK

This book's web resource features a workbook to assist in completing your business plan. It is a guide for gathering the information necessary to write a business plan. Not all of the information gathered in the workbook will appear in your business plan, but the material will help you develop your company's goals, objectives, and strategies.

Once you have researched each area, you will be ready to write your plan.

The presentation format and style is important if you are showing it to lenders, investors, or staff. Remember it is part information and part marketing brochure for your business. Make it easy to read and entertaining. People with money to invest receive many business plans, and you want your opportunity to stand out. If you are the primary user, keep the written descriptions brief or summarize information in point form because you will have all the detailed information on hand.

Allow enough time to write the business plan. It might take weeks or months, but it is time well spent. The online files will reduce the effort required to summarize data and prepare financial forecasts. Business plan software packages are available on the market, but it is unlikely you will find one tailored to your operations. Be prepared to start with a basic template and modify it to meet your specific needs. Many banks provide business-planning software at a nominal charge. An example of a completed business plan is in the web resource.

Once you have drafted your plan, make sure you have avoided some of the common mistakes people make when writing business plans. Many entrepreneurs are disappointed when their carefully crafted business plan fails to secure financing or investment. They may complain that there is too much competition for money or that the business plan process is not worth the effort. But often, it is the plan, not the process that is flawed. To succeed, avoid these mistakes in your business plan:

- *Lack of primary market research*—Yes, you need secondary research showing tourism trends and market characteristics, but you should also talk to prospective customers. Summarize your conversations and surveys; the feedback you get will be important in convincing people you can fill a market need.

- *Erroneous market share assumptions*—Too many entrepreneurs assume that if it is a big market, they will be able to get even a small percentage of that market and they will have large sales. This is tempting in tourism, one of the largest economic activities on the planet, but basing your financial forecasts on assumptions like this will flag you as a business rookie.

- *Wrong length*—Your business plan needs to be the right length for the audience. If you are showing it to external users, make sure there is enough detail to explain the uniqueness of your business pitch, but do not get into jargon or minutiae that might confuse. Aim for 20 to 40 pages. If you have more information, include it in appendices or make it available for review later.

Ask someone to read your business plan before you send it to creditors or investors and give you feedback. If he or she finds information difficult to understand or your presentation boring, you can easily fix it. You will not get the same second chance if you present a badly written business plan to an external audience.

SUMMARY

You have learned a lot about the sustainable tourism business. After reading about the mechanics of starting and running a business with a triple bottom line, you have a better idea of the skills and resources you need to succeed. Use your business plan as a framework to pull together your background research, the best practices you observed, and management strategies suited to your situation. By organizing your thoughts in this way, you will shape your vision for the future and help move your tourism organization toward a sustainable future.

|||||||||||||||||||||||||||||||| **GLOSSARY** ||||||||||||||||||||||||||||||||

commercial loan—A loan of money by a bank to a business. These loans may be secured (backed by collateral) or unsecured. Small or start-up sustainable tourism businesses may find it difficult to obtain a commercial loan.

government subsidy—Usually a grant that does not require repayment, but businesses must meet qualifying requirements.

leasing—Instead of purchasing vehicles or office equipment, a business might lease an asset to use. Usually the business does not assume ownership of a leased asset, but it will be responsible for operating costs and some maintenance. Although the business pays financing costs, leasing preserves cash flow.

line of credit—A more flexible form of bank credit. Businesses only borrow money against their line of credit as they need it. Interest is usually not charged on the unused portion.

mortgage loan—A long-term credit offered on real property such as land or buildings.

trade credit—The amount of time vendors give a business to pay a bill, usually 30 days.

REVIEW QUESTIONS

1. What is a business plan? What are the advantages of completing a business plan?
2. Describe the major sections of a business plan.
3. Identify common mistakes people make when writing a business plan. How might someone avoid these mistakes?
4. Explain how a business plan is different from other business documents. How can the writer make the business plan more convincing to external users?

VIDEO CASE STUDY

Visit the web resource to watch the video "Why Learn Business Planning?" After watching the video, answer the following questions:

1. How can skills in business planning help your sustainable tourism career?
2. What is a business plan? Describe some of the benefits of developing a business plan.
3. Identify some of the challenges you might face as a sustainable tourism manager. How can a business plan help you tackle these challenges?
4. Technology and world events can change quickly. Do you think business planning is more or less important with rapid change? Discuss your reasons.
5. List the skills or knowledge you think are required to prepare a business plan. Compare the list to your training and identify gaps. Where could you find assistance to fill in the gaps? Consider inexpensive sources such as websites, government agencies, and universities and colleges.

REFERENCE

Sustainable Tourism Online. 2014. Business and strategic planning. www.sustainabletourism online.com/business-operations/planning/business-and-strategic-planning.

INDEX

ABOUT THE AUTHOR

Carol Patterson has been an author and consultant of tourism for over 20 years. She has helped numerous small business owners penetrate and advance into North American markets. She has been widely recognized for her pioneering work in tourism, winning awards for cinematography and sound design as well as her vision. Patterson is an adjunct assistant professor of adventure tourism classes at the University of Calgary. She is the author of several books, including *The Business of Ecotourism,* and co-author of *Handle With Care: Developing a Nature Based Tourism Product in the North.* She is also a Travel Media Association of Canada award recipient for the best environmental/responsible tourism feature. Her travel writing has appeared on BBC Travel and Vacay.ca among other publications.

You'll find other outstanding
recreation resources at
www.HumanKinetics.com

In the U.S. call 1.800.747.4457
Australia 08 8372 0999
Canada. 1.800.465.7301
Europe . . . . .+44 (0) 113 255 5665
New Zealand 0800 222 062

HUMAN KINETICS
The Information Leader in Physical Activity & Health
P.O. Box 5076 • Champaign, IL 61825-5076